LOVE TO THE UTTERMOST: EXPOSITIONS OF JOHN XIII.-XXI.

BY

F. B. Meyer

LOVE TO THE UTTERMOST: EXPOSITIONS OF JOHN XIII.-XXI.

Published by Scriptura Press

New York City, NY

First published circa 1929

Copyright © Scriptura Press, 2015

All rights reserved

ABOUT SCRIPTURA PRESS

Scriptura Press is a Christian company that makes Christian works available and affordable to all. We are a non-denominational publishing group that shares the teachings of the Scripture, whether in the form of sermons or histories of the Church.

PREFACE

The former book on the first twelve chapters of this sublime Gospel was called, The Life and Light of Men. The title was naturally suggested by the subject-matter of those chapters. We had little difficulty in finding a title for the present book, which covers, however cursorily, the remainder of the Gospel. It lay open before us in the opening verses of the thirteenth chapter, as translated in the margin of the Revised Version. "Having loved His own which were in the world, He loved them to the uttermost."

It has been impossible, in the limited space at my disposal, to deal with these chapters as I would. Indeed, to do so, it would be necessary to know the length, and breadth, and depth, and height of the Love of God, which passeth knowledge. Time has been allowed to elapse, in the hope that the view would be clearer, and the expression more adequate, of the deep things to which the Lord gave expression. But it is useless to wait till one is satisfied of the adequacy of one's work, else life will have run its course before a beginning has been made. At the end of ten more years, the task would seem still more impracticable.

In the closing chapters I have woven together the narratives of the four evangelists, so as to give a succinct and connected account of the last hours of our Lord's life, and especially of His death. It has been a great delight thus to tread the Via Crucis, which is also the Via Lucis—the Way of the Cross, which is the Way of Life, and Light, and Love.

I

The Laver in the Life of Jesus

"He poureth water into a basin, and began to wash the disciples' feet, and to wipe them with a towel wherewith He was girded."—JOHN xiii. 5.

In the court of the Temple there were two objects that arrested the eye of the entering worshipper—the Brazen Altar, and the Laver. The latter was kept always full of pure, fresh water, for the constant washings enjoined by the Levitical code. Before the priests were consecrated for their holy work, and attired in the robes of the sacred office, they washed there (Ex. xxix. 4). Before they entered the Holy Place in their ordinary ministry, and before Aaron, on the great Day of Atonement, proceeded to the Most Holy Place, with blood, not his own, it was needful to conform to the prescribed ablutions. "He shall bathe his flesh in water" (Lev. xvi. 4).

First, then, the Altar, and then the Laver; the order is irreversible, and the teaching of the types is as exact as mathematics. Hence, when the writer of the Epistle to the Hebrews invites us to draw near, and make our abode in the Most Holy Place, he carefully obeys the Divine order, and bids us "draw near, with a true heart, in full assurance of faith, having our hearts sprinkled from an evil conscience, and our bodies washed with pure water."

In this scene (John xiii. 1-14), on the eve of our Lord's betrayal, we find the spiritual counterpart of the Laver, just as the Cross stands for the Brazen Altar.

I. THE CIRCUMSTANCE THAT LED TO THIS ACT OF LOVE.—In order fully to understand this touching incident, it is necessary to remember the circumstances out of which it sprang. On the way from Bethany to the upper room in which the Supper had been prepared, and on entering therein, our Lord must have been deeply absorbed in the momentous events in which He was to be the central figure; but He was not unmindful of a contention which had engaged His disciples, for they had been disputing one with another as to which of them should be the greatest. The proud spirit of the flesh, which so often cursed the little group, broke out in this awful hour with renewed energy, as though the prince of this world would inflict a parting blow on his great Antagonist, through those whom He loved best. It was as if he said, "See the results of Thy tears and teachings, of Thy prayers and pleadings; the love which Thou hast so often inculcated is but a passing sentiment, that has never rooted itself in the soil of these wayward hearts. It is a plant too rare and exotic for the climate of earth. Take it back with Thee to Thine own home if Thou wilt, but seek not to achieve the impossible." It was heartrending that this exhibition of pride should take place just at this juncture. These were the men who had been with Him in His temptations, who had had the benefit of His most careful instructions, who had been exposed to the full influence of His personal character; and yet, notwithstanding all, the rock-bed of pride, that cast the angels down from heaven, that led to the fall of man, obtruded itself. This occasion in which it manifested itself was very inopportune; already the look of Calvary was on the Saviour's face, and the sword entering His heart. Surely, they must have been aware that the shadow of the great eclipse was already passing over the face of their Sun.

But even this did not avail to restrain the manifestation of their pride. Heedless of three years of example and teaching; unrestrained by the symptoms of our Lord's sorrow; unchecked by the memory of happy and familiar intercourse, which should have bound them forever in a united brotherhood, they wrangled with high voices and hot faces, with the flashing eye and clenched fist of the Oriental, as to who should be first.

And if pride thus asserted itself after such education, and under such circumstances, let us be sure that it is not far away from any one of us. We do not now contend, in so many words, for the chief places; courtesy, politeness, fear of losing the respect of our fellows, restrain us. But our resentment to the fancied slight, or the assumption by another of work which we thought our own; our sense of hurtness when we are put aside; our jealousy and envy; our detracting speeches, and subtle insinuations of low motive, all show how much of this loveless spirit rankles in our hearts. We have been planted in the soil of this world, and we betray its flavor; we have come of a proud stock, we betray our heredity.

II. LOVE'S SENSITIVENESS TO SIN ON THE PART OF ITS BELOVED.—Consider these epithets of the love of Christ:

It was unusually tender.—When the hour of departure approaches, though slight reference be made to it, love lives with the sound of the departing wheels, or the scream of the engine, always in its ear; and there are given a tenderness to the tone, a delicacy to the touch, a thoughtfulness for the heartache of those from which it is to be parted, which are of inexpressible beauty. All that was present with Christ. He was taking that Supper with them before He suffered. He knew that He would soon depart out of this world unto the Father; His ear was specially on the alert; His nature keenly alive; His heart thrilling with unusual tenderness, as the sands slowly ran out from the hour-glass.

It was supreme love.—"Having loved His own that were in the world, He loved them unto the end." Those last words have been thought to refer to the end of life, but it surely were superfluous to tell us that the strong waters of death could not quench the love of the Son of Man. When once He loves, He loves always. It is needless to tell us that the Divine heart which has enshrined a soul will not forsake it; that the name of the beloved is never erased from the palms of the hands, that the covenant is not forgotten though eternity elapse. Of course Christ loves to the end, even though that end reaches to endlessness. We do not need to be assured that the Immortal Lover, who has once taken us up to union with Himself, can never loose His hold. Therefore it is better to adopt the alternative suggested by the margin of the Revised Version, "He loved them to the uttermost." There was nothing to be desired. Nothing was needed to fill out the ideal of perfect love. Not a stitch was required for the needle-work of wrought gold; not a touch demanded for the perfectly achieved picture; not a throb additional to the strong pulse of affection with which He regarded His own.

It is very wonderful that He should have loved such men like this. As we pass them under review at this time of their life, they seem a collection of nobodies, with the exception perhaps of John and Peter. But they were His own, there was a special relationship between Him and them. They had belonged to the Father, and He had given them to the Son as His special perquisite and belonging. "Thine they were, and Thou gavest them Me." May we dare, in this meaning, to apply to Christ that sense of proprietorship, which makes a bit of moorland waste, a few yards of garden-ground, dear to the freeholder?

It was because these men were Christ's own, that the full passion of His heart set in toward them, and He loved them to the utmost bound; that is, the tides filled the capacity of the ocean-bed of possibility.

It was bathed in the sense of His Divine origin and mission.—The curtain was waxing very thin. It was a moment of vision. There had swept across His soul a realization of the full meaning of His approaching triumph. He looked back, and was hardly conscious of the manger where the horned oxen fed, the lowly birth, the obscure years, in the sublime conception that He had come forth from God. He looked forward, and was hardly conscious of the cross, the nail, the thorn-crown, and the spear, because of the sublime consciousness that He was stepping back, to go to Him with whom He realized His identity. He looked on through the coming weeks, and knew that the Father had given all things into His hands. What the devil had offered as the price of obeisance to himself, that the Father was about to give Him, nay, had already given Him, as the price of His self-emptying. And if for a moment He stooped, as we shall see He did, to the form of a servant, it was not because of any failure to recognize His high dignity and mission, but with the sense of Godhead quick on His soul.

The love which went out toward this little group of men had Deity in it. It was the love of the Throne, of the glory He had with the Father before the worlds were, of that which now fills the bosom of His ascended and glorified nature.

He was aware of the task to which He was abandoning these men.—He knew that as He was the High Priest over the house of God, they were its priests. He knew that cleansing was necessary before they could receive the anointing of the Holy Ghost. He knew that the great work of carrying forward His Gospel was to be delegated to their hands. He knew that they were to carry the sacred vessels of the Gospel, which must not be blurred or fouled by contact with human pride or uncleanness. He knew that the very mysteries of Gethsemane and Calvary would be inexplicable, and that none might stand on that holy hill, save those that had clean hands and a pure heart; and because of all this, He turned to them, by symbol and metaphor, to impress upon their heart and memory the necessity of participating in the cleansing of which the Laver is the type.

The highest love is ever quickest to detect the failures and inconsistencies of the beloved. Just because of its intensity, it can be content with nothing less than the best, because the best means the blessedest; and it longs that the object of its thought should be most blessed forever. It is a mistake to think that green-eyed jealousy is quickest to detect the spots on the sun, the freckles on the face, and the marring discords in the music of the life; love is quicker, more microscopic, more exacting that the ideal should be achieved. Envy is content to indicate the fault, and leave it; but love detects, and waits and holds its peace until the fitting opportunity arrives, and then sets itself to remove, with its own tenderest ministry, the defect which had spoiled the completeness and beauty of its object.

Perhaps there had never been a moment in the human consciousness of our Lord, when, side by side with this intense love for His own, there had been so vivid a sense of oneness with His Father, of His unity with the source of Infinite Purity and Blessedness. We might have supposed that this would have alienated Him from His poor friends, but in this our thoughts are not as His. Just because of His awful holiness, He was quick to perceive the unholiness of His friends, and could not endure it, and essayed to rid them of it. Just because of His Divine goodness He could detect the possibilities of goodness in them, and be patient enough to give it culturing care.

The most perfect musician may be most tortured by incompetence; but he will be most likely to detect true merit, and give time to its training. "The powerfullest magnet will pick out, in the powdered dust of the ironstone, fine particles of metal that a second or third-rate magnet would fail to draw to itself." Do not dread the awful holiness of Jesus; it is your hope. He will never be content till He has made you like Himself; and side by side with His holiness, never fail to remember His gentle, tender love.

III. THE DIVINE HUMILITY, THAT COPES WITH HUMAN SIN.—"He riseth from supper, and layeth aside His garments; and He took a towel and girded Himself." This is what the apostle calls taking upon Himself the form of a servant. The charm of the scene is its absolute simplicity. You cannot imagine Christ posturing to the ages. There was no aiming at effect, no thought of the beauty or humility of the act, as there is when the Pope yearly washes the feet of twelve beggars, from a golden basin, wiping them with a towel of rarest fabric! Christ did not act thus for show or pretence, but with an absolutely single purpose of fulfilling a needed office. And in this He set forth the spirit of our redemption.

This is the key to the Incarnation.—With slight alteration the words will read truly of that supreme act. He rose from the throne, laid aside the garments of light which He had worn as His vesture, took up the poor towel of humanity, and wrapped it about His glorious Person; poured His own blood into the basin of the Cross, and set Himself to wash away the foul stains of human depravity and guilt.

As pride was the source of human sin, Christ must needs provide an antidote in His absolute humility—a humility which could not grow beneath these skies, but must be brought from the world where the lowliest are the greatest, and the most childlike reign as kings.

This is the key to every act of daily cleansing.—We have been washed. Once, definitely, and irrevocably, we have been bathed in the crimson tide that flows from Calvary. But we need a daily cleansing. Our feet become soiled with the dust of life's highways; our hands grimy, as our linen beneath the rain of filth in a great city; our lips are fouled, as the white doorstep of the house, by the incessant throng of idle, unseemly and fretful words; our hearts cannot keep unsoiled the stainless robes with which we pass from the closet at morning prime. Constantly we need to repair to the Laver to be washed. But do we always realize how much each act of confession, on our part, involves from Christ, on His? Whatever important work He may at that moment have on hand; whatever directions He may be giving to the loftiest angels for the fulfillment of His purposes; however pressing the concerns of the Church or the universe upon His broad shoulders, He must needs turn from all these to do a work He will not delegate. Again

He stoops from the throne, and girds Himself with a towel, and, in all lowliness, endeavors to remove from thee and me the strain which His love dare not pass over. He never loses the print of the nail; He never forgets Calvary and the blood; He never spends one hour without stooping to do the most menial work of cleansing filthy souls. And it is because of this humility He sits on the Throne and wields the sceptre over hearts and worlds.

This is the key to our ministry to each other.—I have often thought that we do not often enough wash one another's feet. We are conscious of the imperfections which mar the characters of those around us. We are content to note, criticise, and learn them. We dare not attempt to remove them. This failure arises partly because we do not love with a love like Christ's—a love which will brave resentment, annoyance, rebuke, in its quest,—and partly because we are not willing to stoop low enough.

None can remove the mote of another, so long as the beam is left in the eye, and the sin unjudged in the life, None can cleanse the stain, who is not willing to take the form of a servant, and go down with bare knees upon the floor. None is able to restore those that are overtaken in a fault, who do not count themselves the chief of sinners and the least of saints.

We need more of this lowly, loving spirit: not so sensitive to wrong and evil as they affect us, as anxious for the stain they leave on the offender. It is of comparatively small consequence how much we suffer; it is of much importance that none of Christ's disciples should be allowed to go on for a moment longer, with unconfessed and unjudged wrongs clouding their peace, and hindering the testimony which they might give. Let us therefore watch for each other's souls: let us consider one another to provoke to love and good works; let us in all sincerity do as Christ has done, washing each other's feet in all humility and tender love. But this spirit is impossible save through fellowship with the Lamb of God, and the reception of His holy, humble nature into the inmost heart, by the Holy Ghost.

II

Thrice Bidden to Love

"A new commandment I give unto you, That ye love one another; as I have loved you, that ye also love one another."—JOHN xiii. 34.

Anacreon complains that when they asked him to sing of heroic deeds, he could only sing of love. But the love with which he fills his sonnets will bear as much comparison with that of which Jesus spoke in His last discourse, as the flaring oil of a country fair with the burning of the heavenly constellations. Even the love that binds young hearts is too selfish and exclusive to set forth that pure ray which shone from the heart of the Son of Man, and shines and will shine. What word shall we use to describe it?

Charity?—The disposition denoted by this great word does not fulfill the measure of the love of Christ. It is cold and severe. It can be organized. It casts its dole to the beggar and turns away, content to have relieved the sentiment of pity. By being employed for one manifestation of love, charity is too limited and restricted in its significance to become an adequate expression of the Divine love which Drought Jesus from the throne, and should inspire us to lay down our lives for the brethren.

Philanthropy?—This is a great word, "the love of man." And yet the philanthropist is too often content with the general patronage of good works, the elaboration of schemes, the management of committees, to do much personal work for the amelioration of the world. The word is altogether too distant, too deficient in the personal element, too extensive in its significance. It will not serve to represent the Divine compassion with which the heart of Christ was, at the moment of speaking, in tumult.

Complacency?—No; for this is the emotion excited by the contemplation of merit and virtue, which turns away from sin and deformity; and the sentiment denoted by our Master's words is one that is not brought into existence by virtue, nor extinguished by demerit and vice.

Since all these words fail, we are driven to speak of love, as Christ used the word, as being the essence of the Divine nature, for God is love. It is the indwelling of God in the soul. It is the transmitting through our lives of that which we have received in fellowship with the uncreated glory of the Divine Being. That which was in the beginning between the Father and the Son; that which constrained our Emmanuel to sojourn in this world of sin; that which inspired His sacrifice; that which dwells perennially in His heart, vanquishing time and distance; which overflows all expressions, and defies definition—is the love of which these words speak, and which we are commanded to entertain toward each other.

It is a commandment: "These things I command you." "This is His commandment: that we should believe in the name of His Son Jesus Christ, and love one another even as He gave us commandment." Obviously, then, obedience must be possible. Christ had gauged our nature not only as Creator, but by personal experience. He knew what was in man. The possibilities of our nature were well within His cognizance; therefore it must be possible for us to love one another qualitatively, if not quantitatively, as He has loved us. Do not sit down before this great command and say it is impossible; that were to throw discredit on Him who spake it. Dare to believe that no word of His is vain. He descries eminences of attainment which it is possible for us all to reach: let us surrender ourselves to Him, that He should fulfill in us His ideal, and make us experts in the science of love.

It is a new commandment.—Archbishop Ussher on a memorable occasion called it the eleventh. It is recorded that having heard of the simplicity and beauty of the ordering of Rutherford's home, he resolved to visit it for himself. One Saturday night he arrived alone at the Manse, and asked for entertainment over the next day. A simple but hearty welcome was accorded him; and after partaking of the frugal fare, he was invited to join the household in religious exercises which ushered in the Lord's day.

"How many commandments are there?" the master asked his guest, wholly unaware who he was.

"Eleven," was the astonishing reply; at which the very servants were scandalized, regarding the newcomer as a prodigy of ignorance. But the man of God perceived the rare light of character and insight which gleamed beneath the answer, and asked for a private interview. This issued in the invitation to preach on the following day. To the amazement of the household, so scandalized on the previous night, the stranger appeared in the master's pulpit, and announced the words on which we are meditating as his text, adding, "This may be described as the eleventh commandment."

Obedience to this fulfills the rest.—Love is the fulfilling of the law. Do we need to be told to have no other gods but God, to forbear taking His name in vain, and to devote one day in seven to the cultivation of a closer relationship with Him, if we love Him with all our soul and mind and strength? Do we need to be warned against killing our neighbor, stealing his goods, or bearing false witness against his character, if we love him as ourselves? Only let a man be filled with this divine disposition which is the unique characteristic of God; let him be filled with the spirit of love; let him be perfected in love, and, almost unconsciously, he will not only be kept from infringing the prohibitions of the law of Sinai, but will be inspired to fulfill the requirements of the Mount of Beatitudes. Love, and do as you like. You will like to do only what God would like you to do.

There is a very important purpose to be realized in obeying this command.—"By this shall all men know that ye are My disciples, if ye have love one to another." Every Church claims to be the true representative of Christ. The Eastern, because it occupies the lands where Christianity was cradled. The Roman Catholic, because it professes to be able to trace its orders to the apostles. But, amid the hubbub of rival claims, the world, unconvinced, still awaits the emergence of the true Bride of the Lamb. The one note of the true Church is Love. When once men of different nationalities and countries behold its manifestation, they do not hesitate to acknowledge the presence of God, and to admit that those who are animated by perfect love to Him and to one another constitute a unique organization, which cannot have originated in the will or intellect of man, but, like the New Jerusalem, must have come out of heaven from God. So sublime, so transcendent, so unearthly is love, that its presence is significant of the handiwork of God, as the fire that burned in the bush indicated that the "I AM" was there.

Love is a supreme test, not only of the Church, but of the individual. It has been the mistake of every age to make faith rather than love the test of Christianity. "Tell me how much a man believes, and I shall know how good a Christian he is!" The whole endeavor of the mediaeval Church was to reduce the followers of Christ to a uniformity of belief. And in our own time, a man is permitted by consent to be grasping after money, imperious in temper, uncharitable in speech, without losing position in the Church, so long as he assents to all the clauses of an orthodox creed.

With Christ, however, love is all-important. A man may have faith enough to remove mountains, but if he have not love, he is nothing, and lighter than vanity in the estimation of heaven. Faith ranks with hope and love, but it is destined to pass as the blossoms of spring before the fruit of autumn, whilst love shall abide forevermore. A man may have a very inadequate creed; like the woman of old, he may think there is virtue in a garment, or a rite; like Thomas, he may find it impossible to attain to the exuberant confidence of his brethren; but if he loves Christ enough to be prepared to die for Him, if through the narrow aperture of a very limited faith, love enough has entered his soul from the source of love, Christ will entrust him with the tending of His sheep and lambs, and call him into the secret place. Of course, the more full-orbed and intelligent our faith, the quicker and intenser will be our love. But faith, after all, is but the hand that takes, whilst love is the fellowship of kindred hearts that flash each on the other the enkindling gleam.

If you do not love, though you count yourself illumined with the light of perfect knowledge, you are in the dark. "He that hateth his brother is in the darkness, even until now."

If you do not love, you are dead. "He that loveth not, abideth in death." The light sparkle of intellectual or emotional life may light up your words, and fascinate your immediate circle of friends, but there will be no life toward God. Love is the perfect tense of live. Whoso does not love does not live, in the deepest sense. There are capacities for richer existence that never unfold until love stands at the portal and sounds his challenge, and summons the sleeper to awake and arise.

If you do not love, you are under the thrall of the devil, into whose dark nature love never comes. "Herein the children of God are manifest and the children of the devil. Cain was of the wicked one, and slew his brother."

"As I have loved you." Life is one long education to know the love of God. "We have known and believed the love that God hath to us," is the reflection of an old man reviewing the past. Each stage of life, each phase of experience, is intended to give us a deeper insight into the love wherewith we are loved; and as each discovery breaks upon our glad vision, we are bidden to exemplify it to others. Does Jesus forgive to the seventy-seventh time? We must forgive in the same measure. Does Jesus forget as well as forgive? We, too, must forgive after the same fashion. Does Jesus seek after the erring, and endeavor to induce the temper of mind that will crave forgiveness? We also must seek the man who has transgressed against us, endeavoring to lead him to a better mind. The Christian knows no law or limit but that imposed by these significant words, spoken on the eve of Christ's sacrifice, "As I have loved you."

Thus all life gives opportunities for the practice of this celestial temper and disposition. It has been said that talent develops in solitude, whilst character is made in the strain of life. Be it so. Then the character of loving may be made stronger by every association we have with our fellows. Each contact with men, women, and children, may give us an opportunity of loving with a little more of the strength, purity, and sweetness of the love of Christ. The busiest life can find time for the cultivation of this spirit. That which is spent in a crowd will even have greater opportunities than the one which is limited to solitude. The distractions and engagements that threaten to break our lives up to a number of inconsiderable fragments may thus conduce to a higher unity than could be gained by following one occupation, or concentrating ourselves on one object.

Let us gird up the loins of our minds, and resolve to seek a baptism of love from the Holy Ghost, that we may be perfected in love; that we may love God first, and all else in Him, ascending from our failures to a more complete conformity to the love wherewith He has loved us; embracing the sinful and erring in the compass of our compassion, as we embrace the Divine and Eternal in the compass of our adoration and devotion.

III

Heaven Delayed, but Guaranteed

"Simon Peter said unto Him, Lord, whither goest Thou? Jesus answered him. Whither I go, thou canst not follow Me now; but thou shalt follow Me afterward."—JOHN xiii. 36.

These chapters are holy ground. The last words of our dearest, spoken in the seclusion of the death-chamber to the tear-stained group gathered around, are not for all the world, and are recorded only to those whose love makes them able to appreciate. And what are these words that now begin to flow from the Master's lips, but His last to His own? They were held back so long as Judas was there. There was a repression caused by his presence which hindered the interchange of confidences; but, when he was gone, love hastened to her secret stores, and drew forth her choicest, rarest viands to share them, that they might be in after days a strength and solace.

 This marvellous discourse, which begins in chapter xiii. 31, continues through chapters xiv., xv., xvi., and closes in the sublime prayer of chapter xvii. Better that all the literature of the world should have shared the fate of the Alexandrian library, than that these precious words should have been lost amid the fret of the ages.

The Lord commences His discourse by speaking of His speedy departure. "Little children," He said, using a term which indicated that He felt toward them a parental tenderness, and spoke as a dying father might have done to the helpless babes that gathered around his bed, "I am to be with you for a very little time longer; the sand has nearly run out in the hour-glass. I know you will seek Me; your love will make you yearn to be with Me where I am, to continue the blessed intimacy, the ties which within the last few weeks have been drawn so much closer; but it will not be possible. As I said to the Jews, so must I say to you, Whither I go, ye cannot come." He then proceeds to give them a new commandment of love, as though He said: "The cannot which prevents you following Me now is due to a lack of perfect love on your part, as well as for other reasons; it is necessary, therefore, that you wait to acquire it, ere you can be with Me where I am."

Simon Peter hardly hears Him uttering these last words; he is pondering too deeply what he has just heard, and calls the Master back to that announcement, as though He had passed it with too light a tread: "Going away! Lord, whither goest Thou?" To that question our Lord might have given a direct answer: "Heaven! The Father's bosom! The New Jerusalem! The City of God!" Any of these would have been sufficient; but instead He says in effect: "It is a matter of comparative indifference whither I go; I have no wish to feed curiosity with descriptions of things in the heavens, which you could not understand. The main point for you, in this brief life, is so to become assimilated to Me in humility, devotion, likeness, and character, that you may be able to be My companion and friend in those new paths on which I am entering, as you have been in those which I am now leaving. "Whither I go, thou canst not follow Me now; but thou shalt follow Me afterward."

The words staggered Peter; he could not understand what Christ meant; he could not see how much had to be done before he could share in Christ's coming glory. He made the same mistake as James and John had done before, and wanted the throne, without perceiving that it was conditioned on fellowship in the cup and the baptism into death. With deep emotion he persisted in his inquiries: "Why cannot I follow Thee now? There is no place on earth to which I would not go with Thee. Have I not already left all to follow Thee? Have I not been with Thee on the Transfiguration Mount, as well as in Thy journeyings? There is but one experience through which I have not passed with Thee, and that is death; but if that stands next in Thy life-plan, I will lay down my life for Thy sake. Anything to be with Thee."

How little Peter knew himself! How much better did Christ know him. "What! dost thou profess thyself willing to die with Me? Verily, verily, I say unto thee, thou shalt deny Me thrice, between now and cock-crow to-morrow morning." These words silenced Peter for all the evening afterward. He does not appear to have made another remark, but was absorbed in heart-breaking grief: though all the while there rang in his heart those blessed words of hope: "Whither I go, thou canst not follow Me now; but thou shalt follow Me afterward"—words which our Lord caught up and expanded for the comfort of them all, who now with Peter for the first time realized that they were about to be parted from Jesus, and were almost beside themselves with grief: "Let not your heart be troubled. . . ."

I. THE DESIRE TO BE WITH CHRIST.—This was paramount. These simple men had little thought of heaven as such. If Christ had begun to speak of golden pavement, gates of pearl, and walls of chrysolite, they would have turned from His glowing words with the one inquiry, "Wilt Thou be there?" If that question had been answered uncertainly, they would have turned away heart-sick, saying: "If Thou art not there, we have no desire for it; but if Thou wert in the darkest, dreariest spot in the universe, it would be heaven to us."

There were three desires, the strands of which were woven in this one yearning desire and prayer to be with Christ. They wanted His love, His teaching, His leading into full, richer life. And is not this our position also? We want Christ, not hereafter only, but here and now, for these three self-same reasons.

We want His love.—There is no love like His—so pure and constant and satisfying. What the sun is to a star-light, and the ocean to a pool left by the retiring tide, such is the love of Jesus compared with all other love. To have it is superlative blessedness; to miss it is to thirst forever.

We want His light.—He speaks words that cast light on the mysteries of existence, on the dark problems of life, on the perplexing questions which are perpetually knocking at our doors.

We want His life.—Fuller and more abundant life is what we crave. It is of life that our veins are scant. We desire to have the mighty tides of divine life always beating strongly within us, to know the energy, vigor, vitality of God's life in the soul. And we are conscious that this is to be found only in Him.

Therefore we desire to be with Him, to drink deeper into His fellowship, to know Him and the power of His resurrection, to be brought into an abidingness from which we shall never recede. We have known Christ after the flesh; we desire to know Him after the Spirit. We have known Him in humiliation; we want to know Him in His glory. We have known Him as the Lamb of the Cross; we want to know Him as the Divine Man on the throne.

II. THE FATAL OBSTACLE TO THE IMMEDIATE GRANTING OF THESE DESIRES.— "Thou canst not follow Me now." There is thus a difference in His words to His disciples, and those to the Jews. These also were told that they could not follow Him, but the word now was omitted. There was no hope held out to them of the great gulf being bridged. That was the cannot of moral incompatibility; this, of temporary unfitness, which by the grace of God would finally pass away, and the whole of their aspirations be realized (John vii. 34; viii. 21).

It is easy to see why Peter was unfit for the deeper realization of Christ in His resurrection. Our Lord had just spoken of being glorified through death. It was as Judas left the chamber, intent on his betrayal, that Jesus said, "Now is the Son of Man glorified!" He saw that the hidden properties of His being could only be unfolded and uttered through death and resurrection. But Peter had little sympathy with this; he might avow his determination to die, but he had never really entered into the meaning of death, and all it might involve.

He could not detect evil. The traitor was beside him; but he had to ask the beloved disciple to elicit from Jesus who it might be by whom the Master would be betrayed.

He was out of sympathy with the Lord's humiliation, so that he chode with Him for stooping to wash his feet; and if he could not understand the significance and necessity of this lowly deed of love, how could he enter into the spirit of that life which was planted in death, and which bore even in resurrection the print of the nails?

He strove with the rest for the primacy. Who should be the greatest? was the question that agitated them, as the other evangelists tell us, in that solemn hour. And none that was possessed with that spirit of pride and emulation could be in harmony with that blessed world where the greatest are the lowliest, the highest the least, and the King set on the right hand of power, because more capable of humbling Himself than any beside.

But, besides all this, Peter was animated by the strong spirit of self-assertion and determination. Always on the lake shore he had been able to get to the front by his stronger voice, and broader shoulders, and more vehement manner. Why should he not do the same now? Why could he not keep pace with Christ even through the dark valley, and accompany Him through unknown worlds?

✳ It cannot be, said Christ; you are too strong in your carnal strength, too self-reliant, too confident. It is not possible for you to be with Me, in the life that springs from death, and to which death is the door, till you have deeply drunk into the spirit of My death. You are too strong to follow Me when I descend to the lowest on My way to the highest; I must take for My companion now a forgiven malefactor; but I will some day come for you, and receive you to Myself.

So Peter had to be broken on the wheel of a servant-girl's question, and humbled to the dust. In those bitter hours he was thoroughly emptied of his old proud, self-reliant, vain-glorious spirit, and became as a little child.

This must be our path also. We must descend with Christ, if we would ascend to sit at His side. We must submit to the laying of our pride in the very dust. We must accept humiliations and mortifications, the humblings of perpetual failure and shortcoming, the friction and fret of infirmity and pain; and when we have come to an end of ourselves, we shall begin to know Christ in a new and deeper fashion. He will pass by and say, "Live!" The spirit of His life will enter into us; the valley of Achor will become a door of hope, and we shall sing God's glad new song of Hope. The ideal which had long haunted us, in our blood, but unable to express itself, will burst into a perfect flower of exquisite scent and hue.

III. THE CERTAINTY OF THE ULTIMATE GRATIFICATION OF EVERY DESIRE GOD HAS IMPLANTED.—This is an absolute certainty, that God inserts no desire or craving in our nature, for which there is no appropriate gratification. The birds do not seek for food which is not ready for them. The young lions do not ask for prey that is not awaiting them somewhere in the forest glade. Hence the absoluteness of that shall—"Thou shalt follow Me afterward." It is as if Jesus said, "I have taught you to love Me, and long after Me; and I will certainly gratify the appetite which I have created."

Pentecost was the Divine fulfillment of all those conditions of which we have been speaking. It was not enough that Peter should be an emptied and broken man; he must become also a God-possessed, a Spirit-filled man. Thus only could he be fitted to know Christ after a spiritual sort, and to participate in His Resurrection Life. It was surely to the Advent of the Holy Ghost that our Lord referred in that significant afterward.

We too must seek our share in Pentecost. Do not be content with "Not I"; go on to say, "but Christ." Do not be satisfied with the emptying of the proud self-life; seek the infilling of the Holy Spirit. Do not stop at the cross, or the grave; hasten to the upper room, where the disciples are baptized in fire and glory. The Holy Spirit will enable you to abide in Christ, because He will bring Christ to abide in you; and life, through His dear grace, shall be so utterly imbued with fellowship with the blessed Lord, that, whether present or absent, you will live together with Him. It is the man who is really filled with the Spirit of God who can follow Jesus, as Peter afterward did, to prison and to death, who can drink of the cup of which He drank, and be baptized with the baptism with which He was baptized.

"Why should I fear?" asked Basil, of the Roman prefect. "Nothing you have spoken of has any effect upon me. He that hath nothing to lose is not afraid of confiscation. You cannot banish me, for the earth is the Lord's. As to torture, the first stroke would kill me, and to kill me is to send me to glory."

IV

"Many Mansions"

"I go to prepare a place for you."—JOHN xiv. 2.

The cure for heart-trouble, when the future is full of dread, is faith—faith directed to Jesus; and just such faith as we give God, for He is God. He has shown Himself well worthy of that trust; all His paths toward us have been mercy and truth; and we may therefore safely rest upon His disclosures of that blessed life, of which the present is the vestibule. "Let not your heart be troubled," He says, "ye believe in God, believe also in Me." Or it might be rendered, "Believe in God, believe also in Me."

Let us listen to Him, as He discourses of the Father's house and its many mansions.

Heaven is a home.—"My Father's house." What magic power lies in that word! It will draw the wanderer from the ends of the earth; will nerve the sailor, soldier, and explorer with indomitable endurance; will bring a mist of tears to the eyes of the hardened criminal, and soften the heart of stone. One night in the trenches of the Crimea the bands played "Home, sweet Home," and a great sob went through the army.

But what makes home home? Not the mere locality or building; but the dear ones that lived there once, now scattered never to be reunited, only one or two of whom are still spared. It was father's house, though it was only a shepherd's shieling; he dwelt there, and mother, and our brothers and sisters. And where they dwell, or where wife and child dwell, there is home.

Such is Heaven. Think of a large family of noble children, of all ages, from the little child to the young man beginning his business career, returning after long severance to spend a season together in the old ancestral home, situated in its far-reaching grounds, and you can form some idea of what it will be, when the whole Family of the Redeemed gather in the Father's house. All reserve, all shyness, all restraint gone forever. God has given us all the memory of what home was, that we may guess at what awaits us, and be smitten with homesickness. As the German proverb puts it: "Blessed are the homesick, for they shall reach home."

Heaven is very spacious.—There are "many mansions." There is no stint in its accommodation. In the olden Temple there were spacious courts, long corridors, and innumerable chambers, in which a vast multitude could find a home day and night. The children trooped about and sang around their favorite teacher. The blind and lame sheltered themselves from heat or storm. The priests and Levites in great numbers lived there. All of this probably suggested the Master's words.

Heaven too will contain immense throngs, without being crowded. It will teem with innumerable hosts of angels, and multitudes of the redeemed which no man can number. Its children will be as the grains of sand that bar the ocean's waves, or the stars that begem the vault of night. But it can easily hold these, and myriads more. Yet there is room! As age after age has poured in its crowds, still the cry has gone forth, There is still room! The many mansions are not all tenanted. The orchestra is not full. The complement of priests is not complete.

Do not believe those little souls, who would make you believe that

Heaven is a little place for a select few. If they come to you with that story, tell them to begone! tell them that they do not know your Father's heart; tell them that all He does must be worthy of Himself. Jesus shall see of the travail of His soul, and be satisfied.

Heaven is full of variety.—It is not like one great hall; there are myriads of adjacent rooms, "mansions," which will be fitted up, so to speak, differently. One for the sweet singer, another for the little ones and their teachers, another for the student of the deep mysteries of the Kingdom, another for those who may need further instruction in the mysteries of God.

Heaven's life and scenery are as various as the aptitudes and capacities of souls. Its music is not a monotone, but a chorale. It is as a home, where the parents delight to develop the special tastes of their children. This is surely what Jesus meant when He said, "I go to prepare a place for you." He is ever studying our special idiosyncrasies—what we need most, and can do best; and when He has ascertained it, He suits our mansion accordingly.

When a gardener is about to receive some rare exotic, he prepares a place where it will flower and fruit to the best advantage. The naturalist who is notified of the shipment of some new specimen, prepares a habitat as suited as possible to its peculiarities. The mother, whose son is returning from sea, prepares a room in which his favorite books and pictures are carefully placed, and all else that her pondering heart can devise to give him pleasure. So our Lord is anxious to give what is best in us its most suitable nourishment and training. And He will keep our place against our coming. It will not suit another, and will not be given to another.

That all this will be so, is witnessed by the instincts of our hearts, and if it had not been so, He would have told us. That little clause is inimitably beautiful; it seems to teach that where He permits His children to cherish some natural presentiment of the blessed future—its solemn troops and sweet societies; its friendships, recognitions, and fellowships; its holy service, and special opportunities—that He really assents to our deepest and most cherished thoughts. If it had not been so, He would have told us.

The charm of Heaven will be the Lord's presence.—"Where I am, ye shall be also." We shall see His face, and be forever with Him. What would not men give, if some old manuscripts might turn up with new stories of His wondrous life, new parables as charming as those of the Good Shepherd and the Prodigal Son; new beatitudes; new discourses like that on the Vine. God might have permitted this. But what would it be in comparison with all that lies before! The past has lost much; but the future holds infinitely more. We shall see new Gospels enacted before our eyes, behold Christ as a real visible person in the glory of Divine manhood, hear Him speak to us as His friends, and shall know what He meant when He promised to gird Himself, and come forth to serve His servants.

If you are in doubt as to what Heaven is like, is it not enough to know that it will be in accord with the nature and presence and choice of Jesus Christ?

After His resurrection, He spent forty days among His disciples, that men might see what the risen life was like. As He was, and is, so shall we be. His body is the pattern in accordance to which this shall be fashioned. What He was to His friends after His resurrection, we shall be to ours, and they to us. We shall hear the familiar voices and the dear old names, shall resume the dear relationships which death severed, and shall speak again of the holy secrets of our hearts with those who were our twin-spirits.

And He will come again, either in our death hour or in His Second Advent, "to receive us" to Himself. If we only could believe this, and trust Him who says it, our hearts could not be troubled, though death itself menaced us; for we should realize, that to be received at the moment of dissolution by the hands of Jesus, into the place on which He has lavished time and thought and love, must be "far better" than the best that earth could offer.

V

The Reality of which Jacob's Dream was the Shadow

"Jesus saith unto him, I am the way, the truth, and the life; no man cometh unto the Father, but by Me."—JOHN xiv. 6.

We all know more truth than we give ourselves credit for. A moment before the Lord had said, "Whither I go ye know, and the way ye know." Thomas, the pessimist—always inclined to look at the dark side of things—directly contradicted Him, saying, "Master, we are absolutely ignorant of the goal to which Thy steps are bending; it is impossible, therefore, for us to know the path that lies through the gloom, and by which Thou art to come to it." It was a strange collision, the Master's "Ye know," and Thomas's "We know not." Which was right?

There is no doubt that Jesus was right, and they did know. In many a discourse He had given sufficient materials for them to construct a true conception of the Father's house, and the way to it. These materials were lying in some dusty corner of their memory, unused, and Christ knew this. He said, therefore, in effect, "Go back to the teachings I have given you; look carefully through the inventory of your knowledge; let your instincts, illumined by My words, supply the information you need: there are torches in your souls already lighted, that will cast a radiant glow upon the mysteries to the brink of which you have come."

This is true of us all. Christ never conducts to experiences for which He has not previously prepared us. As the great ocean-steamers take in their stores of coal and provision, day and night, for weeks previous to their sailing; so, by insensible influences, Christ is ever anticipating the strain and stress of coming circumstance, passing in words which are spirit and life, though they may stand in their heavy packing-cases in the hold, until we are driven to unpack, examine, and use their contents. Not unseldom sorrow is sent for no other purpose than to compel us to take cognizance of our possessions. Many a fabric of manufacture, many an article of diet, many an ingenious process has been suggested in days of scarcity and famine. So, old words and truths come back in our sore need. Christ often speaks to us, as a teacher to a nervous child, saying, "You know quite well, if you would only think a little." More truth is stored in memory than recollection can readily lay hands upon.

Thomas persisted in his protestations of ignorance, and so the Lord uttered for his further information the royal sentence, which sums up Christianity in the one simple pronoun "I." It was as if He said to His disciples gathered there, and to His Church in all ages, "To have Me, to know Me, to love and obey Me, this is religion; this is the light for every dark hour, the solution for all the mysteries." Christianity is more than a creed, a doctrinal system, a code of rules—it is Christ.

I. CHRIST, AS THE WAY.—"I am the Way," said our Lord. The conception of life as a pilgrimage is as old as human speech. On the third page of our Bibles we are told that "Enoch walked with God." The path of the Israelites through the desert was a pilgrim's progress, and the enduring metaphor for our passage from the cross to the Sabbath-keeping. Isaiah anticipated the rearing up of a highway which should be called the way of holiness, which should not be trodden by the unclean; no lion should be there, or ravenous beast go up thereon; but the ransomed of the

Lord should walk there, and go with singing to Zion. But in the furthest flights of inspired imagination, the prophet never dreamed that God Himself would stoop to become the trodden path to Himself, and that the way of holiness was no other than that Divine Servant who so often stood before Him for portrayal. "I am the way," said Christ.

He fulfills all the conditions of Isaiah's prediction.

He saw a highway. A highway is for all: for kings and commoners; for the nobleman daintily picking his way, and the beggar painfully plodding with bare feet. And Jesus is for every man. "Whosoever will, let him come"; let him step out and walk; let him commit himself to Him who comes to our doors that He may conduct us to the pearly gate.

It was a way of holiness, where no unclean or leprous person was permitted to travel. Neither can we avail ourselves of the gracious help of Christ, so long as we are harboring what He disapproves, or doing what He forbids.

It was so plain and straight, that wayfaring men though fools could not mistake it. And the Master said, that whilst the wise and prudent might miss His salvation, babes would find it. "Hidden from the wise and prudent, but revealed to babes."

It afforded perfect immunity from harm. The wild beasts of the forest might roar around it, but they were kept off that thoroughfare by an invisible and impassable fence. Who is he that can harm us whilst we follow that which is good? The special Divine permission was necessary, before Satan could tempt Job, whose heart was perfect with his God.

It was trodden with song. And who can describe the waves of joy that sometimes roll in on the believing, loving soul. There is always peace, but sometimes there is joy unspeakable and full of glory. The hands of Jesus shed the oil of gladness on our heads, whilst the lamentation and regret that haunt the lives of others are abashed, as the spectres of the night before the roseate touch of morn.

What further thought did Christ mean to convey, when He said, "I am the Way"? We cannot see the other side of the moon. The full import of these words, as they touch His wonderful nature, as it lies between Him and His Father, is beyond us; but we may at least study the face they turn toward our lives.

The true value of a way is never realized until we are following it through an unknown country, or groping along it in almost absolute darkness. I remember, during a tour in Switzerland, on starting for a long day's march, the comfort of the assurance that I had only to keep to one road which was clearly defined, and it would inevitably bring me to my destination. How different this to another experience of making my way, as I might, across the hillsides in the direction which I fancied was the right one! All that had to be done in the first instance was to follow the roadway, to obey its sinuous windings, to climb the hills where it climbed, to descend the valleys where it descended, to cross the rivers and torrents at the precise point with it. It seemed responsible for me as long as I kept to it. Whenever I thought to better myself by wandering right or left, I found myself landed in some difficulty, and when I returned to it, it seemed to say, "Why did you leave me? I know that sometimes I am rough and difficult; but I can do better for you, than you can for yourself, and indeed I am the only possible way. Obey me, and I will bring you home." It is so that Christ speaks to us.

Each day, as we leave our home, we know that the prepared path lies before us, in the good works which God has prepared for us to walk in. And when we are ignorant of their direction, and are at a loss as to where to place our steps, we have only to concern ourselves with Christ, and almost unconsciously we shall find ourselves making progress on the destined way. Christ is the Way: love Christ, trust Christ, obey Christ, be concerned with Christ, and all else will be added. Christ is the Way. When the heart is wrapped up in Him, it is on the way, and it is making progress, although it never counts the rate or distance, so occupied is it with Him.

"I fear I make no progress," sighs the timid soul.

"But what is Christ to thee?"

"Everything."

"Then if He be all in all to thee, thou art most certainly on God's way; and thou art making progress toward thy home, albeit that it is unconsciously. Be of good cheer, Christ is the Way; remember the ancient pilgrims, of whom it is written, that the way was in their hearts."

"But God the Father is so little to me!"

"But to deal with Christ is to deal with God: to be wrapped up in the love of Christ is to make ever deeper discoveries into the heart of God. He is the Way to God: to know Him is to come to the Father."

II. CHRIST AS THE TRUTH.—The thought grows deeper as we advance. Obedience to the Way conducts to the vision of the Truth; ethics to spiritual optics. The truth-seeker must first submit himself in all humility and obedience to Christ; and when he is willing to do His will, he is permitted to know.

(1) Christ is more than a teacher. "We know that Thou art a Teacher, come from God," said Nicodemus. He is more, He is the Truth of God. All truth is ensphered in Him. All the mysteries of wisdom and knowledge are hidden in Him. We fully know truth only as it is in Jesus. When the Spirit of Truth would lead us into all truth, He can do nothing better than take of the things of Christ, and reveal them to us, because to know Christ is to know the Truth in its most complete, most convenient, and most accessible form. If you know nothing else, and know Christ intimately and fully, you will know the Truth, and the Truth will make you free. If you love truth, and are a child of the truth, you will be inevitably attracted to Christ, and recognize the truth that speaks through His glorious nature. "He that is of the truth heareth My voice."

(2) Distinguish between Christ the Truth, and truth about Him. Many true things may be said about Him; but we are not saved by truths about Him, but by Himself the Truth.

Not the indubitable fact that Jesus died; but the Person of Him who died and lives forevermore. Not the certain fact that Jesus lay in the grave; but the blessed Man

Himself, who lay there for me.

Not the incontestable facts of His resurrection and ascension; but that He has borne my nature to the midst of the throne, and has achieved a victory which helps me in my daily struggle.

This is the ground basis of all true saving faith. The soul may accept truths about Christ, as it would any well-authenticated historical fact; but it is not materially benefited or saved until it has come to rest on the bosom of Him of whom these facts are recorded.

(3) To know Christ as Truth demands truth in heart and life. The insincere man; the trifler; the flippant jester who takes nothing seriously; the superficial man who uses the deepest expressions, as counters for society talk; the inconsistent man who is daily doing violence to his convictions, by permitting things which his conscience condemns—must stand forever on the outskirts of the Temple of Truth: they have no right to stand before the King of Truth. If you have never discerned the truth as it is in Jesus, it becomes a serious question whether you are perfectly true, or whether you are not, like Pilate, harboring insincerity in your heart, which blinds your eyes to His ineffable attributes.

(4) Concern yourself with Christ. Be content to let the world and its wisdom alone. "The wisdom of this world is foolishness with God . . . He taketh the wise in their own craftiness." Give yourself to know Christ, who is made unto us wisdom, as well as sanctification and redemption. To know Him is to be at the fountain-head of all truth; and the soul which has dwelt with Him by day and night will find itself, not only inspired by an undying love for the true, but will be able to hold fellowship with truth-lovers and truth-seekers everywhere; nay, will be able even to instruct those who have the reputation of great learning and knowledge in the schools of human thought. "I have more understanding than all my teachers; for Thy testimonies are my meditation. I understand more than the aged, because I have kept Thy precepts." To know and to possess Christ, is to have the Word, that is the Wisdom of God, enshrined as a most sacred possession in the heart.

III. CHRIST AS THE LIFE.—It is not enough to know; we need life. Life is, indeed, the gate to knowledge. "This is life eternal that they should know Thee." It was imperative, therefore, that Jesus should become a source of life to men, that they might know the Truth, and be able to walk in the Way, and more especially since death had infected and exhausted all the springs of the world's vitality.

It was into a world of death that the Son of God came. The spring of life in our first parents had become tainted at its source. At the best Adam was only a living soul. Dead—dead—dead in trespasses and sins; such was the Divine verdict, such the course of this world. Earth resembled the valley in the prophet's vision, full of bones, very many and very dry. All the reservoirs of life were spent; its fountains had died away in wastes of sand.

Then the Son of God brought life from the eternal throne, from God Himself; and became a Life-giving Spirit. His words were spirit and life: He was Himself the Resurrection and the Life: those that believed in Him became partakers of the Divine Nature. The tree of life was again planted on the earth's soil, when Jesus became incarnate. "I give eternal life unto My sheep," He said, "and they shall never perish." "He that believeth on the Son hath eternal life."

If, then, you are wanting life, and life more abundantly, you must have Christ. Do not seek it, but Him: not the stream but the fountain; not the word, but the speaker; not the fruit, but the tree. He is the Life and Light of men.

And if you have Christ you have life. You may not be competent to define or analyze it; you may not be able to specify the place or time, when it first broke into your soul; you may hardly be able to distinguish it from the workings of your own life: but if you have Christ, trust Christ, desire Christ above all, you have the Life. "He that hath the Son hath the Life; he that hath not the Son of God hath not the Life." "We know Him that is true, and we are in Him that is true . . . this is eternal life." "I," said Jesus, "am the Way, the Truth, and the Life."

VI

Christ Revealing the Father

"Philip saith unto Him, Lord, shew us the Father and it sufficeth us. Jesus saith unto him, He that hath seen Me hath seen the Father."—JOHN xiv. 8, 9.

The longing of the universal heart of man was voiced by Philip, when he broke in, rather abruptly, on our Lord's discourse with the challenge that He should answer all questions, dissipate all doubt, by showing them the Father. Is there a God? how can I be sure that He is? what does He feel toward us?—these are questions which men persistently ask, and wait for the reply. And the Master gave the only satisfactory answer that has ever been uttered in the hearing of mankind, when He said in effect, "The knowledge of God must be conveyed, not in words or books, in symbols or types, but in a life. To know Me, to believe in Me, to come into contact with Me, is to know the deepest heart of God. 'He that hath seen Me hath seen the Father; how sayest thou then, Show us the Father?'"

I. PHILIP'S INQUIRY.—It bore witness to the possible growth of the human soul. Only three short years before, as we are told in the first chapter of this Gospel, Christ had found him. At that time he was probably much as the young men of his age and standing. Not specially remarkable save for an interest in, and an earnestness about, the advent of the Messiah; his views, however, of his person and work were limited and narrow: he looked for his advent as the time for the reëstablishment of the kingdom of David, and deliverance from the Roman yoke. But three years of fellowship with Jesus had made a wonderful difference in this young disciple. The deepest mysteries of life and death and heaven seemed within his reach. He is not now content with beholding the Messiah, he is eager to know the Father, and to stand within the inner circle of His presence-chamber.

The highest watermark ever touched by the great soul of Moses was when he said, amid the sublimities of Sinai, "I beseech Thee, show me Thy glory." But in this aspiration Philip stands beside him. There is a close kinship between the mighty lawgiver and the fishermen of Bethsaida. How little there is to choose between, "Show me Thy glory," and "Show us the Father." Great and marvellous is the capacity of the soul for growth!

It truly interpreted the need of man.—"It sufficeth us." From nature, with all her voices that speak of God's power and Godhead; from the page of history, indented with the print of God's footprints; from type and ceremony and temple, though instituted by God Himself; even from the unrivalled beauty of our Saviour's earthly life—these men turned unsatisfied, unfilled, and said, "We are not yet content, but if Thou wouldest show us the Father, we should be."

And would it not suffice us?—Would it not be sufficient to give new zest and reality to prayer, if we could realize that it might be as familiar as the talk of home, or like the petitioning of a little child? Would it not suffice to make the most irksome work pleasant, if we could look up and discern the Father's good pleasure and smile of approval? Would it not suffice to rob pain of its sting, if we could detect the Father's hands adjusting the heat of the furnace? Would it not suffice to shed a light across the dark mystery of death, if we felt that the Father was waiting to lead us through the shadows to Himself? How often the cry rises from sad and almost despairing hearts, "Show us the Father, and it sufficeth us."

But surely this request was based on a mistake.—Philip wanted a visible theophany, like that which Moses beheld, when the majestic procession swept down the mountain pass; or as the elders saw, when they beheld the paved sapphire work; or after the fashion of the visions vouchsafed to Elijah, Isaiah, or Ezekiel. He wanted to see the Father. But how can you make wisdom, or love, or purity visible, save in a human life?

Yet this is the mistake we are all liable to make. We feel that there must be an experience, a vision, a burst of light, a sensible manifestation, before we can know the Father. We strain after some unique and extraordinary presentation of the Deity, especially in the aspect of Fatherhood, before we can be completely satisfied, and thus we miss the lesson of the present hour. Philip was so absorbed in his quest for the transcendent and sublime, that he missed the revelations of the Father which for three years had been passing under his eyes. God had been manifesting His tenderest and most characteristic attributes by the beauty of the Master's life, but Philip had failed to discern them; till now the Master bids him go back on the photographs of those years, as fixed in his memory, to see in a thousand tiny illustrations how truly the Father dwelt in Him, and lived through His every word and work.

Are you straining after the vision of God, startled by every footstep, intently listening till the very atmosphere shall become audible, expecting an overwhelming spectacle? In all likelihood you will miss all. The kingdom comes not with outward show. When men expected Christ to come by the front door, He stole in at the back. Whilst Philip was waiting for the Father to be shown in thunder and lightning, in startling splendor, in the stately majesty that might become the Highest, he missed the daily unfolding of the Divine Nature that was being afforded in the Life with which he dwelt in daily contact.

Philip's request emphasized the urgent need of the ministry of the Holy Spirit.—"If ye had known Me". . . the Saviour said. "Have I been so long time with you, and yet hast thou not known Me?" They failed to know the Father, because they failed to know Christ, and they failed in this because they knew Him only after the flesh. They were so familiar with Him as their Friend, His love was so natural, tender, and human, He had become so closely identified with all their daily existence, that they did not recognize the fire that shone behind the porcelain, the Deity that tabernacled beneath the frail curtains.

Often those who dwell amid the loveliest or grandest scenery miss the beauty which is unveiled to strangers from a distance. Certain lives have to be withdrawn from us before we understand how fair they were, and how much to us. And Jesus had to leave His disciples before they could properly appreciate Him. The Holy Spirit must needs take of the things of Christ, and reveal them, before they could realize their true significance, symmetry, and beauty.

Two things are needful, then: first, we must know Christ through the teaching of the Holy Ghost; and next, we must receive Him into our hearts, that we may know Him, as we know the workings of our own hearts. Each knows himself, and could recognize the mint-mark of his own individuality; so when Christ has become resident within us, and has taken the place of our self-life, we know Him as we know ourselves. "What man knoweth the things of man save the spirit of man which is in him?—but we have the mind of Christ?"

II. THE LORD'S REPLY.—"He that hath seen Me, hath seen the Father."

He did not rebuke the request, as unfit to proffer, or impossible to satisfy. He took it for granted that such a desire would exist in the heart, and that His disciples would always want to be led by Him into the Father's presence. In this His ministry resembled that of the great forerunner, who led His disciples into the presence of the Bridegroom, content to decrease if only He might increase. The Master's answer was, however, widely different from John's. The forerunner pointed to Jesus as He walked, and said, "Behold the Lamb of God"; Jesus pointed to Himself, and said, "I and My Father are One; to have seen Me is to have seen the Father; to have Me is to possess the Father."

It troubled the Lord greatly that He had been so long time with them, and yet they had not known Him; that they had not realized the source of His words and works; that they had concentrated their thought on Him, instead of passing, as He meant them to do, from the stream to the source, from the die to the seal, from the beam of the Divine Glory to its Sun. He bade them, therefore, from that moment realize that they knew and had seen the Father in knowing and seeing Himself. Not more surely had the Shechinah dwelt in the tabernacle of old, than did it indwell His nature, though too thickly shrouded to be seen by ordinary and casual eyes.

Let us get help from this. Many complain that they know Christ, pray to Christ, are conscious of Christ, but that the Father is far away and impalpable. They are therefore straining after some new vision or experience of God, and undervaluing the religious life to which they have already attained. It is a profound mistake. To have Jesus is to have God; to know Jesus is to know God; to pray to Jesus is to pray to God. Jesus is God manifest in the flesh. Look up to Him even now from this printed page, and say, "My Lord and my God."

Jesus is not simply an incarnation of God in the sense in which, after the fashion of the Greek mythology, gods might come down in the likeness of men, adopting a disguise which they would afterward cast aside; Jesus is God. All the gentle attributes of His nature are God's; and all the strong and awful attributes of power, justice, purity, which we are wont to associate with God, are His also.

Happy is the moment when we awake to realize that in Jesus we have God manifest and present; to know this is the revelation of the Father by the Son, of which our Saviour spoke in Matt. xi. 27.

III. A GLIMPSE INTO THE LORD'S INNER LIFE.—This Gospel is the most lucid and profound treatise in existence on His inner life. It is the revelation of the principles on which our Saviour lived.

So absolutely had He emptied Himself that He never spake His own words: "The words that I speak unto you, I speak not of Myself." He never did His own works: "My Father worketh hitherto, and I work. . . . The Father abiding in Me doeth His works." This was the result of that marvellous self-emptying of which the Apostle speaks. Our Lord speaks as though, in His human nature, He had a choice and will of His own. "Not My will, but Thine be done," was His prayer. Perhaps it was to this holy and divine personality that Satan made appeal in the first temptation, bidding Him use His powers for the satisfaction of His hunger, and in independence of His Father's appointment. But however much of this independence was within our Lord's reach, He deliberately laid it aside. Before He spoke, His spirit opened itself to the Father, that He might speak by His lips; before He acted. He stilled the promptings of His own wisdom, and lifted Himself into the presence of the Father, to ascertain what He was doing, and to receive the inflow of His energy (John v. 19; xii. 44, 49).

These are great mysteries, which will engage our further consideration. In the meanwhile, let us reason that if our Lord was so careful to subordinate Himself to the Father that He might be all in all, it well becomes us to restrain ourselves, to abstain from speaking our own words or doing our own works, that Jesus may pour His energies through our being, and that those searching words may be fulfilled in us also, "Striving according to His working, which worketh in Me mightily."

VII

The Great Deeds of Prayer

"Verily, verily, I say unto you, He that believeth on Me, the works that I do shall he do also; and greater works than these shall he do; because I go unto My Father."—JOHN xiv. 12.

Whenever our Lord was about to say something usually important, He introduced it by the significant expression, "Verily, verily"; or, as it is in the original, "Amen, amen, I say unto you." The words well become His lips, who in the Book of Revelation is called "the Amen, the Faithful and True Witness." They are really our Lord's most solemn affirmation of the truth of what He was about to utter, as well as an indication that something of importance is about to be revealed.

Indeed, it was necessary in the present case that the marvellous announcement of the text should receive unusual confirmation, because of its wide extent. If our Lord had ascribed this power of doing greater works than Himself in His earthly life, to apostle, prophet, or illustrious saint, we should have required no special assurance of its deliberate truth; but to learn that powers so transcendent are within the reach of any ordinary believer, to learn that any one who believes may outdo the miracles on the outskirts of Nain, and at the tomb of Bethany, is as startling as it is comforting. There is no reason why the humblest soul that ponders this page should not become the medium and vehicle through which the Christ of the glory shall not surpass the Christ of Galilee, Jerusalem, and Judea.

The best method of treating these words is to take them clause by clause as they stand.

I. THE FIRST NOTE IS FAITH.—"He that believeth on Me." Three varieties of faith are alluded to in the context. Faith in His works: "Believe the works." Faith in His words: "Believe Me." Faith in Himself, as here. In the Greek the preposition translated in, would be better rendered into, as though the believer was ever approaching the heart of Christ in deeper, warmer, closer fellowship; perpetual motion toward, combined with unbroken rest in. Each of these three forms of faith plays an important part in the Christian life.

Arrested by the works of Christ—His irresistible power over nature, His tender pity for those who sought His aid, the blessed and far-reaching results of His miracles—we cry with Nicodemus, "Verily, this is a Teacher come from God; for none can do such miracles, except God be with him." The Master perpetually appealed to the witness borne by His works to His Divine mission, as when He said, "If I had not done among them the works which none other did, they had not had sin, but now have they both seen and hated both Me and My Father." And again, "The very works that I do bear witness of Me." But at the best the works of Christ are only like the great bell ringing in the church-tower calling attention to the life being unfolded within, and are not calculated to induce the faith to which the greater works are possible.

Next we come to the words of Christ. They are spirit and life: they greatly feed the soul. He speaks as none other has ever spoken of the mysteries of life, death, God, and eternity. It is through the words that we come to the Speaker. By feeding on them we are led into vital union with Himself. But His words, as such, and apart from Him, will not produce works that shall surpass those He wrought in His earthly ministry.

Therefore from works and words we come to the Lord Himself with a trust which passes up beyond the lower ranges of faith; which does not simply receive what He waits to give, or reckon upon His faithfulness, but which unites us in indissoluble union with Himself. This is the highest function of faith; it is unitive: it welds us in living union with our Lord, so that we are one with Him, as He is one with God.

We are in Him in the Divine purpose which chose us in Him before the foundation of the world; grafted into Him in His cross; partaking of a common life with Him through the regeneration of the Holy Ghost. But all these become operative in the union wrought by a living faith; so that the strongest assertions which Jesus made of the close relationship between His Father and Himself become the current coin of holy speech, as they precisely describe the union which subsists between us and Jesus. The living Saviour has sent us, and we live by the Saviour. The words we speak are not from ourselves, but the Saviour within us, He doeth His works. We are in Him and He in us, all ours are His, and His ours.

Stay, reader, and ask thyself whether thou hast this faith which incorporates thee with the Man who died for thee on the cross, and now occupies the Throne, the last Adam who has become a life-giving Spirit.

II. A TRUE FAITH ALWAYS WORKS.—"He that believeth in Me, the works that I do shall He do also."

There are many counterfeits of faith in the world. Electroplate! veneer! They will inevitably fail in the last supreme test, if not before. James especially calls attention to the distinction between a living and a dead faith. It becomes us to be on our guard.

The test of genuine faith are twofold. In the first place, a genuine, living faith has Christ for its object. The hand may tremble, but it touches His garment's hem; the eye may be dimmed by doubt, but it is directed toward His face; the feet may stumble, but as the fainting pilgrim staggers onward, this is his repeated cry, "Thou, O Christ, art all I want."

In the second place, a true faith works. Its works approve its nature, and show that it has reached the heart of Christ, and becomes the channel through which His life-forces pour into the soul. Jacob knew that Joseph was alive and that his sons had opened communications with him, because of the wagons that he sent; and we may know that Jesus lives beyond the mist of time, and that our faith has genuinely connected us with Him, because we feel the pulse of His glorious nature within our own. And when this is so, we cannot but work out what He is working within.

Ask me why a true faith must work! Ask why the branch can do no other than bear clusters of ruddy grapes; its difficulty would be to abstain from bearing; the vitality of the root accounts for its life and productiveness. Blame the lark, whose nature vibrates in the sunshine, for pouring from its small throat acres of sound; blame the child, full of bounding health, for laughing, singing, and leaping; blame the musician, whose soul has caught some fragments of the music of eternity, for pouring it forth in song, before you wonder why it is that the true faith which has opened the way from the believer to his Lord produces those greater works.

III. THERE ARE TWO KINDS OF WORK INDICATED.—(1) "The works that I do shall he do also."—What a blessing Christ's ministry must have been to thousands of sufferers! He passed through Galilee as a river of water of life. In front of Him were deserts of fever blasted by the sirocco, and malarious swamps of ague and palsy, and the mirage of the sufferer's deferred hope; but after He had passed, the parched ground became a pool, and the thirsty land springs of water, the eyes of the blind were opened, and the ears of the deaf unstopped, the lame man leaped as a hart, and the tongue of the dumb sang.

How glad the sick of any district must have been when it was rumored that He was on His way to it! What eager consultations must have been held as to the best means of conveying them into His presence! What sleepless nights must have been spent of speculation as to whether, and how, He would heal!

Such results followed the labors of the apostles. The lame man at the beautiful gate of the Temple; the palsied Aeneas; the dead Dorcas; the crowds in the streets over-shadowed by Peter's passing figure; the miracles wrought by Paul at Paphos, Lystra, Philippi, and Malta—all attested the truth of the Master's words, "The works that I do shall ye do also." There is no doubt that, if it were necessary, such miracles might be repeated, if only the Church exercised the same faith as in those early days of her ministry to the world. But there are greater works than these.

(2) "Greater works than these shall ye do."—The soul is greater than the body, as the jewel than the casket. All work, therefore, which produces as great an effect on the soul-life as miracles on the physical life, must be proportionately greater, as the tenant is greater than the house, as the immortal than the mortal. It is a greater work to give sight to the blind soul than to the blind body; to raise the soul from its grave than Lazarus from his four days' sleep.

Again, eternity is also greater than time, as the ocean is greater than a creek. The ills from which the miracles of Christ delivered the suppliant crowds, were at the most limited by years. The flesh of the leper became wrinkled with old age; Jairus' daughter fell again on sleep; the generation which had been benefited by the mighty works, passed away without handing on a legacy of health to succeeding time! But if a sinner is turned from the error of his ways, if salvation comes to a nature destined for immortality, and lifts it from the slough of sin to the light of God, the results must be greater because more permanent and far-reaching.

Moreover, the pain from which the word of the Gospel may save, is infinitely greater than that which disease could inflict. Men have been known to brave any physical torture rather than endure the insupportable anguish of a sin-laden conscience. The worm that never dies is more intolerable than cancer; the fire that is never quenched keener than that of fever. To save a soul from these is, therefore, a greater work.

Christ hinted at this distinction in one of His earliest miracles, when He proposed to forgive the sick of the palsy his sins, before bidding him walk; and bade the seventy rejoice more that their names were written in heaven than that the devils were subject to them. The apostles bear witness to a growing appreciation of this distinction, by the small space given in the Acts of the Apostles to their miracles, compared with the greater attention concentrated on their discourses; and surely the history of Christendom bears witness to the great and permanent character of spiritual work. The Church could not have influenced the world as she has done, had she been nothing more than a healer of diseases and an exorciser of demons.

IV. THE SOURCE OF THESE GREATER WORKS.—"Because I go to the Father." Clearly the Church has had an argument to present to men which even her Master could not use. He could not point, except indefinitely, to the cross, its flowing blood, its testimony to a love which the cold waters of death could not staunch. Through the ages this has been the master-motive, the supreme argument.

Then, again, the Master could not count upon the coöperation of the Spirit in His convicting power, as we can. "When He is come, He will convict the world of sin"; but He did not come till after that brief career of public ministry had closed. Speaking reverently, we may say that the Church has an Ally that even her Master had not.

But the main reason is yet to come. Perhaps an illustration will best explain it. Supposing the great painter, Raphael, were to infuse his transcendent power, as he possessed it during his mortal life, into some young brain, there is no reason why the genius of the immortal painter should not effect, through a mere tyro in art, results in form and color as marvellous as those which he bequeathed to coming time. But suppose, further, that after having been three hundred years amid the tones, forms, and colors of the heavenly world, he could return, and express his thoughts and conceptions through some human medium, would not these later productions be greater works than those which men cherish as a priceless legacy? So if the Lord were to work in us such works only as He did before He ascended to His glory, they would be inferior to those which He can produce now that He has entered into His glorified state, and has reassumed the power of which He emptied Himself when He stooped to become incarnate. This is what He meant when He said, "Because I go unto the Father."

Open your hearts to the living, risen, glorified Saviour. Let Him live freely in your life, and work unhindered through your faith; expect Him to pour through you as a channel some of those greater works which must characterize the closing years of the present age. Remember how the discourses and miracles of His earthly life even increased in importance and meaning; for such must be the law of His ministry in the heavenlies. According to our faith it will be unto us. The results which we see around us are no measure of what Christ would or could do, they indicate the straitening effect of our unbelief. Lift up your heads, O ye gates, and be ye lifted up, ye low-browed doors of unbelief; and the King of Glory shall come in with His bright and mighty retinue, and shall go out through human lives to do greater works by the instrumentality of His people than ever He wrought in the course of His earthly ministry.

VIII

How to Secure More and Better Prayer

"And I will pray the Father, and He shall give you another Comforter, that He may abide with you forever."—JOHN xiv. 16.

The great lack of our life is that we do not pray more. And there is no failure so disastrous or criminal as this. It is very difficult to account for it. If in all times of discouragement and vicissitude we could have access to one of the wisest and noblest of our fellow creatures, or to some venerated departed saint, or to the guardian angel deputed to attend our steps, or to the archangel that presides as vicegerent over this system of worlds, how strong and brave we should become! Whatever our need, we would at once seek His august presence, and obtain His counsel and assistance. How extraordinary is our behavior then with respect to prayer, and that we make so little of our opportunities of access into the presence of our Father, in whom wisdom, power, and love blend perfectly, and who is always willing to hear us—nay, is perpetually urging us to come!

The reason may lie in the very commonness of our opportunities. The swing-door of prayer stands always waiting for the least touch of faith to press it back. If our Father's presence-chamber were opened to us only once a year, with how much greater reverence would we enter it, how much more store would we set on it! We should anticipate the honor and privilege of that interview for the whole year, and eagerly avail ourselves of it. Alas, that familiarity with prayer does not always increase our appreciation of its magnificence!

The cause of our apathy is probably also to be sought in the effort which is required to bring our sensuous and earth-bound natures into true union with the Spirit of God. True prayer is labor. Epaphras labored in his intercessions. Our feet shrink from the steep pathway that climbs those heights; our lungs do not readily accustom themselves to the rare air that breathes around the summit of the Mount of Communion.

But there is a deeper reason yet: we have not fully learned or obeyed the laws and conditions of prayer. Until they are apprehended and complied with, it is not possible for us to pray as we might. They are not, however, very recondite. The least advanced in the Divine school may read them on this page, where Christ unbares the deepest philosophy of devotion in the simplest phrases.

It is evident that He expected that the age which Pentecost was to inaugurate, and to which He so frequently refers as "in that day," would in a special sense be the Age of Prayer. Mark how frequently in this last discourse He refers to it—(xiv. 13, 14; xv. 7, 16; xvi. 24, 26). Clearly the infilling of the Holy Spirit has a special bearing on the prayerfulness of the individual and the Church. But this will unfold as we proceed.

I. THE PRAYING CHRIST.—"I will pray the Father." It is true that He sat down at the right hand of the Majesty on high, because He had completed the work for which He became man. That session indicated a finished atonement. As the Father rested from the work of creation, so the Son entered into His rest, having ceased from the work of redemption, so far as it could be effected in His death, resurrection, and ascension. But as in His rest the Father worked in Providence, sustaining that which He had created, so did the Saviour continue to work after He had entered into His Sabbath-keeping.

We have already dealt with one branch of His twofold activity, in His work through those who believe. The greater works which the risen Saviour has been, and is, achieving through His people bear witness to the perpetual energy streaming from His life in the azure depths. "The apostles," Mark tells us, "went forth and preached everywhere, the Lord working with them, and confirming their word with signs following."

The other branch of His twofold ministry is His intercession on our behalf. He says, "I will pray the Father" for you.

(1) What a contrast to the assertions which we have already pondered of His oneness with the Father, and to His assurance in almost the same breath that He would Himself answer His people's prayers! It is inexplicable, save on the hypothesis that He has a dual nature, by virtue of which, on the one hand, He is God, who answers prayer, and on the other the Son of Man, who pleads as the Head and Representative of a redeemed race.

(2) It is, however, in harmony with Old Testament symbolism. The High Priest often entered the Presence of God with the names of the people on his breast, the seat of love, and on his shoulder, the seat of power; and once a year, with a bowl of blood and sprig of thyme in his hands, pleaded for the entire nation. What more vivid portrayal could there be of the ceaseless intercession of that High Priest who was once manifested to bear the sin of many, and who now appears in the presence of God for us.

(3) In the days of His flesh, He pleaded for His Church, as in the sublime intercessory prayer of chapter xvii.; for individuals, as when He said, "Simon, Simon, Satan hath desired to have you that he may sift you as wheat; but I have prayed for thee"; and for the world, as when He first assumed His High-priestly functions, saying from His cross, "Father, forgive them; they know not what they do." Thus He pleads still. For Zion's sake He does not hold His peace, and for Jerusalem's sake He does not rest. For His Church, for individual believers, for thee and me, He says in heaven, as on earth, "Father, I pray for them." Perennially from His lips pours out a stream of tender supplication and entreaty. This is the river that makes glad the city of God. Anticipating coming trial; interposing when the cobra-coil is beginning to encircle us; pitying us when the sky is overcast and lowering; not tiring or ceasing, though we are heedless and unthankful; He pleads on the mountain brow through the dark hours, whilst we sleep.

(4) These intercessions are further stimulated by our love and obedience. "If ye love Me, keep My commandments, and I will pray the Father." He looks on us, and where love is yearning to love more fully, and obedience falters in its high endeavors, He prays yet more eagerly, that grace may be given us to be what we long to be. He prays for those who do not pray for themselves; but He is even more intent on the perfecting of those who are the objects of His special interest, because of their loyalty and love—"I pray for them; I pray not for the world."

(5) His special petition is that we may receive the gift of Pentecost. "I will pray the Father, and He shall give you another Comforter." It would almost seem as though He spent the mysterious

ten days between His ascension and Pentecost in special intercession that His Church might be endued with power from on high. The pleading Church on earth and the pleading Saviour in heaven were at one. The two voices agreed in perfect symphony, and Pentecost was the Father's answer. The Saviour prayed to the Father, and He gave another Comforter. Nor has He ceased in this sublime quest. It is not improbable that every revival of religion, every fresh and deeper baptism of the Spirit, every new infilling of individual souls, has been due to our Saviour's strong cryings on our behalf. It may be that at this hour He is engaged in asking the Father that He would dower the universal Church with another Pentecost; and if so, let us join Him in the prayer.

II. THE PRAYING CHURCH.—"Whatsoever ye shall ask in My name."

(1) Prayer must be addressed to the Father. As soon as we utter that sacred name, the Divine nature responds; and, to put it vividly, is on the alert to hear what we desire. A little child cannot utter a sigh however slight, a sob however smothered, without awakening the quick attention of its mother; and at the first whisper of our Father's name, He is at hand to hear and bless. Alas! we have too often grieved His Holy Spirit by a string of selfish petitions, or a number of formal platitudes! To the wonderment of angels, we thus fritter away the most precious and sacred opportunities. Be still, then, before you pray, to consider what to ask; order your prayers for presentation: and be sure to begin the blessed interview with words of sincere and loving appreciation and devotion.

(2) The conditions of successful prayer are clearly defined in these words. There must be love to Christ and to all men; obedience to His will, so far as it is revealed; recognition of His mediation and intercession, as alone giving us the right to draw nigh; identification with Him, so as to be able to use His name; passionate desires for the Father's glory. Where these five conditions exist, there can be no doubt as to our receiving the petitions which we offer. Prayer that complies with them cannot fail, since it is only the return tide of an impulse which has emanated from the heart of God.

(3) Note how the Saviour lives for the promotion of His Father's glory. How often, during His earthly ministry, He declared that He was desiring and seeking this beyond all else! Though His prayer could only be granted by His falling into the ground to die, He never flinched from saying, "Father, glorify Thy Name." But here He tells us that through the ages as they pass He will still be set on the same quest. By all means He must glorify His Father; and if, in any prayer of ours, we can show that what we ask will augment the Father's glory, we are certain to obtain His concurrence and glad acquiescence. "That," He says, "will I do."

(4) We must pray "in His Name." As the ambassador speaks in the name of queen and country; as the tax-collector appeals in the name of the authorities; both deriving from their identification with their superiors an authority they could not otherwise exercise; so our words become weighted with a great importance when we can say to our Father, "We are so one with Jesus that He is asking in and through us; these words are His; these desires His; these objects those on which His heart is set. We have His sanction and authority to use His name." When we ask a favor in the name of another, that other is the petitioner, through us; so when we approach

God in the Name of Jesus, it is not enough to append His sacred name as a formula, but we must see to it that Jesus is pleading in us, asking through our lips, as He is asking through His own in the heart of the sapphire throne.

III. THE LINK BETWEEN THESE TWO.—"He will give you another Comforter." The word Comforter might be rendered Advocate. We have two Advocates; one with the Father, Jesus Christ the Righteous, and one with us. As the one went up, the other came down. As the one sat down at the right hand of God, the other rested on the heads and hearts of the company in the upper room. As the one has compassion on our infirmities, so the other helps our infirmities. As the one ever liveth to intercede for us in heaven, so the other maketh intercession in us for the saints with groanings that cannot be uttered.

This is the clue to the mystery of prayer. It is all-important that the Church on earth should be in accord with its Head in His petitions before the Throne. Of what avail is it for a client and advocate to enter an earthly court of justice unless they are in agreement? Of what use is it to have two instruments in an orchestra which are not perfectly in tune? And how can we expect that God will hear us unless we ask what is according to His will, and, therefore, what is in the heart and thought of Jesus?

This, then, is the problem that confronts us. How can we ascertain what Jesus is pleading for? We may guess it generally, but how be assured of it particularly? Who will tell us the direction in which the current of His mighty pleadings is setting, that we may take the same direction? These inquiries are answered in the ministry of the Holy Spirit. On the one hand, He fills and moves the Head, and on the other, His members. There is one Spirit of life between Jesus in the glory and His believing people everywhere. One ocean washes the shores of all natures in which the life of God is found.

Be still, therefore, and listen carefully to the voice of the Spirit of God speaking in thine heart, as thou turnest from all other sounds toward His still small whisper, and He will tell thee all. Coming, as He does, from the heart of Jesus, He will tell thee His latest thought. In Him we have the mind of Christ. Then, sure that we are one with Him, and therefore with the Father, we shall ask what is according to His will to give. Prayer goes in an eternal circle. It begins in the heart of God, comes to us through the Saviour and by the Spirit, and returns through us again to its source. It is the teaching of the raindrops, of the tides, of the procession of the year; but wrought out and exemplified in the practice of holy hearts.

IX

The Other Paraclete

"He shall give you another Comforter."—JOHN xiv. 16.

There was no doubt in our Lord's mind that His asking would be at once followed by the Father's giving. Indeed, the two actions seemed, in His judgment, indissolubly connected—"I will ask, and He shall give." From which we learn that prayer is a necessary link in the order of the Divine government. Though we are assured that what we ask is in God's purpose to communicate—that it lies in the heart of a promise, or in the line of the Divine procedure, yet we must nevertheless make request. "Ye have not," said the Apostle James, "because ye ask not." "Ask," said the Master, His eye being open to the laws of the spiritual world, "and it shall be given you."

The prayer of the Head of the Church was heard, and He received the Holy Spirit to bestow Him again. "Having received of the Father the promise of the Holy Spirit," said the Apostle Peter, "He hath shed forth this, which ye now see and hear." Thus the Holy Spirit is the gift of the Father, through the Son, though He is equal with each of the blessed Persons in the Trinity, and is with them to be worshipped and glorified.

I. THE PERSONALITY OF THE HOLY GHOST.—That word, "another"—"He shall give you another Comforter"—is in itself sufficient to prove the Divinity and Personality of the Holy Ghost. If a man promises to send another as his substitute, we naturally expect to see a man like himself, occupying his place, and doing his work. And when Jesus foreannounced another Comforter, He must have intended a Person as distinct and helpful as He had been. A breath, an afflatus, an impersonal influence could not have stood in the same category with Himself.

There are those who think that the Holy Spirit is to the Lord Jesus what a man's spirit is to his body; and imagine that our Lord simply intended that the spirit of His life-teaching and self-sacrifice would brood over and inspire His followers; but this could not have fulfilled the promise of "the other Comforter." It would simply have been Himself over again, though no longer as a living Person; rather as the momentum and energy of a receding force which gets weaker and ever weaker as the ages pass. Thus the spirit of Napoleon or of Caesar is becoming little more than a dim faint echo of footsteps that once shook the world.

Jesus knew how real and helpful He had been to His followers—the centre around which they had rallied; their Teacher, Brother, Master; and He would not have tantalized them by promising another Paraclete, unless He had intended to announce the advent of One who would adjust Himself to their needs with that quickness of perception, and sufficiency of resource, which characterize a personal Leader and Administrator. There were times approaching when the little band would need counsel, direction, sympathy, the interposition of a strong wise Hand— qualities which could not be furnished by the remembrance of the past, fading like the colors on clouds when the sun has set; and which could only be secured by the presence of a strong, wise, ever-present Personality. "I have been one Paraclete," said the Lord in effect; "but I am now going to plead your cause with the Father, that another Paraclete may take My place, to be My other self, and to abide with you forever."

There is no adequate translation for that word Paraclete. It may be rendered Comforter, Helper, Advocate, Interpreter; but no one word suffices. The Greek simply means one whom you call to your side, in a battle, or a law-court, to assist you by word or act. Such a One is Christ; such a One is the Holy Spirit. He is a definite Person whom you can call to, and lean on, and work with. If a man were drowning, he would not call to the wandering breath of the wind; but to any person who might be on the bank. The Spirit is One whom you can summon to your side; and it is therefore quite in keeping with Scripture to pray to the Holy Spirit. On the whole we are taught to direct prayer to the Father, through the Son, and as prompted by the Holy Spirit; but as a matter of practice and habit, it is indifferent which Person in the Holy Trinity we address, for each is equally God. As the Father is God, so also is the Son, and so the Holy Spirit. In her hymns and liturgies the Church has never hesitated to summon the Holy Spirit to her help.

It is in recognition of the Personality of the Holy Spirit that the historian of the Acts of the Apostles quotes His solemn words, "Separate Me Barnabas and Saul"; tells us that Ananias and Sapphira lied to Him; and records that the Church at Jerusalem commenced its encyclical letter with the words, "It seemed good to the Holy Ghost and to us." Happy that body of Christians which has come to realize that the Holy Ghost is as certainly, literally, and personally present in its midst, as Jesus Christ was present when, in the days of His flesh, He tarried among men!

II. A SEVENFOLD PARALLEL BETWEEN THE ADVENTS OF THE TWO PARACLETES.—(1) Each was in the world before His specific advent.—Long before His incarnation the delights of the Son of God were with men. In Angel-form, He visited their tents, spoke with them face to face, calmed their fears, and fought on their behalf. He trod the holy fields of Palestine with noiseless footfall that left no impress on the lightest sands, long before He learned to walk with baby-feet, or bore His cross up Calvary.

So with the Holy Spirit. He brooded over chaos, strove with men before the deluge, moved holy men to write the Scriptures, foreshadowed the advent of the Messiah, equipped prophets and kings for their special mission. In restraining evil, urging to good, preparing the way for Christ, the Holy Spirit found abundant scope for His energies. But His influence was rather external than internal; savored rather of gift than grace; and dealt more often with the few than with the many—with the great souls that reared themselves to heaven like Alpine summits touched with the fires of dawn, rather than with the generality of men, who dwelt in the valley of daily commonplace, enwrapped in the mists of ignorance and unbelief. It was to be the special prerogative of this age, that He should be poured out on all flesh, so that sons and daughters should prophesy, whilst servants and handmaidens participated in His gracious influences.

(2) The advent of each was previously announced.—From the Fall, the coming of the great Deliverer was foretold in type and sign, in speech and act, in history and prophecy. Indeed, as the time of the Incarnation drew nigh, as Milton tells us in his sublime ode on the Incarnation, surrounding nations had caught from the chosen people the spirit of expectancy, and the world was in feverish anticipation of the coming of its Redeemer. He was the Desire of all nations. All the ages, and all the family of man, accompanied Mary to Bethlehem, and worshipped with the

Magi.

So with the Holy Spirit. Joel distinctly foretold that in the last days of that dispensation. God would pour out of His Spirit; and His message is echoed by Isaiah, Zechariah, Ezekiel, and others; till Jesus came, who more specifically and circumstantially led the thoughts of His disciples forward to the new age then dawning, which should be introduced and signalized by the coming and ministry of the Spirit.

(3) Each was manifested in a body.—The Lord Jesus in that which was prepared for Him by the Father, and born of a pure Virgin. We are told, that He took on Him the form of a servant, and was made in the likeness of man. Similarly the Holy Spirit became, so to speak, incorporate in that mystical Body, the Church, of which Jesus is the Head.

On the day of Pentecost, the hundred and twenty who were gathered in the upper room, and who, up to that time, had had no corporate existence, were suddenly constituted a Church, the habitation and home of the Divine Spirit. What the human body of Jesus was to the second Person of the Holy Trinity, that the infant Church was to the third; though it did not represent the whole body, since we must add to those gathered in the upper room many more in heaven and on earth, who by virtue of their union with the risen Christ constituted with them the Holy Catholic Church, which is His body, the fullness of Him who filleth all in all. "This," said the Blessed Spirit, "is My rest forever; here will I dwell, for I have desired it."

(4) Each was named before His advent.—"Thou shalt call His name
Emmanuel." "His name shall be called Wonderful, Counsellor, the Mighty
God, the Everlasting Father, the Prince of Peace." Thus was the Lord
Jesus designated to loving hearts before His birth.

So also with the Holy Spirit. The last discourses of Jesus are full of appellatives, each setting forth some new phase of the Holy Spirit's ministry; some freshly-cut facet of His character. The Spirit of Truth; the Holy Spirit; the Paraclete; the Spirit of Conviction—such are some of the names by which He was to be known.

(5) Each was dependent on another.—Our Lord said distinctly, "The Son can do nothing of Himself, but what He seeth the Father do"; and He said of the Holy Spirit, using the same preposition, "He shall not speak of Himself, but whatsoever He shall hear, that shall He speak."

What a conception is here! It is as though the Holy Spirit were ever listening to the Divine colloquy and communion between the Father and the Son, and communicating to receptive hearts disclosures of the secrets of the Deity. The things which eye hath not seen, nor ear heard, God hath revealed unto us by His Spirit; "for the Spirit searcheth all things, yea, the deep things of God."

(6) Each received witness.—The Father bore witness to His Son on three separate occasions. On the first, at His baptism, He said, "This is My beloved Son, in whom I am well pleased"; on the second, when the three apostles were with Him on the holy mount, and He received from the Father glory and honor; and on the third, when the inquiry of the Greeks reminded Him of His approaching death, and the voice from heaven assured Him that glory would accrue to the Father through His falling into the ground to die.

So in regard to the Holy Spirit. Seven times from the throne the ascended Lord summons those that have ears, to hear what the Spirit saith to the churches; as though to emphasize the urgent importance of His message, and the necessity of giving it our most earnest heed, lest we should drift past it.

(7) The presence of each is guaranteed during the present age.—"I am with you," saith the Lord, and they were among the closing words of His posthumous ministry, "all the days, even unto the end of the age"; and here it is foretold that the Comforter would abide during the age, for so the phrase might more accurately be rendered.

This is specially the age of the Holy Spirit. He may be grieved, ignored, and rejected; but He will not cease His blessed ministry to the bride, till the Bridegroom comes to claim her for Himself. Oh, let us avail ourselves of His gracious presence to the utmost of our opportunity, that He may realize in us the full purpose of His ministry. Let us not pray for Him, as if in any degree He had been withdrawn, but as believing that He is as much with the Church of to-day as on the day of Pentecost; as near us as when awe-struck eyes beheld Him settling in flame on each meekly-bowed head.

The Lord said, "He shall remain with you to the end of the age." The age is not closed, therefore He must be with us here and now. There can be no waning of His grace or power. The pot of oil is in the Church, only she has ceased to bring her empty vessels. The mine is beneath our feet, but we do not work it as of yore. The electric current is vibrating around, but we have lost the art of switching ourselves on to its flow. It is not necessary then for us to pray the Father that He should give the Holy Paraclete in the sense in which He bestowed Him on the Day of Pentecost in answer to the request of our Lord. That prayer has been answered: the Paraclete is here; but we need to have the eyes of our heart opened to perceive, and the hand of our faith strengthened that we may receive, Him.

The work of the Holy Spirit in and through us is conditioned by certain great laws, which call for our definite and accurate obedience. Not on emotion, nor on hysteric appeals, nor on excitement, but on obedience, does the power of God's Spirit pass into human hearts and lives. Therefore, let us walk in the Paracletism of the Paraclete, continually in the current of His gracious influences, which will bear us on their bosom ever nearer to our Lord. Oh to glorify Him; to know and love Him; to become passionately eager that all hearts should enthrone Him regardless of the personal cost it may involve! Glory be to the Father, and to the Son, and to the Holy Ghost; as it was in the beginning, is now, and shall be forevermore. Amen.

X

The Three Dispensations

"The Spirit of truth; whom the world cannot receive, because it seeth Him not, neither knoweth Him: but ye know Him; for He dwelleth with you, and shall be in you."—JOHN xiv. 17.

They are lofty themes which we have been discussing in the foregoing pages; and just because they touch the highest matters of the spiritual life, they involve us in profound responsibility. It was because Capernaum had been exalted to heaven in privilege, that she could be cast down to hell. Of those to whom much is given, much is required. Better not to have known these truths of the inner life, if we are content to know them only by an intellectual apprehension, and make no effort to incorporate them into the texture of our character. Few things harden more certainly than to delight in the presentation of the mysteries of the kingdom, without becoming the child of the kingdom.

The object, therefore, which now engages us is less one of elucidation than of self-examination. Let us discern ourselves. Let us see whether we be in the faith. Let us expose soul and spirit to the discrimination of the Word of God, which is a discerner of the thoughts and intents of the heart.

I. THERE ARE TWO AVENUES OF KNOWLEDGE.—"Whom the world cannot receive, because it seeth Him not, neither knoweth Him." Three things are specified as beyond the range of the world's power: it does not receive, it does not know, it does not see, the things of the unseen and eternal world. It cannot see them, therefore it does not know them, and therefore does not receive them, and this is especially true of its attitude toward the Holy Ghost.

When the world hears talk of the Holy Spirit it brings to bear upon Him those organs of cognition which it has been accustomed to apply to the objects of the natural world, and even to the human life of Christ. But, as might have been expected, these are altogether useless. It is as absurd to endeavor to detect the presence of the spiritual and eternal by the faculties with which we discern what is seen and temporal, as it would be to attempt to receive the impression of a noble painting by the sense of taste, or to deal with the problems of astronomy by the tests that are employed in chemical analysis. The world, however, does not realize its mistake. It persists in applying tests to the Spirit of God which may be well enough in other regions of discovery, but which are worse than useless here. "The natural man receiveth not the things of the Spirit of God, neither can he know them, because they are spiritually discerned." "Whom the world cannot receive, for it beholdeth Him not, neither knoweth Him."

There was a touch of this worldly spirit even in Thomas, when he said, "Except I see in His hand the print of the nails, and thrust my hand into His side, I will not believe"; and in so far as the world-spirit is permitted to hold sway within us, our powers of spiritual perception will be blunted, and become infected with the tendency to make our intellect or imagination our sole means of apprehending Divine truth.

There is a better way than this; and our Lord indicates it when He says, "Ye know Him, for He abideth with you, and shall be in you." Pascal said, "The world knows in order to love: the

Christian loves, in order to know." The same thought underlies these words of Christ. The world attempts to see the Spirit, that it may know and receive Him; the child of God receives Him by an act of faith that he may know Him.

An illustration of this habit is given in the story of Naaman. The spirit of the world whispered to him of the desirability of knowing that the waters of Israel possessed curative properties, before he committed himself absolutely to the prophet's directions; and if he had waited to know before bathing in them, he would have remained a helpless leper to the end of his days. His servants, however, had a clearer perception of the way of faith, and persuaded him to dip seven times in the Jordan. He acted on the suggestion, dipped seven times, and his flesh came as that of a little child. Similarly we are called to act upon grounds which the world would hold to be inadequate. We hear the testimony of another; we recognize a suitability in the promise of the Scripture to meet the deep yearnings of our soul; we feel that the words and works of Jesus Christ constitute a unique claim for Him, and we open our hearts toward Him. In absolute humility and perfect obedience we yield to Him our whole nature. Though the night be yet dark, we fling wide our windows to the warm southwest wind coming over the sea. The result is that we begin to know, with an intuitive knowledge that cannot be shaken by the pronouncements of the higher criticism. We have received the Spirit, and our after life is too short to unfold all that is involved in that unspeakable gift. We know Him because He abideth with us, and is in us. No man knoweth the things of a man, save the spirit of man which is in him; and we can only know the Spirit of God when He has taken up His residence within us, and witnesses with our spirit, as One who is interwoven with the very texture of the inner life.

Consecration is therefore the key to this higher knowledge, and if any who read this page are yearning after a discernment of the things of God on which they may build the house of their faith amid the swirl of the storm and the beat of the wave of modern doubt, let them open their entire nature, humbly to receive, diligently to obey that Spirit whom Christ waits to give to all who seek.

II. THE CHARACTERISTIC OF THIS DISPENSATION.—"He shall be in you." It has been repeatedly said that creation is the work of the Father, redemption of the Son, and regeneration of the Holy Spirit. It may also be said, that there are three dispensations: that of the Father, in the earlier history of mankind; that of the Son, culminating in our Lord's ascension; and that of the Holy Spirit, in which we are now living. In the history of the world these were successive. In the history of souls they may be the contemporaneous. In the same house one member may be in the dispensation of the Father, another in that of the Son, and a third in that of the Holy Ghost. It is highly necessary, says the saintly Fletcher, that every good steward of the mysteries of God should be well acquainted with this fact, otherwise he will not rightly divide the word of life. There is peril lest we should give the truth of one order of dispensation to those who are living on another level of experience.

There is a remarkable illustration of this in the life of John the Baptist, who clearly realized the distinction on which we are dwelling, and used it with remarkable nicety, when approached by various classes of character. When Gentile soldiers came to him, in Roman regimentals, he merely bade them do violence to no man, and be content with their wages. When Jews came he said, "Behold the Lamb of God!" To his eagle eye a further dispensation was unveiled to which he alluded when he said, "He shall baptize you with the Holy Ghost, and with fire." Similarly they to whom inquirers address themselves should diagnose their spiritual standing, that they may lovingly and wisely administer the truth suitable to their condition.

The dispensation of the Father includes those who hope that He has accepted and forgiven them, but have no clear perception of the atoning work of Christ; are governed rather by fear than love; tremble beneath the thunders of Sinai more often than they rejoice at the spectacle of Calvary; are tossed to and fro between hope and despair; desire the favor of God, but hesitate to speak confidently of having attained it. Such are to be found in churches where the Gospel is veiled beneath heavy curtains of misconception and formalism. In the same class we might put men like Cornelius, who in every nation fear God and work righteousness.

The dispensation of the Son includes those who clearly perceive His Divine nature, and rejoice in His finished propitiation; they know that they are accepted in the Beloved; they receive His teachings about the Father; they submit to the rule of life which He has laid down; but they know comparatively little of the inner life, or of their oneness with Christ in resurrection and ascension; they understand little of what the apostle meant by speaking of Christ being formed in the soul; and like the disciples at Ephesus they know but little of the mission and in-filling of the Holy Spirit.

The dispensation of the Holy Spirit includes those who have claimed their share in Pentecost. In their hearts the Paraclete dwells in sanctifying grace, on their heads He rests in mighty anointing. The previous class resemble Ruth the gleaner; the latter, Ruth the bride. The one dwells in Romans vii. and Hebrews iii.; the other in Romans viii. and Hebrews iv. For those the water has to be drawn from the well, in these it springs up to everlasting life. Oh to know the "in-ness" of the Holy Ghost. Know ye not that Jesus Christ is in you by the Spirit, unless ye be reprobate!

III. THE SYMPTOMS OF THE INDWELLING.—We must distinguish here, as Dr. Steele suggests, between what is variable, and what is constant.

These vary—(1) The joy of realization, which is sometimes overpowering in its intensity, at other times like the ebbing tide.

(2) Agony for souls, which would be insupportable if it were permanent. Christ only asks us to watch in Gethsemane for one hour.

(3) Access in prayer. Sometimes the vision is face to face; at others, though we grasp as in Jacob's night-wrestle, we cannot behold. Like Esther, we seem to wait in the ante-chamber. As the lark of which Jeremy Taylor speaks, we rise against the east wind.

(4) The openings of Scripture. The Bible does not seem to be always equally interesting. At times it is like the scented letter paper, smelling of aloes and cassia, bearing the handwriting we love; at others it resembles the reading book of the blind man, the characters in which, by constant use, have become almost obliterated, so as hardly to awake answering thought.

(5) The pressure of temptation. We sometimes think that we are getting out of the zone of

temptation. The pressure is so reduced that we think we shall never suffer again as we have done. Then, all suddenly, it bursts upon us, as the fury of the storm, when, after an hour's cessation, it takes the mariner unawares.

All these symptoms are too variable to be relied upon for a diagnosis of our spiritual condition, or an evidence of the dispensation to which we belong.

These are constant—(1) The consciousness of being God's. This is to be distinguished from the outgoing of our faith and love toward God. At the beginning of our experience we hold Him, but as the Holy Spirit dwells more fully we realize that we are held by Him. It is not our love to God, but His love to us; not our faith, but His faithfulness; not the sheep keeping near the Shepherd, but the Shepherd keeping the sheep near to Himself. A happy sense steals over the heart, as over the spouse, "I am my Beloved's, and His desire is toward me."

(2) The supremacy of Jesus in the heart. There is no longer a double empire of self and Christ, as in the poor Indian who said to the missionary, "I am two Indians, good and bad"; but there is the undivided reign of Christ, who has put down all rule and authority and power—as in the case of Martin Luther, who said, "If any one should ask of my heart, who dwells here, I should reply, not Martin Luther, but Christ."

(3) Peace, which looks out upon the future without alarm, because so sure that Christ will do His very best in every day that lies hidden beneath the haze of the future; which forbears to press its will too vehemently, or proffer its request too eagerly, because so absolutely certain that Jesus will secure the highest happiness possible, consistently with His glory and our usefulness to men.

(4) Love. When the Spirit of God really dwells within, there is a baptism of love which evinces itself not only in the household, and to those naturally lovable, but goes out to all the world, and embraces in its tenderness such as have no natural traits of beauty. Thus the soft waters of the Southern Ocean lap against unsightly rocks and stretches of bare shingle.

Where love reigns in the inner chamber of the soul, doors do not slam, bells are not jerked violently, soft tones modulate the speech, gentle steps tread the highways of the world, bent on the beautiful work of the messengers of peace, and the very atmosphere of the life is warm and sunny as an aureole. There is no doubt of the indwelling Spirit where there is this outgoing love.

(5) Deliverance from the love and power of sin, so that it becomes growingly distasteful, and the soul turns with loathing from the carrion on which it once fed contentedly. This begets a sense of purity, robed in which the soul claims kinship to the white-robed saints of the presence-chamber, and reaches out toward the blessedness of the pure in heart who see God. There is still a positive rain of smut and filth in the world around; there is a recognition of the evil tendencies of the self-life, which will assert themselves unless graciously restrained; but triumphing above all is the purity of the indwelling Lord, who Himself becomes in us the quality for which holy souls eagerly long.

XI

Three Paradoxes

"I will not leave you comfortless: I will come to you."

"The world seeth Me no more; but ye see Me."

"Because I live, ye shall live also."—JOHN xiv. 18, 19.

The Bible and Christian life are full of paradoxes. Paul loved to enumerate them; they abound also in the discourses of our Lord. Here are three.

The Master had declared His purpose of leaving His apostles and friends and returning to His Father: but in the same breath He says, "I will not leave you desolate; I come to you."

Again, He had forewarned them that He would be hidden from them; yet now He tells them that they would still behold Him.

Further, with growing emphasis and clearness, He had unfolded His approaching death by the cruel Roman method of the cross; yet He claims the timeless life of an ever-present tense and insists that their life will depend on His.

Absent, yet present; hidden, yet visible; dying, yet living and life-giving—such are the paradoxes of this paragraph in His marvellous farewell discourse; and they reveal three facts of which we may live in perpetual cognizance.

I. WE MAY ENJOY THE PERPETUAL RECOGNITION OF THE ADVENT OF CHRIST.— "I will not leave you orphans, or desolate, I come unto you" (R. V.). Note the majesty of those last words; they are worthy of Deity; He speaks as though He were always drawing nigh those He loves: "I come unto you."

Christ is always present, yet He comes.—The Creator had been always immanent in His universe, but He came in each creative act; the Lawgiver had been ever-present in the Church in the wilderness, but He came down on Sinai, and His glory lit up the peaks of sandstone rock; the Deliverer was never for a moment absent from the side of the Shepherd-King, but in answer to His cry for help He came down riding upon a cherub, flying on the wings Of wind; the Holy Spirit had been in the world from the earliest days of prayer and inspired speech, but He came down from the throne to sit on each bowed head in lambent flame. So Christ is with us all the days, yet He comes. He will come at last to receive His own to Himself, and to judge the world; but He comes in dark and lonely hours that we may not be desolate.

He comes when we need Him most.—When the storm is high, and the water is pouring into the boat; when the house is empty because the life that made it home has fled; when Jericho has to be attacked on the morrow, and the Jordan crossed; when lover and friend stand aloof; when light is fading before dimming eyes, and names and faces elude the grasp of the aged mind; when the last coal is turning to grey ash; when the rush of the river is heard in the valley below—Jesus says, I come. It is in the hour of desolation, when Lazarus has been in the grave four days already, that the glad tidings are whispered in the ear of the mourner, "The Master is come." "I will not leave you orphans," He said, "I come unto you." Oh, blessed orphanhood, it were well to be bereaved, to have such comforting!

He pays surprise visits.—He does not always wait to be invited; but sometimes, when we lie sleeping with wakeful hearts, we hear His gentle voice calling to us, "Arise, My love, and come away." Then as we lift the door-latch, our hand drops with the sweet-smelling myrrh which betrays His presence. How often when we have been losing ground, getting lukewarm and worldly, we have suddenly been made aware of His reviving presence, and He has said, I come. He comes, as the wood-anemones and snowdrops (the most fragile and tender flowerets of spring) penetrate the hard ground to announce that the winter is over and gone, and that the time of the singing of birds is come.

It is well to put ourselves in His way.—There are certain beaten tracks well-worn by His feet, and if we would meet Him we must frequent their neighborhood. Olivet, where He used to pray; Calvary, where He died; Joseph's garden, where He rose, are dear to Him yet. When we pray or meditate; when we commemorate His dying love at the memorial feast; when we realize our union with Him in death and resurrection; when we open our hearts to the breathing of the Holy Spirit—we put ourselves in His way, and are more likely to encounter Him when He comes. "To them that look for Him shall He appear." "Behold the Bridegroom cometh, go ye out to meet Him"—but take the path by which He is sure to travel. Be in the upper room, with the rest of the disciples, so that you may not, like Thomas, miss Him when He comes.

His footsteps are noiseless.—It is said of old, "Thy footsteps are not known," therefore we need not be surprised if He steal in upon us as a thief in the night, or as spring over the wolds. There is no blare of trumpet or voice of herald; we cannot say, Lo here, or Lo there; when the King comes there is no outward show; "He does not strive, nor cry, nor lift up, nor cause His voice to be heard in the street."

"He entered not by the eyes," says St. Bernard, "for His presence was not marked by color; nor by the ears, for there was no sound; nor by the touch, for He was impalpable. How then did I know that He was present? Because He was a quickening power. As soon as He entered He awoke my slumbering soul. He moved and pierced my heart, which before was stony, hard, and sick. He began also to pluck up and destroy, to build and plant, to freshen the inner drought, to enlighten the darkness, to open the prison-house, to make the crooked straight and the rough smooth; so that my heart could bless the Lord with all that was within me."

Oh, lonely, desolate soul, open thy door to Him; wait not on the alert to detect His entrance, only believe that He is there; and presently, and before ever thou art aware, thou wilt find a new fragrance distilling through the heart-chamber, a new power throbbing in thy pulse.

II. WE MAY ENJOY THE PERPETUAL RECOGNITION OF THE PRESENCE OF CHRIST.—"The world beholdeth Me no more, but ye behold Me." Nothing makes men so humble and yet so strong as the vision of Christ.

It induces humility.—When Isaiah beheld His glory more resplendent than the sheen of the sapphire throne, he cried that he was undone; when Peter caught the first flash of His miraculous power gleaming across the waves of Galilee, just when the fish were struggling in the full net, he besought Him to depart, because he felt himself a sinful man; and when John saw Him on the Isle of Patmos, he fell at His feet as dead, though, surely, if any of the apostles could have faced

Him unabashed, it had been he.

This is specially noticeable in the Book of Job. Few books are so misunderstood. It is supposed to contain the description of the victory of Job's patience; in reality it delineates its testing and failure. It shows how he who was perfect, according to the measure of his light, broke down in the fiery ordeal to which he was exposed; and finally was forced to cry, "I have heard of Thee by the hearing of the ear, but now mine eye seeth Thee; wherefore I abhor myself and repent, in dust and ashes."

Wouldst thou be humble, wouldst thou know thyself a worm and no man, wouldst thou see that thou art verily undone, defiled, and helpless? Then ask the blessed Spirit to reveal Jesus in all His matchless beauty and holiness, eliciting the confession that thou are the least of saints and the chief of sinners. This is no forced estimate, when we take into account the opportunities we have missed, the gifts we have misused, the time we have wasted, the light which we have resisted, the love which we have requited with neglect.

It produces strength.—See that man of God prone on the floor of his chamber, shedding bitter tears of godly sorrow, not forgiving himself, albeit that he knows himself forgiven; bowing his head as a bulrush, crying that he is helpless, broken, and at the end of himself—Will he be able to stand as a rock against the beat of temptation, and the assault of the foe? Yes, verily, for the same presence which is a source of humility in private, will inspire to great deeds of faith and heroism when he is called to stand in the breach or lead the assault.

It is this vision of the present Lord that, in every age of the Church, has made sufferers strong. "The Lord is on my right hand, I shall not be moved," said one. "The Lord stood by me, and strengthened me," said another. In many a dark day of suffering and persecution; in the catacombs; in the dens and caves where Waldenses hid; on the hillsides where the Covenanters met to pray; in the beleaguered cities of the Netherlands; in prison and at the stake—God's saints have looked to Him, and been lightened, and their faces have not been ashamed. "Behold," said the first martyr, "I see the heavens opened, and the Son of Man standing on the right hand of God."

Oh for more of the open vision of Jesus, ministered to us by the gracious Spirit! Would that His words were oftener verified in our experience: "Ye behold Me!" He is always with us; and if only our eyes were not holden, we should behold Him with the quick perception of the heart. Indeed, the race can only be rightly run by those who have learned the blessed secret of looking off unto Him. "We see Jesus."

It is a most salutary habit to say often, when one is alone, "Thou art near, O Lord." "Behold, the Lord is in this place." We may not at first realize the truth of what we are saying. His presence may be veiled, as the forms of mountains swathed in morning cloud. But as we persist in our quest, putting away from us all that would grieve Him, and cultivating the attitude of pure devotion, we shall become aware of a Divine presence which shall be more to us than a voice speaking from out the Infinite.

III. WE MAY ENJOY THE PERPETUAL RECOGNITION OF THE LIVING CHRIST.— "Because I live, ye shall live also." There are many life-verses in this Gospel which shine like stars in the firmament of Scripture. Amongst them, in the first chapter, that, in the Word as manifested to men, was life; and in the fifth chapter, that, "as the Father had life in Himself He gave to the Son to have life also in Himself." The Father is the fountain of life. Eternal life is ever rising up in His infinite Being with perennial vigor; and all things living, from the tiny humming-birds in the tropical forest to the strongest archangel beside the sapphire throne, derive their being from Him. Thus we have seen ferns around a fountain, nourishing their fronds on its spray. All things owe their existence and continued being to the unmeasured life, which has been from all eternity treasured up in God, and is ever flowing out from God.

This life was Christ's, in the mystery of the eternal Trinity, before the worlds were made; but it was necessary that He should receive it into His human nature, so as to become the reservoir and storehouse from which all who were one with Him might receive grace on grace. "I am come," He said, "that they might have life, and that they might have it more abundantly." This life dwelt in Him during His earthly ministry, though comparatively few availed themselves of it; His death set it abroach for all the world; the smitten rock yielded streams of living water; the last Adam became a life-giving Spirit; from His throne He proclaimed Himself as He that liveth, though He became dead, and is alive forevermore.

We live by His life.—Our life is as dependent upon Him as a babe's on its mother. Could ought happen to Him, we should instantly feel the effect. Long before He succumbed, we must. We have no independent, self-derived, or self-sustained life. Apart from Him we wither.

We live in His life.—The tiny streamlet of our being has joined His, is merged in it, and flows on together with it, to the great ocean of eternity. To us to live is Christ, both here and hereafter. Our aims and purposes are merged in His; we are enriched in all that enriches Him; gladdened by all that promotes His happiness and glory; made more than conquerors through our oneness with Him, in the victory that has overcome the world.

We live because He lives in us.—At the moment of regeneration He came to indwell. He that hath the Son hath life; he that hath life hath the Son. It has pleased God to reveal His Son in us. We have found Him of whom Moses in the law and the prophets did write, and we have found Him in our hearts. Where dwellest Thou? we asked Him; and He replied, Come and see; and He manifested Himself as having become to us the inward principle of an endless life. Christ dwells deep in our heart, and we are beginning to comprehend the immensity of the Divine love of which He is the exponent.

Let us draw on this life more confidently, availing ourselves of it perpetually in all our time of need—in all time of our sickness and of our wealth, in adversity and prosperity, in the hour of mortal anguish and the day of judgment; and finding what we could not do or bear or encounter, Jesus can do and bear and meet in and through us, to the Father's eternal glory.

XII

Many Mansions for God

"If a man love Me, he will keep My words: and My Father will love him; and we will come unto him, and make our abode with him."—JOHN xiv. 23.

The Immanence of God! That God should be willing to make His home with man is much; but that He should be willing to come in—to indwell, occupy, and possess our nature—this is incomprehensible to the intellect, though it may be received and rejoiced in by the heart. This is no subject for light and thoughtless speech. We touch on the profoundest mysteries of the Being of the Infinite, and the capacity of human nature. Be reverent, O my soul, in the consideration of such a theme, and take the shoes from off thy feet, for the Bush burns with fire!

It was owing to the question of Jude, that the universal application of our Master's words is so clear. A day or two before, our Lord had entered Jerusalem amid the enthusiasm of the crowds, and the disciples fondly thought the long-expected time had arrived when He would manifest Himself to the world as the Messiah. "This is the beginning of the Messianic reign," said each apostle in his secret heart, as the great procession passed over the shoulder of Olivet; and each began to wonder what special post would be allotted to him in the new empire that seemed so close at hand. These nascent hopes, however, had been rudely dissipated by our Lord's declaration that the world was to see Him no more, accompanied by the promise, "But ye see Me."

The apostles therefore were inclined to think that in some special form the manifestations of His grace and glory would be confined to them. Hence Jude's question, "What is come to pass, Master, that Thou wilt manifest Thyself unto us, and not unto the world?" Jesus answered in effect, "Think not that thou and thy fellows are to have the exclusive right of beholding and communing with Me. What I offer to you is open to all who believe, love, and obey. The gate which I throw open shall stand wide for all who choose to enter. The veil shall be rent, that any who fulfill the spiritual conditions may see the light, and hear the voice, and stand in the inner court. If a man love Me . . ." Note those emphatic words, "a man,"—any man; thou and I.

I. THE DIVINE IMMANENCE.—"We will make our abode." The word "abode" is here a translation of the Greek word which is rendered "mansions" in a former part of this chapter. "We will make our mansion with Him." God is willing to become the mansion of the soul that believes in Christ, but asks in return that such a one should prepare a guest-chamber, and become a mansion in which He may dwell. As He steals with noiseless tread into the loving, believing heart, I hear Him say, "This is My rest forever; here will I dwell, for I have desired it."

(1) It is the Immanence of the Father.—Consider who this is of whom the Saviour speaks. The infinite God! Time with all its ages is but the flash of a moment in His eternity! Space, "beyond the soar of angel wings," is but a corner in His dwelling-place; matter, with its ponderous mass, but the light dust that will not affect the level of the scale! The mighty sun, which is the centre of all worlds, but a mote floating in the beam of His being! All the gathered wisdom of man, stored in the libraries of the world, but as a glow-worm's spark compared with the meridian light

of His wisdom! O souls of men, consider how marvellous that such a One, whom the heavens cannot contain, who overflows their limits, asking for room that He may dwell, will yet become the resident of our nature!

Its motive is Love.—"The Father will love him." This is wonderful! The more so as we are told that His love toward us is identical with that which He has toward our Lord. Speaking of those who shall believe through His apostles' words, Jesus said, "That the world may know that Thou lovest them even as Thou lovest Me." That God should condescend to think about our planet, which is as a leaf in the forest of being! That He should deign to regard mankind, who, in size at least, are less than a colony of ants that may have built their home at the foot of the Himalaya! That He should pity our race! This were much. But that He should love the world, that He should love individuals belonging to our race, that He should love them with the love He has toward the Only-begotten—we could not have believed this unless we had been assured by the lips of infallible Truth. But the supreme revelation which towers above the rest, like some great banyan tree amid the slender growth of the Indian forest, is that the Creator should indwell and find a mansion in the heart of His creatures.

It is dual, yet one.—"We will come." We! Then, is there more than One? Who is this who dares class Himself with the supreme God within the limits of a common pronoun, that challenges the love and trust and obedience of man, that poses as King? The meekest and humblest of men. The One who, above all others of the human family, seemed to have least to disturb or darken the incidence of the rays of truth upon His soul; who has cast a light on all the dark problems of human life, and could not possibly have been deceived in respect to His own nature. His conceptions of the holiness, greatness, and purity of God have stood out in unrivalled magnificence from all others whatsoever; yet it is He who couples in one small word His humanity with Deity, His meekness with the Infinite Majesty, His personality with God's. Is not this proof enough that He was conscious of His Divine nature? Is not the fact of His not counting it robbery to be equal with God evidence that He was God? What can they make of this We, who hold that He was only a good man and a great teacher? Good men are humble men, great teachers know best their own limitations!

It is in, and with, and through the Son, and by the Spirit, that the Father comes to indwell.

(2) It is the Immanence of the Son. To be loved by Him were much!—"I will love Him." His love is of the rarest quality. Most free of the soil of selfishness, of any human love. True and tender, strong and sweet, inexorable in its demands upon Himself, inexhaustible in its outflow toward the objects of His affectionate regard. Such love as He gave to John, who grew like Him beneath the magic power of that environment; as He gave to Mary, who perhaps most deeply understood Him; as He gave to Peter, winning him back from his waywardness—brings with it a heaven of bliss, for which a man may well be prepared to count all things but loss. But there is a bliss beyond all this. The Lover of men would indwell them.

It were much that He should seek our love.—"He that loveth Me." We might have supposed that He would have been satisfied with the vastness of His dominion, and the myriad bright spirits that wait on His word! But no, the thirst for love cannot be satisfied with gold, or bright angelic servants. As Isaac could not find a companion among those who tended the cattle that browsed over the wolds of Canaan, or the troops of slaves that gathered round his father's tents, but Eliezer must bring a bride from across the desert; so the Son of God must needs come as a suitor to our world to find His Bride, who can share His inner thoughts and purposes. Here is a marvel indeed. As the village becomes famous which provides the emperor's bride, so earth, though it be least among her sister-spheres, shall have the proud preëminence of having furnished from her population the Spouse of the Lamb. But, great as this marvel is, it is followed by the greater, that the Immortal Lover is willing to tenant the poor hearts, whose love at the best is so faint and cold.

It were much that He should give us manifestations of His love.—"I will manifest Myself unto him." Have you not sometimes taken up a daisy, and looked into its little upturned eye, and thought and thought again, till through the gate of the flower you have passed into an infinite world of life, beauty, and mystery? There are moments when even a flower is transfigured before us, and manifests itself to us as a thought of God, a ray of His glory, the frail product of His infinite mind, the wick around which trembles the fire of the Shekinah! Have you not sometimes stood alone amid mountains, glaciers, wooded valleys, and rushing streamlets, till nature has dropped her veil, and revealed herself in a phase of beauty and a depth of meaning which struck you as altogether unique and singular? So there are moments in the life of the believer, when Christ, who is ever with us, manifests Himself as He does not to the world. There is borne in upon the spirit a consciousness that He is near; there is a waft of His breath, a savor of His fragrant dress, fresh from the ivory palaces.

All this is much: but how much more to be told that this glorious Christ, the Fellow of Jehovah, who with the Father and the Spirit is God; the Organ of creation; the Mouthpiece of the Godhead; the Mediator of Redemption; the Monarch of all worlds; the Supreme Teacher, Guide, and Saviour of men—is prepared to repeat the experiences of Bethlehem, and make His abode in man! "We will come unto Him, and make our abode with Him."

(3) Learn to revere the work of God in the souls of others.—"For thy meat," said the apostle, "destroy not the soul for whom Christ died." He might have added, "and in whom Christ lives." Weak and erring, trying and vexatious, that fellow-believer may be, yet there is a chamber in his nature in which God has already taken up His abode. The conflict between the light and darkness, the Christ-spirit and the self-spirit, may be long and arduous, but the issue is certain. Help, but do not hinder the process. Be reverent, careful, mindful of the presence of God.

Be hopeful for thyself.—When an art-student asked Mr. Ruskin whether he would ever be able to paint like Turner, the great critic replied, "It is more likely that you will become Emperor of all the Russias!" But God never daunts a soul with such discouragement. He first sets before it a great ideal—the faith of Abraham, the meekness of Moses, the prayer of an Elijah, the love of a John—and then, as the source of all perfection, enters the soul, to be in it all that He has taught it to desire.

Count on the indwelling of His power.—The merchant of to-day has facilities granted to no previous age. The cablegram, telegram, and telephone put him in communication with the markets of the world: steam and electricity are his willing slaves in manufacture: machinery with its unwearying iron fingers toils for him. A single human brain, which knows how to avail itself of these resources, can multiply its conceptions indefinitely. How vast the space between the untutored savage, doing everything with his hands, and the merchant prince, who has but to press the ivory-plated pushes fixed upon the walls of his room! But not less is the difference between the work we can accomplish by our natural resources, and that which we achieve when we recognize that what is impossible to us is possible to Him who has come in to abide. I cannot; but God is within me, and He can.

II. THE CONDITIONS OF THE DIVINE IMMANENCE.—(1) Love to Christ.—"He that loveth Me shall. . . ." We would love Him, but how? Do not think of your love, but of His. "Love is of God." Open the shutters of your being toward the love of God; we love because He first loves. Love is the reflection from us of what we have first received from God.

Love is shed abroad in the heart by the Holy Spirit. The fruit of the Spirit is Love. Seek the in-filling and in-working of the Spirit; be careful to obey His promptings to love; avoid grieving Him by bitterness, wrath, or evil speaking; sit as His willing pupil in the school of love; cast on Him the responsibility of securing in your nature obedience to the primal law which is fulfilled in the one word, "Thou shalt love."

Beneath the nurturing grace of the Spirit, we shall be led to meditate much on the love of Jesus to us, especially as manifested in the death of the cross; and as we muse, the fire will burn, love will glow, and afford the condition of soul which is infinitely attractive to the Divine Lover, who requires our love, and produces the love which He requires.

(2) Obedience to Christ.—Where there is true love, there will be obedience. This rather than emotion. Many a sincere soul who questions its love, because its emotions are low or fluctuating, would rather die than disobey the least jot or tittle of His commandments. Such a one loves. "He that hath My commandments" (treasured in memory and heart), "he it is that loveth Me." Why do ye call Him, Lord, Lord, and do not the things that He says? There may be the luscious language of the lip, but it does not deceive Him. He looks under the leaves for fruit.

Disobedience robs the soul of the sweet sense of Christ's indwelling. Nothing can compensate for failure to obey. Whatever the protestations, there is no real love to Christ where His commands are knowingly disregarded and set at nought. But each time we dare to step out in simple obedience to His will, it seems as though the inner light shines deeper down into the hidden places of our being, and the residence of Christ extends to new chambers of the heart.

XIII

Christ's Legacy and Gift of Peace

"Peace I leave with you, My peace I give unto you: not as the world giveth give I unto you. Let not your heart be troubled, neither let it be afraid."—JOHN xiv. 27.

It seems a little anomalous to talk of peace at a time when the war-clouds are being swiftly blown up from the horizon, the sea roaring, and men's hearts failing them for fear: and yet, in the deepest aspects, this is of all times the most suitable. It is when the storm rattles on the window-panes that the family draws closer round the fire, and the mother clasps her babe to her breast.

The word Peace is the Eastern salutation and benediction. When one stranger encounters another, as they meet and part, they wish each other peace. It was befitting, therefore, that at Christ's entrance into our world, the first salutation to men, as conveyed by the angels, should be, "Peace on earth"; and that His parting words should be, "Peace be unto you." But with what a wealth of meaning does the Lord invest familiar words when they issue from His lips! Let us draw nigh, and allow His sweet and soothing consolations to have their full effect.

I. LET US DISTINGUISH BETWEEN "PEACE" AND "MY PEACE."—"Peace I leave with you, My peace I give unto you." There is a distinction between these two. The former refers to the result of His work for us on the cross: "Being justified by faith, we have peace with God through our Lord Jesus Christ"; the latter refers to His indwelling, who is our Peace. The one He has bequeathed as a legacy to all men: the testator died, and left in His will a perfect reconciliation between God and man, which is for all who are willing to avail themselves of it; the other is a gift, which must be appropriated and used, or it will be ineffectual.

The order of these two varieties of peace is invariable.—We must have peace with God before we can enjoy the peace of God. We must receive the atonement, with all its blessed comfort, before we can enter upon our heritage in Christ Jesus. A believer, whose feet were dipping in the chill waters of the river, said to me recently, when speaking of her enjoyment of some of the deeper aspects of Christian experience, "I am afraid I have been building from the top. I see now, as I come near eternity, that one's foundations must be strong and sure before one can build on them. I need now more than ever the blood of Christ." This, perhaps, is one of the perils of the present day. The Church is arraying herself in her beautiful garments. The gold pieces of Christian thought and life are becoming current coin, taken from the coffers, where they have too long lain, and distributed broadcast. Treatises and tractlets on the innermost aspects of the blessed life are plentiful as flowers in May. There is a danger, therefore, of young converts and others occupying themselves with such themes, and not paying sufficient attention to the Divine order.

Christ dying for us on the cross must precede Christ living in us by His Spirit; justification with its evidences must be well apprehended before sanctification with its fruits; the peace with God must shed its benediction over the soul before it can enter upon the peace of God. Ah soul! thou hast experienced the former; dost thou know the latter? Dost thou know what it is for Christ to enter into the closed doors of the inner chamber of the heart, and say, "Peace be unto thee"? what it is to hear His voice speaking above the tumult of the inland lake of thy soul, and making a great calm? what it is for Him to deal with the springs of the inner life, which lie deeper than emotion or fancy, and pour in His infinite serenity, so that the outflow may be pellucid and tranquil?

Christ lays stress on His peace. He must mean the very peace that filled His own heart; not something like it, but the same, always keeping the heart with the affections, and the mind with its thoughts. This being so, we infer—

That His peace is consistent with a perfect knowledge of coming sorrow.—He knew all things that awaited Him (John xviii. 4): the treachery of Judas, the denial by Peter, the forsaking by all, the shame and spitting, the cross and grave; and yet He spoke serenely of His peace. It is therefore consistent with the certain outlook toward darkness and the shadow of death. You may know from certain symptoms that cancer has struck its fangs into your flesh, and that paralysis has begun to creep along your spine, that your dearest is barked by the Woodsman for felling, that your means of subsistence will inevitably dry up; but, facing all these, as Jesus faced the cross, you may still be conscious of a peace that passeth understanding.

That it is consistent with energetic action.—Men are disposed to think that peace is one of the last fruits of the tree of life, which drops into the hand of the aged. A man says to himself, I shall have to relinquish this active life, to settle in some quiet country home in the midst of nature, and then perhaps I shall know what peace means. A snug home and a competence, the culture of flowers, the slow march of the seasons, tender home-love, far away from the hustling throng of the world—these are the conditions of peace. Not so, says Christ: "Arise, let us go hence." Let us leave this quiet harbor, and launch out into the stormy deep. Let us leave this still chamber, around the windows of which the vines cling, and go forth into the garden where the cedars fight with the tempest, and amidst it all we shall find it possible to enjoy the peace that passeth knowledge. Let men and women immersed in the throng of daily toil, young men, busy men, understand that Christ's peace is for those who hear the bugle note of duty summoning them to arise, and go hence.

That the chief evidence of this peace is in the leisureliness of the heart.—Christ's possession of peace was very evident through all the stormy scenes that followed. With perfect composure He could heal the ear of Malchus, and stay the impetuosity of Peter; could reason quietly with the slave that smote Him, and bid the daughters of Jerusalem not to weep; could open paradise to the dying thief, and the door of John's home to the reception of His mother. Few things betray the presence of His peace more than the absence of irritability, fretfulness, and feverish haste, which expend the tissues of life.

Oh that you may now receive from Christ this blessed gift! Let the peace of Christ rule in your heart; it is your high privilege, be not backward in availing yourself of it. It will be as oil to the machinery of life.

II. THE SOURCES OF CHRIST'S PEACE.—(1) The vision of the Father.—"If ye loved Me, ye would rejoice because I said, I go unto the Father."

Throughout these closing chapters He seems able to speak of nothing else. His mind ranges from the disciples whom He was leaving to the Father to whom He was going. Almost unconsciously He gives us a glimpse of His self-repression in staying so long away from His Father's manifested presence, when He says that if we loved Him we would be glad to lose His bodily presence because He had gone to be with the Father. He gives us to understand how real and near the Father was to Him, and how He longed to be again in His bosom! He was so occupied with this thought, that He reckoned little of what lay between. Hail! ye stormy waters of death, stormy winds, and boisterous waves, ye do but waft my soul nearer its haven in the Father's love!

It is the thought of the Father that gives peace, because it robs life of its terrors and death of its sting. Why fear what life may bring when the Father has arranged each successive step of its pathway! Why dread Judas or Caiaphas, Herod or Pilate since the Father lies between the soul and them as a rampart of rock! Why lose heart amid the perplexities and discouragements, whose dark shadows lie heavily on the hills, when in the green pastures of the valley the Father's love tends the sheep! Ask Christ to reveal the Father to you. Live in His everlasting love, and learn what He can be amid the storm and tumult as a very present help.

(2) Disentanglement from the world.—"The prince of this world cometh, and hath nothing in Me." He came first at the beginning of the Saviour's life, with temptations to his ambitions; he came again at its close, with temptations to that natural shrinking from pain which is characteristic of a highly organized nature. "Back, Son of Man! Thou canst not bear the cross and spear, the nail and thorn! Thy tender flesh will ill sustain Thee when the sorrows of death and the pains of hell get hold upon Thee!" So Satan came; but there was no response in the heart of Christ, no answering voice from the depths of His soul, no traitor within to join hands with the tempter without. There was no square inch of territory in all Christ's nature which the devil could claim, or from which he could operate.

This is a clue to Christ's peace, which we do well to follow till it lead us out into the open. As long as we are entangled with this world, peace evades us, just as sleep, which comes easily to the laboring man who has nothing beyond his daily wage, vanishes from the pillow of the merchant, who on stormy nights thinks uneasily of the vessels which carry his wealth far out at sea. We must stand clear of the ambitions of the world, of the fear or favor of man, of the avaricious craving for wealth, or the fear of poverty. We must put the cross of Christ between us and the world, which was judged at Calvary. We must be able to say truly that our treasure is in heaven and our heart also, and that we seek the things where Christ sitteth at the right hand of God. Then the stock-market may fluctuate, riches go or come, men praise or hate, nought will affect our peace, any more than the tumults of a continental city, in which we are spending a night in transit, can cause us serious disturbance.

(3) Supreme love.—"I love the Father." I have so often noticed how a supreme love in a young girl's life seems to calm and quiet her, because it draws the whole of her nature in one strong flow toward the man of her choice. Before that, there was a waywardness, a vacillation, a nervous excitement, which passed away as soon as love dawned upon her soul. So long as the heart is subject to every influence, it quivers and wavers as the magnet needle when swept by

streams of electricity. A strong uniting love does for us what the strong attraction of the pole does for the needle. Christ loved the Father. There was no difficulty in bearing what He sent, or doing what He bade. There were no rival claimants, no questionings or debate within the palace of His heart. Every passion and emotion of His human nature was quieted and stilled in the set of His whole being toward the Father. If you too would have peace, you must love; you must love supremely Him who alone is worthy, who can never disappoint or fail. And in proportion as you love God, you will find pleasure in all beautiful things, in all lovely persons, in all the fair gifts of nature and life. Oh, love the Lord, O my soul, and all that is within me, love His holy name!

(4) A supreme source of authority.—"As the Father gave Me commandment, even so I do." Every soul must have a supreme source of authority in its life, if it is to have peace. Its own whim, the suggestion of passion, the vagrant impulse of the moment, are inconsistent with tranquillity. There must be for each of us one voice which is imperative, one command which is indisputable, one authority which admits of no gainsaying. If you will search your heart you will see that this is so. Compare the restlessness of the Book of Judges with the tranquillity of the reign of Solomon, and you will have an apt illustration of your own experience before consecration put Christ on His throne, and afterward. When the true Melchizedek established his reign within you, at once your heart became Salem, the city of peace. When you put the government upon His shoulder, He set up His reign within you as the Prince of Peace. Happy for you, if to the increase of His government there is no end; for of the increase of your peace there will be no end either.

Combine these four—the sense of God's presence and providence in the details of life; detachment from the world; a supreme love to God; the recognition in everything that you are His slave—and you will comply with the conditions of participating in the peace of Christ which He offers. Some persons have a marvellous faculty of imparting their own tranquillity in an accident, a storm, an illness; their aspect, tones, manner, are like the repose of a summer's evening after a sultry day: so shall Christ be to you, and you to others.

III. CHRIST'S GIVING CONTRASTED WITH THE WORLD'S.—"Not as the world giveth, give I unto you."

The world wishes peace, but lightly speaks the word; frequently wishing it when there is least warrant for it; wishing it without doing anything to produce it; wishing it whilst glorying over a wrong, healing slightly a wound, covering with the turf the crater of a volcano. Christ, on the other hand, lays the foundations of peace in suitable conditions of a holy and healthy life.

With the world, peace is a passing emotion; with Christ, a settled principle of action—the perfect balance and equilibrium of the soul, out of which comes all that is fair, strong, wholesome.

The world's peace consists in the absence of untoward circumstances; Christ's is altogether independent of circumstances, and consists in the state of the heart. It matters nothing to Him that in the world we have tribulation. He bids us be of good cheer, because in Him we shall have peace. The wildest conjunction of outward things cannot break the perfect peace which nestles to His heart, as Noah's dove to the hand which plucked it in from the weltering waters.

"Let not your heart be troubled," the Master says again. You may be troubled on every side, but be not troubled. Do not let the trouble come inside. Watch carefully against its intrusion, as you would against that of any other form of temptation. Let My peace, like a sentinel, keep you; and as you look forward to the unknown future, out of which spectral figures emerge, do not be afraid. There is a part for you to do, as well as for Me. I can give you My peace, but you must avoid any and everything that will militate against its possession and growth.

XIV

The Story of the Vine

"I am the true Vine, and My Father is the Husbandman."—JOHN xv. 1.

We have now a story to tell which, in the eye of heaven, will make our world forever memorable and wonderful among her sister spheres. It is the story of the Vine, and how it was the Divine purpose our earth should be its fruitful soil, and our race intimately associated with its growth and history.

"I am the true Vine," said our Lord. Not improbably, as He was passing forth with His disciples into the moonlit air, He perceived a vine clustering around the window or door; and with an eye ever awake to each touch of natural beauty, and a heart always alert for spiritual lessons, He turned to them and said, What that vine is in the world of nature I am in relation to all true and faithful souls. I am the true Vine—true, not as opposed to false, but true in the sense of real, substantial, and enduring. The essential, as distinguished from the circumstantial; the eternal, as distinct from the temporary and transient.

Nature is a parable of God. In each of her forms we have a revelation of God. Not so complete as that given through the mind of prophets, or the life of Jesus Christ, but still a revelation of the Divine. Each natural object, as it stood in Eden's untainted beauty, displayed some aspect of Him, whom no man can see and live. The apple-tree among the trees of the wood; the rose of Sharon: the lily of the vale; the cedar, with its dark green foliage; the rock for strength; the sea for multitudinousness; the heaven with its limpid blue, like the Divine compassion, overarching all—these are some of the forthshadowings in the natural world of spiritual qualities in the nature of God. The vine was made the clinging, helpless plant it is, that it might forever remind men of certain deep characteristics of the Divine nature.

I. THE VINE AND ITS BRANCHES.—The unity of the vine. The vine and its branches constitute one plant. Some branches may be trailed along the trellis-work outside the cottage door, others conducted through hothouse after hothouse; yet one life, one stream of sap, one essential quality and character pervades them all, from the dark root, buried in the soil, to the furthest twig or leaf. Yonder branch, waving its fronds high up against the hothouse glass, cannot say to that long leafless branch hidden beneath the shelf, You do not belong to me, nor I to you. No twig is independent of another twig. However different the functions, root and branches, leaves and cluster, all together make one composite but organic whole. So is it with Christ. All who are one with Him are one with each other. The branches that were nearest the root in the days of Pentecost are incomplete without the last converts that shall be added in the old age of the world. Those without these will not be made perfect.

This is the underlying truth of the holy Catholic Church. Men have tried to show that it must be an outward and visible organization, consisting of those who had received, through a long line of apostolical succession, some mystic power for administering rites and conferring absolution, together with those who came beneath the touch of their priestly hands. That theory has notoriously broken down. But the truth of which it is a grotesque travesty is presented in our

Lord's conception of the vine, deeply planted in the dark grave of Joseph's garden, which had reached down its branches through the ages, and in which every believing soul has a part. Touch Christ, become one with Him in living union, abide in Him, and you are one with the glorious company of the apostles, the goodly fellowship of the prophets, the noble army of martyrs and the Church of the First-born, whose names are written in heaven.

The pliancy of the vine.—More than most plants it needs a husbandman. It cannot stand upright like other fruit-trees, but requires a skillful hand to guide its pliant branches along the espaliers, or to entwine them in the trellis-work. It suggests a true thought of the appearance presented to the world by Christ and His Church.

Mrs. Hamilton King, in her description of the sermon preached in the hospital by Ugo Bassi, on the eve of the great movement which, by the expulsion of the Austrians, gave Italy to the Italians, specially dwells on this. Down five wards the prisoners are lying on the hospital-beds from which they will never rise again. To them the deep voice of the hero-preacher tells the story of the vine: how "it is tied to a stake, and if its arms stretch out, it is but cross-wise; they are also forced and bound."

Thus it was with Christ. Never following His own way; always bound to the imperative must of the Father's will; yielded to the cross as a willing Sufferer. And so it has been with His followers. Not strong to stand alone, but always yielded to the Father's will, that He should lead them whither He would—to a cross, if needs were; to persecution and shame, if this would better serve His purpose; to a Gethsemane, if that were the only gate to life.

Yield thyself to those loving hands. They may lead thee afar from thy original purpose—twisting thee in and out with many a contortion; fixing thee with nail and fastening; trailing thee over the wall, to droop thy clusters to the hands of strangers. Nevertheless, be sure to let Him have His way with thee; this is necessary for the accomplishment of His purpose.

The suffering of the vine.—When, in the spring, "the grace of the green vine makes all the land lovely, and the shoots begin to wind and wave in the blue air," the husbandman comes in with pruning-hook and shears, and strips it bare of all its innocent pride. Nor is this all. Even in the vintage it is not allowed to glory in the results of the year, "the branches are torn down and trodden in the wine-press, while the vine stands stripped and desolate."

So it has always been. The well-being of the world has been greatly promoted through the Church, but always at an infinite cost to herself. Christ's people have always been a suffering people, and it is in exact proportion to their anguish that they have enriched mankind. They have saved others, but not themselves. The red stream of blood that has vitalized the world, has flowed from broken hearts.

The interdependence of vine and branches.—In God from eternity dwelt a wealth of love, pity, and yearning over the souls of men, that could not express themselves directly. There was no language for the infinite passion of the Divine heart. Hence the gift of the Son, through whom, when He had become flesh, the Infinite might express Himself. But even this was not sufficient. The vine-root is not enough in itself, it must have branches to carry its rich juices to the clusters, so that these may hang free of each other in the sun and air. Christ must have branches—long lines of saved souls extending down the centuries—through which to communicate Himself to men.

We have seen how necessary the root is to the branches. Only from it can our fruit be found. But let us humbly, yet gladly, believe that we are also necessary to Christ. He cannot do without us. The Son wants sons; angels will not suffice. Through redeemed men alone can He achieve His eternal purpose. I hear the Root pleading for more and yet more branch-life, that it may cover the world with goodly shadow and fruit.

II. FRUIT OR NO FRUIT.—From all that has been said, it is clear that the one purpose in the vine is fruit-bearing. See, here, how the Divine Teacher accentuates it. "Fruit," "much fruit," "more fruit." Nothing less will content Him in any one of us. For this we were taken out of the wild vine in which we were by nature, and grafted into Him; for this the regeneration of the Holy Ghost, and the discipline of life; for this the sunshine of His love, and the dew of the Holy Ghost. It becomes each seriously to ask, "Am I bringing forth fruit unto God? There may be orthodoxy of doctrine, correctness in life, and even heartiness of service; but is there fruit, much fruit, more fruit?"

Fruit!—This is the only condition of being retained in living union with the Vine.

Much fruit!—Only thus will the Father be glorified.

More fruit.—Otherwise there must be the repeated use of the knife.

Nowhere does the Lord contemplate a little fruit. A berry here and there! A thin bunch of sour, unripened grapes! Yet it is too true that many believers yield no more than this. He comes to us hungry for grapes, but behold a few mildewed bunches, not fit to eat!

Where there is no fruit, there has been no real union with the Vine. Probably you are a professor, but not a possessor; a nominal Christian, an attendant at church or chapel, but not really one with Christ. True union with Him produces a temper, a disposition, a ripe and mellow experience which certainly indicates that Christ is within. You cannot simulate the holy joy, the thoughtful love, the tranquil serenity, the strong self-control, which mark the soul which is in real union with Jesus; but where there is real abiding, these things will be in us and abound, and we shall be neither barren, nor unfruitful in the knowledge of our Lord Jesus Christ.

III. THE KNIFE AND THE FIRE.—"Every branch in Me that beareth fruit," the Father who is the Husbandman "purgeth it that it may bring forth more fruit." Too many children of God, when passing through great physical and other suffering, account it punishment. Nay, it is not punitive, but purgative. This is the pruning-knife, cutting away the shoots of the self-life, that the whole energy of the soul may be directed to the manifesting of the life of the Lord Jesus. It may seem a grievous waste to see the floor of the hothouse or vineyard littered with fronds and shoots and leaves, but there need be no lament: the branches of the autumn will well repay each stroke of that keen edge with fuller, richer fruit. So we gain by loss, we live as we die, the inward man is renewed as the outer decays.

The knife is in the Father's hand; let us never forget that. He will not intrust this delicate and difficult work to man or angel. Shall we not be in subjection to the Father of our spirits and live? Blessed be the Father of our Lord Jesus, and our Father in Him. He that spared not Christ may be trusted to do the best for us.

Employing the same word, the Master said, "Now ye have been pruned through the word that I have spoken to you." Perhaps if we were more often to yield ourselves to the pruning of the Word, we should escape the pruning of sore pain and trial. If the work were done by the golden edge of Scripture, it might make the iron edge of chastisement needless. Therefore, when we take the Word of God in hand, let us ask the great Husbandman to use it for the pruning away of all that is carnal or evil, so that His life may have unhindered sway.

But if we will not bear fruit we must be taken away. We shall lose our sphere of Christian service, and be exposed as hollow and lifeless professors. The vine-branch that has no wealth of purple clusters is good for nothing. Salt which is savorless is fit neither for the land nor the dunghill. Vine-branches that bear no fruit are cast into the fire. Professors that lack the grace of a holy temper, and the beauty of a consistent life are taken away. "Men cast them into the fire and they are burned."

These three years the Divine Husbandman has come hungrily seeking fruit of thee, yet in vain. Nevertheless, He will spare thee for this year also, that thou mayest mend thy ways. This is the reason of thy multiplied anxieties; He is pruning thee. If thou bearest fruit, it will be well, eternally well; but if not, then it is inevitable that thou shalt be cut away as dead and useless wood.

XV

"Abide in Me, and I in you"

"Abide in Me, and I in you. As the branch cannot bear fruit of itself, except it abide in the vine; no more can ye, except ye abide in Me."—JOHN xv. 4.

These words are so familiar by constant repetition, that their power to awaken the soul is greatly lessened. They go and come through ear and mind, as a lodger who has gone and come with exactly the same appearance and at precisely the same hours for years, and no one notices him now, because there is nothing novel about him to awake notice or remark. How good would it be if we could hear this tender injunction for the first time. Next to this, let us ask the Divine Spirit to rid it of the familiarity of long use, to re-mint it, and to make it fresh and vital, that it may seem to us that we have never before realized how much Jesus meant, when He said, Abide in Me.

Perhaps it may assist us, if we adopt another English word for abide, and one which, in some respects even more neatly, and certainly in sound, resembles the Greek. It is the word remain; so that we may read the Master's bidding thus: Remain in Me, and I in you.

This word is often employed in the New Testament in connection with house and home. "Mary abode [or remained] with Elizabeth for three months"; and "There abide [or remain]," said our Lord, when giving His disciples direction for their preaching tour, and referring to some hospitable house which has been opened to welcome them. It is used three times in that memorable colloquy which introduced John and Andrew to their future Teacher and Lord; "Master," they said, "where abidest [or remainest] Thou; He saith unto them, 'Come and ye shall see.' They came therefore, and saw where He is remaining, and they remained with Him that day." And again: "Zacchaeus, make haste and come down, for to-day I must remain in thy house." We are to remain in Christ as a man stays in his home.

It is inferred, of course, that we are in Christ.—It would be absurd to bid a man remain in a house unless he were already within its doors. We must be sure that we are in Christ. Naturally we were outside—"Remember," says the Apostle, "that aforetime ye were separate from Christ, alienated from the commonwealth of Israel, strangers from the covenants of promise, having no hope, and without God in the world." We were shoots in the wild vine, partaking of its nature, involved in its curse, threatened by the axe which lay at its root. But all this is altered now. The Father, who is the Husbandman, of His abundant grace and mercy, has taken us out of the wild vine and grafted us into the true. "Of God are ye in Christ Jesus."

It is quite true that we repented of our sins, and turned toward God; that we have believed in Christ, and taken His yoke; that we have found rest under the shelter of His cross, and joy in expecting His advent; but we must never forget that behind all these movements of our will, and choice, and faith, were the willing and doing of God Himself. It is the Lord's doing, and it is marvellous in our eyes. "Blessed be the God and Father of our Lord Jesus Christ, who hath begotten us again unto a living hope." What confidence this gives us! We are in Christ by the act of God's grace and power, and surely He who put us in, can keep us there. Did He not shut

Noah into the ark, and keep him there amid all the crash of the pitiless deluge! We have only to consent to remain, and allow God to perfect that which concerneth us. Be confident of this very thing, that He who began a good work in you, will perform it until the day of Jesus Christ.

The stress which the Master lays on our abiding in Him.—He appears to summon all His forces to accentuate His parting message. You always reserve your most important injunctions to the last, that they may remain fresh and impressive, as the train steams out of the station, as the boat leaves the landing-stage; so Christ left this entreaty to the last, that it might carry with it the emphasis of a parting message forevermore. But note how He drives it home. Its keyword occurs eleven times in eleven consecutive verses. He depicts the terrible result if we do not abide: we shall wither, be taken away, and consigned to the fire. He shows how utterly we shall miss the one end of our existence, the glorification of the Father by fruit-bearing, unless we strenuously and continuously abide. He allures by the thought of the much fruit; by the assurance of success in prayer; by the promise of fullness of joy, of love, and of blessedness. He entreats, commands, exhorts, all in one breath. It is as though He were to say, "Children, I am leaving you; there are many things I desire for you, many commands to utter, many cautions, many lessons; but I am content to leave all unsaid, if only you will remember this one all-inclusive bidding, Abide in Me, remain in Me; stay where God has put you; deepen, emphasize, intensify the union already existing between you and Me. From Me is your fruit found. Without Me ye can do nothing. Abide in Me, and I in you. Grow up into Me in all things, which am the Head, rooted and built up in Me, and stablished by your faith, even as ye were taught."

There are many analogies to this appeal.—The sun says to the little earth-planet, Abide in me. Resist the temptation to fly into space, remain in the solar sphere, and I will abide in the formation of thy rocks, the verdure of thy vegetation, and all living things, baptizing them in my fire.

Abide in me, says the ocean to the alcove, that shows symptoms of division from its waves. Keep thy channel unsilted and open, and I will pour my fullness up to thy farthest shore, twice in every twenty-four hours.

Abide in me: the vine says it to the branch, that it may impart supplies of life and fruit; the air says it to the lung, that it may minister ozone and oxygen to its cells; the magnet says it to the needle, that it may communicate its own specific quality, and fit it to guide across the ocean the mighty steamer, laden with the freight of human life.

Abide in me: the artist says it to the novice; Edison would say it to some young Faraday; the preacher to the student. Any man who is eager to impart his ideas to coming time is glad when some young life, eager, quick to receive formative impressions, presents itself. Here, says he, is my opportunity of incarnating myself afresh, and still living, speaking, painting, when my life is done. "Stay with me, young soul, share my home, saturate yourself with my ideas and methods of expression, go to no other fields to glean, and I will give my best self in return."

So, also, the mother speaks to the child. If she is wise she will be chary of handing it over to the nurse, or sending it away to the care of strangers, except for the hours necessary for education. Companions and games, books and studies, shall be within the influences of her mother's love; and she, in return, will gladly bestow herself to the eager life that waits on her every movement, look, and word.

In all these cases, it is always the stronger that pleads with the weaker to abide, promising the communication to fuller life. Each, in measure, says, in the words of the glorious Christ, "I am stronger, wiser, fuller, better than you; all is mine that it may be yours, therefore, abide in Me, and I will abide in you."

Notice Christ's consciousness of sufficiency for the needs of men.—It were blasphemous audacity to speak thus, if He were not more than man. He affirms that there can be no life apart from Him; that souls not united with Him wither on the forest floor. He says, that fruit-bearing is only possible to those who receive from His fullness grace for grace. He says, that to be in union with Him will secure union with all holy souls. He says, that if His words are carefully pondered and obeyed, we shall make no petition which His Father will not grant. He says, that His love, in quality and quantity, is like the love that God has toward Himself; that His commands take rank with those of Deity. He offers Himself to all mankind in coming ages, as their contemporary, and as the one sufficient source of life and godliness. All these assumptions are made in the range of these verses; and as we ponder them, we feel that the Speaker must be conscious of being other than human, and as possessing those infinite attributes which are the sole property of the Eternal.

Yet, who shall say that He has offered more than He can give? Have not we tested Him in each of these particulars, and do not we, who have come to Him by faith, know that in no one item has He been guilty of exaggeration? We were dead, but behold, we live! We spent our energies in profitless work; but now we bear fruit unto God. We were lonely and isolated, but now have come to the heavenly Jerusalem, to the innumerable company of angels, and to the Church of the Firstborn. Our prayers were aimless and ineffective; but now we have the petitions we desired. New hope and joy have filled our hearts, as the ruddy clusters hang full and ripe in the autumn. Prove Him for yourself and see if this shall not be so for you also. Only give yourself entirely up to Christ. Abide in Him. Remain in Him. Let thought and speech and life be bathed in the influences of His Holy Spirit; Let the sap of His life flow where the sap of the self-life was wont to flow; and lo! old things will pass away, and all things will become new.

The law and method of abiding.—There are two currents always flowing within our reach:
The Not I, and the I.
The last Adam, and the first.
The Spirit, and the flesh.

God has put us by His grace into the first of these. The Master says, "Stop there." Much as when a father puts his little boy in the railway carriage, en route for home, and says, "My boy, stop where you are. Do not get out; no change is necessary." We are in Christ by regeneration and faith. We may not always be thinking about Him; but we remain in Him, unless by unfaithfulness or sin we consciously and voluntarily leave Him. And if we have left Him for a single moment, it is always possible by confession and renewal to regain our old position.

This is confessedly an inadequate figure of speech. There is a sense in which the member cannot be amputated from the body, and the soul cannot be divorced from its union with Christ. But we are not dealing now with our integral oneness with Christ for life, but with our abiding union with Him for fruit-bearing and service. And again we say, for those who are so immersed in daily business, as to be unable for long together to keep their minds fixed on Christ, that their abiding in Him does not depend on their perpetual realization and consciousness of His presence, but on the faith that they have done and said nothing inconsistent with the holy bond of fellowship.

You are in a lift until you step out of it, though you may not be thinking of the lift. You keep on a road until you take a turning right or left, although, engrossed in converse with your friend, you do not think of the road. You are in Christ amid the pressure of daily care, and the haste of business, so long as your face is toward the Lord, your attitude that of humble submission, and your conscience void of offence. During the day it is therefore possible at any moment to say, "I am in Thee, O blessed Christ. I have not all the rapture and passion of more radiant hours, but I am in Thee, because I would not by a single act, leave Thy secret place." If at such a moment you are conscious that you are not able to say as much, instantly go back over the past few hours, discover the place when you severed yourself from your Lord, and return.

Study Godet's beautiful definition of abiding: "It is the continuous act by which the Christian lays aside all he might draw from his own wisdom, strength and merit, to desire all from Christ by the inward aspiration of faith."

Whenever, therefore, temptation arises to leave the words of Christ (ver. 7), for the maxims of the world, step back, remain in Him, deny yourself.

Whenever you are tempted to leave the narrow path of His commandments (ver. 10), to follow the impulses of your own nature, reckon yourself dead to these that you may run in those.

Whenever you are tempted to forsake the holy temper of Christ's love, for jealousy, envy, hatred, step back and say, I will not go out of my hiding-place, I elect to remain in the love of God.

The one effort of life is therefore reduced to a persistent resistance to all the suggestions of the world, the flesh and the devil; that we should step out of that Blessed Man into whom the Father has grafted us.

Then He abides in us. He is strong where we are weak, loving and tender where we are thoughtless, holy where we fail. He is in us as wisdom, righteousness, sanctification, and redemption; and as the hope of glory.

XVI

Prayer that Prevails

"If ye abide in Me, and My words abide in you, ye shall ask what ye will, and it shall be done unto you."—JOHN xv. 7.

Christ expected answers to His prayers, and in all His teaching leads us to feel that we shall be able to obtain, through prayer, what otherwise would not come to our hand. He knew all that was to be known of natural law and the Father's heart; but notwithstanding His perfect acquaintance with the mysteries of the Father's government, He said, "Ask what ye will, and it shall be done unto you."

A careful comparison between the confident assurances of the Master, and the experience of Christians, as detailed in their biographies or personal confessions, discloses a wide difference between His words and the findings of His disciples. Many have become accustomed to disappointment in prayer. They have asked so many things which they have never received; have sought so much without finding; have knocked so repeatedly, but the door has remained closed. We are in the habit of accounting for our failure by saying that probably our prayer was not according to the will of God, or that God withheld the less that He might give us something better. In some cases there may be even an unspoken misgiving about the harmony of prayer with our Father's love and wisdom, or with a perfect confidence in Him as doing the best for us in the world. We forget that if we prayed as we should, we should ask what was according to His will. We evade Christ's definite words, "Whatsoever ye shall ask in My Name, that will I do."

When we consider the lives of some who have wrought mightily for God, it is clear that they had learned a secret which eludes many of us. Take this, for instance, from the biography of Dr. Burns Thomson. "When much together as students," writes his friend, "we agreed on special petitions, and the Lord encouraged us by giving answers, so early and so definite, as could only have come from Himself, so that no room was left for the shadow of a doubt that God was the Hearer and Answerer of prayer. Once the answer came the same day, and at another time, whilst we were yet speaking. My friend often spoke of our agreement, to the glory of Him who fulfilled to us His promise, and I refer to it, to encourage others." This is but one leaf out of the great library of prayers, intercessions, and supplications for all saints, which stand recorded before God.

We naturally turn to our Lord's last utterances in which His instructions about prevailing prayer are fuller than those of the Sermon on the Mount; and than those given in the mid-passage of His earthly life, which depict the importunity of the widow with the unjust judge, and of the friend with his friend at midnight. The words spoken in the chapter we are now considering are particularly pertinent to our purpose, because they deal exclusively with the age to which our Lord frequently referred as "that day," the day of Pentecost, the age of the Holy Ghost, the day of this dispensation.

OUR LORD TEACHES THAT ANY PRAYER WHICH IS TO PREVAIL WITH GOD

MUST PASS

FIVE TESTS, though these are but different phases of the same attitude.

(1) The glory of the Father.—"That the Father may be glorified in the Son" (John xiv. 13). The one purpose of Christ on earth was to glorify the Father; and at the close of His life here He was conscious that He had not striven in vain. "Now," said He, "is the Son of Man glorified, and God is glorified in Him." This was the purpose of His earthly career, and it was perfectly consistent with that of His eternal being; for each person of the Holy Trinity is ever intent on unfolding and displaying the moral beauty of the other twain. Having sat down at the right hand of the Majesty on high, Christ still pursues His cherished purpose of making His Father known, loved, and adored. No prayer, therefore, can hope to succeed with Him, or can claim His concurrent intercession, which is out of harmony with this sublime intent.

Whatever petition we offer should be submitted to this standard. Can we establish it in the presence of Christ, that our request will promote the glory of the Father? Bring in your evidence—establish your pleas—adduce your strong reasons. If you can make good your claim, your prayer is already granted. But be sure that it is impossible to seek the glory of God consistently with selfish aims. These two can no more coexist than light and darkness in the same cubic space. The glory of God will ever triumph at our cost. It is equally certain that none of us can truly pray for the glory of God, unless we are living for it. It is only out of the heart that has but one purpose in life and death, that those prayers emanate which touch the tenderest chord in the Saviour's nature, and awaken all His energies to their highest activity, "That will I do."

(2) In Christ's Name.—"Whatsoever ye shall ask in My Name" (John xiv. 13). Throughout the Holy Scriptures, name stands for nature. The Master says, "You must ask My Nature." In other words, when we pray, it must not be as the self-nature, but as the Christian-nature dictates. We always know when that is paramount. It excludes boasting; it is pure, peaceable and loving; it is far removed from the glare and gaud of the world, it is full of Calvary, Olivet, and Pentecost. There are days in our life when we feel borne along on its tidal current; when Christ is in us, the hope of glory; when a power is working within us beyond what we can ask or think; when we live, yet not we, but Christ in us—these are the times most propitious for prayer. Pour out your heart before God. Let Christ, who is in you by the Holy Spirit, speak to the Christ who is above you on the throne. Let the living water, which has descended from the eternal city, return back to its source through the channel of your heart. This is praying in His Name, and according to His Nature.

Before we can expect our prayers to prosper, let us sit quietly down, and, putting aside all other voices, permit the Christ-nature to speak. It is only in proportion as it countersigns our petitions that they will reach the audience-chamber of eternity. Surely, if this test were properly applied, many of the petitions we now offer so glibly would never leave our lips, and we should be satisfied about the fate of many another prayer which, like some ill-fated barque, has left our shores, and never been heard of again. But again let it be remembered that none can pray in the name of Christ who do not live for that name, like those early evangelists of whom John says that for the sake of the Name they took nothing of the Gentiles. The name of Christ must be predominant in life, if it is to be efficacious in prayer.

(3) Abide in Christ.—"If ye abide in Me, . . . ask what ye will" (John xv. 7). We are in Christ, by the grafting of the great Husbandman, who took us out of the wild vine of nature, and incorporated us with Christ. That union is forever, but its conscious enjoyment and helpfulness arise only in so far as we keep His commandments. A limb may be in the body, and yet be dislocated and useless. If you are in a train running through to your destination at the terminus, all that is necessary is to resist the temptation to alight at the stations en route, and to remain where you are. If, then, God the Father has put you into Christ, and is seeking to establish you in Him, be careful to resist every temptation or suggestion to depart from living fellowship by any act of disobedience or unbelief.

If you abide in Christ in daily fellowship, it will not be difficult to pray aright, for He has promised to abide in those who abide in Him; and the sap of the Holy Ghost, securing for you fellowship with your unseen Lord, will produce in you, as fruit, desires and petitions similar to those which He unceasingly presents to His Father. Throughout the ages Christ has been asking of God. This is the perpetual attitude of the Son to the Father. He cannot ask what the Father may not give. To get then into the current of His prayer is to be sure of success. Abide in Him, that He may abide in you; not only in the activities of holy service, but in the intercessions and supplications of the hour of private prayer.

(4) Submit prayer to the correction of the Word.—"If My words abide in you" . . . (John xv. 7). Christ's words have been compared to a court of solemn and stately presences, sitting to try our prayers before they pass on into the Master's presence.

Here is a prayer which is selfish and earth-born, grasping at the prizes of worldly ambition and greed. But as it enters it encounters that solemn word, "Seek ye first the kingdom of God and His righteousness," and it turns back surprised and ashamed.

Here is another prayer, full of imprecation and unkindness toward some one who has maligned or injured the petitioner. But it is met by that solemn word of the Master, "Love your enemies, pray for them that despitefully use you," and it hastens to retire.

Here is another prayer full of murmuring regret because of the pressure of the cross, the weight of the restraining yoke. But forthwith that notable word of Christ forbids its further progress, saying, "In the world ye shall have tribulation; but be of good cheer, I have overcome the world." In the presence of that reminder and rebuke, the prayer, abashed, turns away its face and departs. Like the accusers of the woman taken in the act of sin, prayers like these are inwardly convicted of unfitness, and go forth.

The words of Christ forbid unsuitable prayer, but they also stir the heart with great desire for the realization of those good things which Christ has promised to them that love Him. In this sense prayer becomes a dialogue between the Master who says, "Seek ye My face," and the disciple who responds, "Thy face, Lord, will I seek."

(5) Fruit-bearing.—"I appointed you that ye should bear fruit that . . ." (John xv. 16). In other words, answers to prayers depend very largely on our ministry to others. If we are prompted by

desire for our own comfort, peace, or enjoyment, we shall stand but a poor chance of audience in the secret of His presence. If, on the other hand, our prayers are connected with our fruit-bearing—that is, with our ministry to others, with the coming of the kingdom, and the accomplishment of God's purpose of salvation—the golden sceptre will be extended to us, as when Ahasuerus said to Esther, "What is thy request? Even to the half of the kingdom it shall be performed."

Is sun needed to ripen the fruit? Ask for it. The Father waits to give it. Is dew or rain needed that the pitchers may be filled to the brim with water which is to be made wine? Ask for it. God is not unrighteous to forget your work and labor of love. Ask for all but pruning; this the Father will administer, according to the good pleasure of His goodness. The fruit-bearing branches have a right to claim and appropriate all that is needed for the sweetening and ripening of their precious burden.

The temple of prayer is thus guarded from the intrusion of the unprepared footstep by many tests. At the foot of the marble steps, we are challenged for the watchword; and if we do not speak in harmony with God's glory, our further passage is peremptorily stayed. The key, engraven with the name of Jesus, will only obey the hand in which His nature is throbbing. We must be in Him, if He is to plead in us. His words must prune, direct, and control our aspirations; His service must engage our energies. We must take part in the camp with His soldiers, in the vineyard with His husbandmen, in the temple-building with His artificers. It is as we serve our King, that we can reckon absolutely on His answer to our prayers.

XVII

The hatred of the World

"They shall put you out of the synagogues: yea, the time cometh, that whosoever killeth you will think that he doeth God service. And these things they will do unto you, because they have not known the Father, nor Me."—JOHN xvi. 2, 3.

How near love and hate dwell in these words of Jesus! He had been urging His disciples to cultivate perfect love, the love of God; He now turns to describe the inevitable hatred with which they would be assailed in the world that knew neither the Father nor Himself. And if an additional motive were needed to induce that love, it would surely be given by the consideration of that hate.

This is no unimportant theme. It touches, very nearly, the lives of thousands of believers amongst us. Though they have not to face the thumbscrew and the stake, they discover painfully enough that the offence of the Cross has not ceased. There are amongst us many who daily quiver under the venomous gibe of neighbor and fellow-workman, and find that their acceptance of Jesus Christ as Saviour and Master has suddenly changed their family and working-life from a garden of roses into a bed of thorns. Many a young man in the city counting-house, many a mechanic at the bench, many a traveller in the commercial-room, many a student on the college-benches, is doomed to discover that the world does not love the Church better than in those days when the fires gleamed in Smithfield, and men and women were burned to death for loving God. But how sweet to know that all this verifies the Master's words: Ye are not of the world, even as I am not of the world. If ye were of the world, the world would love his own; but because ye are not of the world, but I have chosen you out of the world, therefore the world hateth you.

I. WHAT THEN IS THE WORLD?—It consists of those who are destitute of the life and love of God, as contrasted with those who have received and welcomed the unspeakable gift which is offered to all in Jesus Christ. The great mass of the unregenerate and unbelieving, considered as a unity, is the world, as interpreted by our Lord and His apostles.

The world has its god and its religion, which was first instituted by Cain at the gates of Eden; its prince, and court, and laws; its maxims and principles; its literature and pleasures. It is dominated by a peculiar spirit which the apostle calls a lust or fashion, and resembles the German Zeit-Geist: an infection, an influence, a pageantry, a witchery; reminding us of the fabled mountain of loadstone which attracted vessels to itself for the iron that was in them, and presently drew the nails from the timbers, so that the whole fabric fell a helpless, shapeless mass into the waves. The votaries of the world attach themselves to the objects of sense, to the things which are seen and temporal. They have the utmost horror of poverty, suffering, and humiliation; these they consider their chief evils to be avoided at any cost; whilst they regard as the chief good, riches, pleasure, and honor.

The world is thus a great unity and entity; standing together as a mighty kingdom; united and compacted together as Nebuchadnezzar's image; environing the Church, as the great kingdoms of Assyria and Egypt did the chosen people of God in the days of the kings. It resembles a pack of wolves. "Behold," said Christ, "I send you forth as sheep in the midst of wolves." Between such irreconcilable opposites as the Church and the world, there cannot but be antagonism and strife. Each treasures and seeks what the other rejects as worthless. Each is devoted to ends that are inimical to the dearest interests of the other. Each follows a prince, who met the prince of the other, in mortal conflict. Let us thank Him, who out of this world chose us for Himself.

II. LET US TRACE THE STORY OF THE WORLD'S HATRED.—It was foretold in Eden. "I will put enmity," so God spoke to the serpent, "between thee and the woman, and between thy seed and her seed." We are not disposed to treat that ancient record with which our Bible opens as romance or fairy story, but to regard it as containing a true and authentic record of what actually transpired. That declaration is the key to the Bible. On every page we meet the conflict, the bruising of the Church's heel by the dark powers, and the increasing area of victory covered by our Emmanuel, the Virgin's Child. This hatred is then in the very nature of things, for this is but another name for God. It is, like others of the deepest facts in the experience of man, fundamental and inevitable, the outcome of mysteries which lie beyond the ken of man.

And it has characterized every age.—Abel is slain by Cain, who was of the evil one, and slew his brother. Joseph is put into a pit by his brethren, and into a prison by his master's wife; the Hebrew is smitten by the Egyptian; David is hunted by Saul as a partridge on the mountains; Micaiah is hated by Ahab because he always testifies against him; Jeremiah lives a very suffering stricken life, until he is slain in Egypt for remonstrating against a policy he could not alter; each of the little company then listening to Christ is forecast for a martyr's death, with, perhaps, the exception of John himself, whose life was martyrdom enough; Stephen sheds the blood of his pure and noble nature, and from that day to this the blood of the saints has poured in streams, until the last harrowing records, which have come to light, only of recent years, of the indescribable tortures and death of Armenian martyrs.

Each age has had its martyr-roll. They have been tortured, not accepting deliverance, have had trial of mockings and scourgings, yea, moreover of bonds and imprisonment; have been stoned, sawn asunder, tempted, and slain with the sword; wandering in deserts and mountains and caves, and the holes of the earth: of whom the world was not worthy.

The root or ground of hatred is not due to the evil discovered in the persons, who are the objects of the world's hate.—"They hated Me without a cause," our Saviour sorrowfully said. There might have been some cloke for the shamelessness of the world's sin, if He had not spoken words and done works among them such as none other ever said and did; but in the face of the perfect beauty of His character, the grace and truth of His words, and the loveliness of His deeds, it was by their perfidy He was crucified and slain. In vain He challenged them to convince Him of sin, and to bear witness to any evil which might justify their malicious cruelty. They knew it was innocent blood; but this knowledge, so far from mollifying them, only exasperated them the more.

The world hates the Church, not for the evil that is in it, but for the good. It hates without cause. The holier and purer a life is, the more certainly it will attract to itself malignity and dislike. The more Christlike we are, the more we must suffer the relentless hate that drove the nails into His hands, and the spear into His side. Do not be surprised at this. Think it not strange concerning the fiery trial which cometh to prove you, as though a strange thing happened unto you; but doubt and question and be in fear, if you meet only smiles and flattery and such honors as the world can give. You may then ask yourselves whether you are not one of the world's own.

The real origin and fountain of the hatred of the world is due to Satan's antagonism to God.— In his original creation, he was doubtless as fair as any of the firstborn sons of light; but in his pride he substituted himself for God, and love faded out of his being, making way for the unutterable darkness of diabolic hate. Satan hates God with a hatred for which there are no words; and therefore when the Father sent the Son to be the Saviour of the world, Satan gathered up every energy and resource of his nature to dog His steps, and make His course through the world as painful as possible. Do you wonder that the life of Jesus was so full of suffering? It could not have been otherwise. Directly God, in the person of Jesus, stepped down into the time-sphere, and assumed the conditions of earth and death, He came within the range of the utmost that Satan could do to molest and injure Him. Similarly, when the blessed Lord becomes the tenant of the heart, and in proportion as He is so, that heart attracts to itself the hatred with which the devil from the beginning has hated God. "If they have persecuted Me, they will also persecute you. If they have kept My saying, they will keep yours also. And these things will they do unto you, because they have not known the Father nor Me."

It is natural for the evil to hate the good.—First, the sinner has an uneasy conscience, and it hurts him to come in contact with those whose character reminds him of what he ought to be, and might be, and perhaps once was. The diseased eye dreads the light. The uncanny, slimy things that lurk beneath stones, and in dark caves, squirm in pain when you let in the day. The Turkish Sultan dislikes the presence of British representatives, and correspondents of the Daily Press, amid the dark deeds of blood and lust by which he is making Armenia a desert. "Every one that doeth evil hateth the light, neither cometh to the light, lest his deeds should be reproved."

In addition to an uneasy conscience, the sinner has an unbroken will. He stoutly resists the impression of a superior and condemning goodness. He hardens his heart, and strengthens its defences. "Who is the Lord, that I should obey His voice? Double the tale of bricks: summon the choice chariots and veteran soldiers of Egypt, that we may pursue, overtake, and divide the spoil." Such are the successive boats and challenges of the hardened heart.

Is it to be wondered at, under such conditions, that the wicked plotteth against the just, and gnasheth upon him with his teeth, that he draws his sword and bends his bow, to shoot privily at the upright of heart? "The wicked watcheth the righteous, and seeketh to slay him. The Lord will not leave him in his hand, nor condemn him when he is judged."

The great object of this hatred is to overcome the good.—In this respect the hate of the world is like the love of the Church. The child of God loves, that he may overcome the evil in the world, by converting evil-doers from the error of their ways and assimilating them to holiness; the child of the devil hates, that he may overcome the good of the world, by arresting their goodness, and assimilating to evil. Ah, how thankful we may be that we are not of the world, but have been chosen out of it; for it lieth in the wicked one, and is infected with the hatred of hell.

It is not difficult, therefore, to go through the world, and escape its hate. We have only to adopt its maxims, speak its language, and conform to its ways. In the well-known picture of the Huguenots, the young girl, with pleading, upturned face, seeks to tie the Royalist scarf around her lover's arm. She will secure his safety if she succeeds! Ah, how many pleading glances are cast at us to induce us to spare ourselves and others, by toning down our speech, and covering our regimentals by the disguising cloke of conformity to the world around! "If you do not approve, at least you need not express your disapproval." "If you cannot vote for, at least do not vote against." If you dissent, put your sentiments in courtly phrase, and so pare them down that they may not offend sensitive ears. Such is the advice, which is freely proffered. But those who follow it quickly discover that the compromise of principle involves certainly and awfully the loss of influence for good.

III. OUR BEHAVIOR AMID THE WORLD'S HATRED.—We have fallen on evil days. The world has been coated over with a Christian veneer, whilst the Church has become leavened with the subtle spirit of the world. It is hard to come out and be separate, because in the dim twilight one is apt to mistake friend and foe. The bribes are so rich for those who conform, the dissuasive so strong for those who refuse to bow to the great golden image. But our duty is clear. We must be true to the spirit of Christ. We must live a holy and unworldly life; we must avoid all that might be construed as an unworthy compromise of the interests of our Master's Kingdom.

And through all the pitiless storm of hate that beats in our faces, we must be glad. "Blessed are ye," said our Lord, "when men shall revile you, and persecute you, and shall say all manner of evil against you falsely for My sake: rejoice and be exceeding glad." And why rejoice? Because your reward is great in heaven; because you know that you are not of the world; because you are shown to be on the path trodden by the saints before you, every step of which has been trodden amid similar manifestations of the devil's hate.

Moreover, abound in love. Let there be no slackening of the patient, tender, pitying love, which heaps coals of fire on the head of the wrongdoer, and will never rest content until it has subdued the evil of his heart, overcoming it with good. Love must ultimately conquer hate, as surely as tomorrow's sun will conquer the darkness that now veils the landscape.

XVIII

The Work of the Holy Spirit on the World

"He will reprove the world of sin, and of righteousness, and of judgment."—JOHN xvi. 8.

Three facts forced themselves home on the apostles during the Lord's parting words. First, that they were to be bereaved of their Master's presence (ver. 5). Second, that they were to be left alone, amid the world's hatred—"Whosoever killeth you" (ver. 2). Third, that their mission would be witness-bearing to the unseen Lord (xv. 27).

And as they fully realized all that these facts involved, they became too absorbed in their own sorrowful conclusions to inquire what bourn the Master sought as He set sail from these earthly shores. "O Master," they said in effect, "why canst Thou not stay? Our orphaned hearts will never be able to endure the blank which Thy absence will cause. Easier could a flock of sheep withstand the onset of a pack of wolves than we the hatred of the world! And as for our witness-bearing, it will be too feeble to avail aught."

And the Master, in effect, answered thus: "I will not leave you without aid. I shall still be with you, though unseen. My presence shall be revealed to your spirits, and made livingly real through the blessed Comforter. He will be with you, and in you. He will authenticate and corroborate your witness. He shall testify of Me; and when He is come, He will convince the world of sin, of righteousness, and of judgment. You see then that I shall be able to help you better by sending the Holy Spirit than by staying with you Myself. It is expedient for you that I go away; for if I go not away the Comforter will not come to you, but if I depart I will send Him unto you."

We may not be able to fathom all the reasons for Christ's withdrawal before the Spirit's advent was possible. But some of them are obvious enough. The full union of the Son of God with our race must be secured through death and resurrection, and His full union with the Father must be indicated in His glorification with the glory He had or ever the worlds were made, before He could be the perfect channel of communicating the Divine fullness to our human nature. The Head must be anointed before the Body. There must be no physical distraction arising from the outward life of Jesus to compete with the spiritual impression of His unseen presence. The text must be completed before the sermon can be preached. Christ must die, or there can be no witness to His atonement; must rise, or there can be no testimony to His resurrection; must ascend, or there can be no declaration as to His finished work and eternal intercession. Since the Spirit reveals Christ, all that was appointed unto Christ to do must be completed ere the Spirit can commence His ministry.

The work of the Spirit on the world is through the Church, and is described by our Lord as threefold. By His revelation of Christ He creates three convictions. Each of these is necessary to the regeneration of man. There must be the sense of sin, or he will not seek the Saviour. There must be a belief that righteousness is possible, or the convicted sinner will die of despair. There must be the assurance that sin is doomed, and shall be finally vanquished, or the baffled warrior will give up the long conflict as hopeless.

I. THE CONVICTION OF SIN.—We are constantly meeting people who are perfectly indifferent to Christianity, because they say they do not feel their need of it. Why should they trouble about it, when they suppose themselves able to do perfectly well without it?

In dealing with these, it is a great mistake to entice them toward the gospel by describing the moral grandeur of Christ's character and teaching. We should at once seek to arouse them to a sense of their great sinfulness. When a man realizes that his life is being eaten out by some insidious disease, he will need no further urging to go to a physician. This is the weakness of modern preaching—that we expatiate on the value of the remedy to men who have never realized their dire necessity.

But what is the truth most appropriate for producing the conviction of sin in the human breast? "Preach the Ten Commandments in all their stern and uncompromising 'shalts' and 'shalt-nots,'" cries one. "Read out the descriptions given in Scripture of the evil things that lurk in the heart of man as filthy things in darksome caves," says another. "Show men the results of sin, take them to the edge of the bottomless pit," insists a third. But not one of these is the chosen weapon of the Holy Spirit. He convicts men of the sin of refusing to believe in Jesus Christ.

There stands the Cross, the evidence and symbol of God's love; and there stands the risen Christ, offering Himself to men. There is nothing which more certainly proves the innate evil of the human heart than its refusal of that mystery of grace. Disbelief is the creature, not of the intellect, but of the will. It is not the result of inability to understand, but of stubborn obstinacy and stiffneckedness. Here is the supreme manifestation of moral beauty, but man has no eyes for it. Here is the highest revelation of God's desire for man to be reconciled with Him, and be at one with Him, His happy child; but man either despises or spurns His overtures. Here is the offer of pardon for all the past, of heirship of all the promises, of blessedness in all the future, but man owns that he is indifferent to the existence and claims of God, and is quite willing to accept the sleeping retribution of bygone years, and to risk a future irradiated by no star of hope. Here is God in Christ beseeching him to be reconciled, declaring how much the reconciliation has cost, but the frail child of yesterday absolutely refuses to be at peace. No trace of tears in his voice, no shame on his face, no response to God's love in his heart.

This is sin at its worst. Not in a Nero drenched with the blood of relatives and saints; nor in an Alva expert to invent new methods of torture; nor in the brutalized expression of the felon; nor in the degradation of the heathen: but in those beside you, who have heard of the love of Jesus from their earliest childhood, and who know that He died for them, and waits to bless them, but who deliberately and persistently refuse Him, you will find the most terrible revelations of what man is capable of. "This is the condemnation, that Light is come into the world, and men loved darkness rather than light, because their deeds were evil."

Conviction in itself is not enough. Many have been convicted who have never gone on to conversion. They have dropped to the ground as untimely fruit, blighted before its maturity.

Conviction of sin does not come to all in the same manner or to the same extent. Indeed, those who have come to Christ in early life are in a degree exempt from drinking this bitter cup, though they have much tenderness of conscience afterward.

Do not wait for more conviction, but come to Jesus as you are, and tell Him that the saddest symptom in your case is your inability to feel as you know you should. Do not tarry to be convinced of sin. Do not stay away till you feel more deeply. Do not suppose that strongly roused emotions purchase His favor. His command is absolute—Believe. But whenever that true repentance is wrought which needs not to be repented of, or those tears of penitence fall from the eyes of the suppliant, the means will always be the person and work and love of Jesus Christ. This is the burning-glass through which the Spirit focuses the rays of God's love on ice-bound hearts.

II. THE CONVICTION OF RIGHTEOUSNESS.—The aggravation of sin of which the Spirit convicts the sinner seems to present a gloom too dark for any ray to penetrate. He cannot forget. The dead past will not bury its dead. The wind of eternity blows away the leaves with which he tries to hide the corpses of murdered opportunities, broken hearts, and dissipated years. He cannot forget. He may close his eyes, but still the memories of the past will haunt him, the deeds he would undo, the words he would recall, the dark ingratitude toward the love of Jesus. Conscience is a flaming terror till a man finds Christ as his Saviour. Her brow is girt with fire, her voice peals with doom.

"Can I ever be cleansed?" cries the convicted soul. "Can these awful gnawings be silenced, and these terrors laid? Can I rise from this ruin and become a new, righteous, God-like man?" These questions are answered by the Spirit who induced them. "There is righteousness," He says, "because Christ is gone to the Father, and ye see Him no more."

He is gone to the Father; and the seal of Divine authenticity has therefore been placed on all He said and did in the Father's name.

He is gone to the Father; and it is clear, therefore, that He has been accepted as the Saviour and Redeemer of men.

He is gone to the Father in the likeness and nature of men; evidently, then, man is an object of God's love, is reconciled to God, and is admitted to the rights and privileges of a son and heir.

The work of Jesus on man's behalf finished at the Cross, accepted by the Father—of which the resurrection is witness—presented by our Great High Priest within the veil, is the momentous truth which the Holy Spirit brings home to the convinced sinner. And inasmuch as we are unable to see within the veil and discern the Divine marks of approval and acceptance, the Holy Spirit descends, and in His advent proves that Jesus has gone where He said, and done what He promised.

How do we know that the work of Jesus Christ has been accepted in the courts of eternity? On this wise. Before He died the Master said that He went to the Father, and that when He was glorified He would ask and receive the Spirit in His fullness. After days had elapsed and the second week from His ascension was already passing, the Spirit in pentecostal fullness fell upon the waiting Church, giving it an altogether new power to combat with the world. What the wagons were to Jacob, proving that Joseph lived and thought of him still, and was indeed supreme in Egypt, that the day of Pentecost was in declaring that Christ's personal righteousness had been vindicated, and that the righteousness He had wrought out for man had received the hallmark of the Divine assay. Therefore the apostle says, "The Holy Ghost also is a witness to us that He hath perfected forever by one offering them that are sanctified." And again, "Him hath God exalted with His right hand to be a Prince and a Saviour; and the Holy Ghost, whom God hath given to them that obey Him, is witness of these things."

III. THE CONVICTION OF JUDGMENT.—When we have been freed from sin, and made righteous in Christ, we are left face to face with a tremendous struggle against sin. The sin of the past is indeed forgiven, the voice of conscience has been hushed, the sinner rejoices to know that he is accepted on the ground of righteousness; but the old temptations still crop up. Passion prompts us to live for present gratification; the flesh deadens the burning aspirations of the spirit. We ask in sad earnestness, How shall we be able to survive the terrible struggle and to come off victorious? It appears a vain hope that we should ever rise to perfect and victorious purity.

At such a time the Comforter convinces us of judgment. Not, as the words are so often misquoted, of judgment to come, but in the sense in which our Lord spoke of judgment to the inquiring Greeks: "Now is the judgment of this world; now shall the Prince of this world be cast out." Our Lord's references to the existence and power of Satan are always distinct and unhesitating. It is impossible to accept Him as our supreme Teacher without accepting His statements concerning His great antagonist, to undo whose work brought the Son of God to earth.

The whole Gospel is a story of the duel in which our Lord forever worsted and mastered Satan. The conflict began with the lonely struggle of the temptation in the wilderness; it pervaded Christ's earthly career; it culminated in the Cross. Its first note was, "If Thou be the Son of God, command that these stones be made bread"; its last note was, "If Thou be the Son of God, come down from the Cross." But when our Lord cried, "It is finished," with the shout of a conqueror, He proclaimed to the universe that, though tempted to the uttermost, He had not yielded in one particular, that evil was not an eternal power, that wrong was not omnipotent. The Cross was the crisis of this world's history: the prince of this world measured himself for one final wrestle with the Son of God. Had he succeeded, evil would have reigned; but since he failed he fell as lightning from heaven.

On this fact the Holy Spirit loves to dwell. He unfolds its full meaning. "See," He says, "Christ has conquered for you, and in your nature. You meet a foe who is not invincible. Christ conquered, not for Himself, but for all who believe. The prince of this world has been judged and found wanting. He is condemned forevermore. Only abide in the last Adam, the Lord from heaven, and let Him abide in you, and He will repeat through you His olden victories."

What a majestic thought is here! The world comes to us first with its fascinations and delights. She comes to us next with her frowns and tortures. Behind her is her prince. But since he has been cast out by a stronger than himself, and exists only on sufferance, his most potent bribes and lures, his most violent onsets, his most unscrupulous suggestions, must collapse. Believer, meet him as a discredited and fallen foe. He can have no power at all over thee. The Cross bruised his head. Thou hast no need to fear judgment. It awaits those only who are still in the devil's power. But thou mayest rejoice that for thee a victory waits, the measure of which will only be explored when thou seest the devil cast into the bottomless pit, and thence into the lake of fire.

XIX

Christ's Reticence Supplemented by the Spirit's Advent

"I have yet many things to say unto you; but ye cannot bear them now."—JOHN xvi. 12-15.

How confidently our Lord speaks of the Spirit's advent; not more so did the prophets foretell His own. Repeatedly He returns to the phrase, When He is come. The advent of the Spirit to the heart of the Church on the Day of Pentecost, was as distinct and marked an event as the advent of the Son of God Himself to the manger-bed of Bethlehem. Let every reader of these words be sure of having taken the full advantage of His Presence, just as we would wish to have availed ourselves to the uttermost of the physical presence of Christ, had our lot so befallen.

I. THE THEME OF THIS PARAGRAPH IS THE INCOMPLETENESS OF OUR LORD'S TEACHING.—For three and a half years He was perpetually pouring forth His wonderful words; in many different places—the market-place, the home at Bethany, the hillside, the Temple cloister; to many different audiences—now in thronging crowds, and again to the secret disciple whose footfall startled the night, or the lone woman drawing water from the well; on many different themes—to mention all of which would be impossible, though He never spoke on any subject, common as a wayside flower, without associating with it thoughts that can never die. We have but a small portion of His words recorded in the Gospels, it is therefore the more remarkable that He left anything unsaid, and that at the close of His ministry He should have to say, I have yet many things to say unto you. Many parables, fair as His tenderest, woven in the productive loom of His imagination, remained unuttered; many discourses, inimitable as the Sermon on the Mount, or as this in the upper room, unspoken; many revelations of heavenly mystery not made.

A comparison between the Gospels and the Epistles will indicate how much our Lord had left unsaid. The relation of the law of Moses to His finished work was left to the Epistle to the Romans: the relation between His Church and the usages of the heathen world, for the Epistle to Corinth: the effect of His resurrection on the sleeping saints for the Epistle to the Thessalonians. He said nothing about the union of Jew and Gentile on terms of equality in His Church; this mystery, hidden from ages and from generations, was only fully unveiled in the Epistle to the Ephesians. It was left for the Epistle to the Hebrews to disclose the superseding of the Temple and its ritual by the realities of the Christian dispensation. The practical precepts for the right ordering of the Churches were left for the pastoral Epistles; and the course of the Church through the ages of the world's history, for the Apocalypse of the beloved Apostle. When we perceive the many things, taught in the Epistles, which were not unfolded by the Lord, we discern a fresh meaning in His assurance that He left much unsaid.

We are perpetually assailed by the cry, "Back to Christ," which is significant of men's weariness of theological system, and organized ecclesiasticism, and of a desire to get away from the accretions of the Middle Ages and the dead hand of Church Tradition, into the pure, serene, and holy presence of Jesus of Nazareth. It always seems to us as if the cry should be Up to Christ, rather than Back to Him. To put it as men generally do, suggests the inference that Christ lies far in the wake of human progress, and behind the haze of eighteen centuries; that He was, but is no longer, a potent factor in the world's life; whereas He is here, now, with us, in us, leading us as of old through rugged passes, and to mountains of transfiguration.

If the endeavor to get back to Christ means the Synoptic Gospels to the exclusion of the fourth, or the Epistles; or the Sermon on the Mount to the exclusion of the Epistle to the Romans; or Jesus to the exclusion of His Apostles, we feel it is but half the truth. Our Lord Himself protested that His teachings were incomplete, that there was much left unsaid which would be said by the Comforter, as even He could not, because the Spirit of God speaks in the inner shrine of the soul, uttering to the inner ear, truths which no voice could speak or ear receive. Let us always remember therefore that the Gospels must be completed by the Epistles, and that the Spirit who spake in the Son, spake also in those whom the Son had prepared to be His mouthpieces to men.

II. THE PARTIAL MEASURE OF HUMAN ABILITY TO KNOW.—"Ye cannot bear them now." Our Lord's reticence did not arise from ignorance, He could have said so much had He not been able to say more. All things were naked and open to His eye, but He had a tender regard for these men whom He loved.

Their bodies could not bear more. When the mind is strongly wrought upon, the delicate organism of the body is deeply affected. On the banks of the river Hiddekel, words of such wondrous importance were uttered to the lonely exile, that Daniel fainted, and was sick many days. "When I saw Him," says John, "I fell at His feet as dead." Flavel, on more than one occasion, asked that the excessive revelation might be stayed. Our Lord, therefore, feared that in their weakened state, torn by anxiety and sorrow, His followers would collapse if further strain were imposed upon their powers of spiritual apprehension.

Their minds could not bear more. The mind cannot receive more than a certain amount. After a while its eye gets weary, it ceases to receive, and even to remember. There are multitudes of cases in which, when too great a weight has been crowded on the delicate organism through which thoughts move, its balance has been upset, and it has drivelled into idiocy. Against this danger, also, our Lord guarded, for His disciples were already excited and over-strained. Their brains were so exhausted that in a few moments they would be sleeping on the cold ground of Gethsemane. Had He poured the light of the other world in full measure upon them, the tide of glory had submerged them, like spent swimmers.

Their affections could not bear more. Because He had spoken to them, sorrow had filled their heart, and He forbore to describe the valley of shadow through which they were still to pass, lest their hearts should break. They had hardly commenced to drink its cup: what would its dregs be? The footmen had wearied them: how would they contend with horses? The brink had terrified them: how would they do in the swellings of Jordan?

It is thus that He deals with us still. He knows our frame, and proportions our trials to our strength. He carefully feels our pulse before commencing the operation through which He would lead us to perfect health. He tempers His discipline to our spiritual capacity. We desire to know many things: the reason why sin has been permitted, the fate of the impenitent; the state of the great masses of men who have passed into eternity without a true knowledge of God. Peter asks for John, "What shall this man do?" Each wants to know the secret plans, whether for himself, or his beloved, which are lying in the mind and purpose of the Eternal. What will the end be? Where does that path lead by which I am going, and which descends steeply into the ravine? Will the fight between evil and good be much prolonged? What are hell, and the bottomless pit, and the meaning of Christ's references to the undying worm and unquenchable flame? And Christ says, "My child, you cannot bear it; you could not sleep at night, you could not play with the merry children by day, you could not perform your slender tasks, if you knew all that I know, and see as I see. Be at rest. Trust Me. I will tell you as soon as you are strong enough. Nothing shall be kept back from you, all shall be revealed." And surely the sufferings and limitations of this present time will not be worthy to be compared with the exceeding weight of glory, when in the presence of our Lord we shall see eye to eye, and know even as we are known.

In the light of these words we may get comfort. When some crushing trouble befalls us, He who only spoke as they were able to bear, will not permit the flame to be hotter, the tide stronger, or the task more trying than we have strength for. We often do not know our strength nor the power of His grace. Sorrow may be sent to reveal us to ourselves, and show how much spiritual energy we have been silently acquiring. Do not, therefore, run to and fro, and say, "It is too much, I cannot bear it." But know and be sure that Christ has ascertained your resources, and is sure of your ability, before He permits the extreme ordeal to overtake you. Dare to say with the apostle, "I can do all things through Christ who strengtheneth me."

III. THE TEACHING OF THE DIVINE SPIRIT.—His personality is unmistakable; though the Greek word for Spirit is neuter, a masculine pronoun is used in conjunction with it when Jesus says, "He, the Spirit of Truth." The personal Christ sent as a substitute for Himself no mere breath or influence, but the personal Spirit. The Advocate before the Throne is well represented by the Advocate in the heart of the Church, and these two agree in one. Distinct as different Persons, but one in the mystical unity of the Holy Trinity.

Note the method of the Holy Spirit. He teaches truth by taking of the things of Christ and revealing them. There are two methods of teaching children, by precept, and by example. I go into a schoolroom one summer afternoon, and remark the hot cheeks and tired eyes of the little ones. Outside the open window the bees are droning past, the butterflies flit from flower to flower, and nature seems to cry to the little hearts, "Come and play with me." Does a garden ever look so beautiful as to children shut up to their studies? "What are you learning, little ones?" I say. "Botany," is the sad answer "We've got to learn all these hard names, and copy these diagrams." "Well," I say, "shut up your books, and come with me." And presently I teach them more botany by contact with the flowers themselves, than they would have learned by hours of poring over lesson-books. It is so the Spirit teaches. Is gentleness or purity, self-sacrifice or prayer, the lesson that we are set to acquire? There is no need for Him to make a new revelation to us. It is enough if He but bring us face to face with Jesus, and show these qualities shining through His words and deeds. The truth certainly, but the truth as it is in Jesus.

The condition of proficiency in the Spirit's school is obedience. "He will guide you into all truth." This word is very significant. Literally it means, Show the way. Ordinarily men ask to know the truth before they obey. The Spirit demands that they should obey before they know. Let me know the outcome of this act; its philosophy, its reasonableness, its result, then I will obey. But the Spirit answers, "It is enough for thee, O child of man, to know Me. Canst thou not trust? Wilt thou not obey? And as thou obeyest thou shalt know. Take this path, plod along its difficult way, climb where it climbs, so shalt thou ascend the steep of obedience, and at each step a further horizon of the truth will open outspread beneath thee."

Let us be more sensitive to the guidance of the Spirit, following whithersoever He clearly indicates, as when the Spirit said to Philip, "Go, join thyself to this chariot." We shall know when we follow on to know the Lord. His going forth is prepared for those who are prepared to obey whatsoever He may appoint.

The aim of the Spirit is to glorify our Lord. "He shall glorify Me, for He shall receive of mine." The Spirit's presence, as such, should not be a subject of our close scrutiny, lest we conflict with His holy purpose of being hidden, that Jesus may be all in all before the gaze of saint and sinner. He is so anxious that nothing should divert the soul's gaze from the Lord whom He would reveal, that He carefully withdraws Himself from view. "There must be nothing, not even God Himself, to distract the heart from Jesus, through whom we come to God. But remember that when you have the most precious views of your dear Lord, it is because the Holy Spirit, all unseen, is witnessing and working within you."

The authority of the Holy Spirit appears in the words, "He shall not speak of Himself; but whatsoever He shall hear, that shall He speak." Where does He hear the truths He utters? Where? There is only one place. In the depths of the eternal throne, in the heart of Deity itself, in the secret place of the Most High. Oh, marvel! surpassing thought, yet true! that things which pass between the Father and the Son, in the depths which no angel can penetrate, may be disclosed and made known to those humble and contrite hearts who are willing to make a space and pause for the Divine Spirit to speak the deep things of God.

May it be ours to be patient and willing pupils in this heavenly school in which the Holy Spirit is Teacher, and Jesus the Text-Book, and character the essential condition of knowledge.

XX

The Conqueror of the World

"In the world ye shall have tribulation: but be of good cheer; I have overcome the world."—JOHN xvi. 33.

It was the road between Jerusalem and the Gate of the Garden. Behind, lay the city bathed in slumber; before, the Mount of Olives with its terraced gardens; above, the Passover moon, pouring down floods of silver light that dropped to the ground through the waving branches of the trees. The Lord was on His way to betrayal and death, along that path flecked by checkered moonlight.

The farewell talk had been prolonged until the disciples had grasped something of the Master's meaning. With many a comforting assurance it had borne them forward to the magnificent but simple declaration, "I came forth from the Father, and am come into the world; again, I leave the world, and go to the Father" (ver. 28). At that announcement light seems to have broken in upon their hearts, and they said unto Him, "Lo, now speakest Thou plainly, . . . by this we believe that Thou camest forth from God." Jesus replied, not as translators render it, "Do ye now believe"; but as it should be rendered, "At last ye believe"; and He proceeded to formulate three paradoxes:

First, That within an hour or so He would be alone, yet not alone.

Secondly, That they would have tribulation, and yet be in peace.

Thirdly, That though He was going to His death, He was certainly a conqueror, and had overcome the world, whose princes were about to crucify Him.

That word overcome appears to have been used only this once by our Lord; but it made a lasting impression on the Apostle John, who constantly makes use of it in his Epistle. We meet with it six times in his brief first Epistle, and sixteen times in the Book of Revelation. Who can forget the sevenfold promise spoken by the risen Lord to those who overcome; or the sublime affirmation concerning the martyrs, that they overcame by the blood of the Lamb and by the word of their testimony?

I. CHRIST AND HIS DISCIPLES HAVE A COMMON FOE—"The world."—And what is the world? It is well to take the inspired definition given in 1 John ii. 16. After enumerating her three daughters—the lust of the flesh, the lust of the eyes, and the pride of life—the apostle goes on to say: "All that is in the world is not of the Father," i.e., does not originate or proceed from Him, but has its source in the world itself. We might reverse this proposition and say: "All that does not emanate from the Father, which you cannot trace back to His purpose in creation, is that mysterious indefinable influence or spirit which makes the world." The world, in this sense, is not primarily a thing, or a collection of people, but a spiritual influence poured out into the very atmosphere of our lives.

The spirit of the world insinuates itself everywhere. It is what we call society; the consensus of fashionable opinion; the spirit which finds its satisfaction in the seen and transient; the ambition that is encircled by the rim of an earthly horizon; the aims, plans, and activities which are comprehended, as the Preacher says, "under the sun." You meet it in the school, where little children judge each other by their dress and the number of horses their fathers keep; in the country town, where strict lines are drawn between the professional or wholesale man and the retailer; in gatherings of well-dressed people, stiff with decorum and the punctilious observance of etiquette.

The world has formulated its Beatitudes, thus:

"Blessed are the rich, for they shall inherit the earth."

"Blessed are the light-hearted, for they shall have many friends."

"Blessed are the respectable, for they shall be respected."

"Blessed are they who are not troubled by a sensitive conscience, for they shall succeed in life."

"Blessed are they who can indulge their appetites to the full, for they shall be filled."

"Blessed are they who have no need to conciliate their rivals, for they will be saved from anxiety."

"Blessed are they who have no poor relations, for they shall be delivered from annoyance."

"Blessed are they of whom all men speak well."

The world's code says, "Do as others do; don't be singular; never offend against good taste; have a tinge of religiousness, but remember too much is impracticable for daily life; whatever you do, don't be poor; never yield an inch, unless you are going to make something by the concession; take every advantage of bettering your position, it matters not at what cost to others—they must look after themselves, as you to yourself."

But it was reserved for John Bunyan to draw Madame Bubble's portrait: "This woman is a witch. 'I am mistress of the world,' she says, 'and men are made happy by me.' She wears a great purse at her side; and her hand is often in her purse fingering her money. Yea, she has bought off many a man from a pilgrim's life after he had fairly begun it. She is a bold and impudent slut also, for she will talk to any man. If there be one cunning to make money, she will speak well of him from house to house. None can tell of the mischief she does. She makes variance betwixt rulers and subjects, 'twixt parents and children, 'twixt a man and his wife, 'twixt the flesh and the heart. Had she stood by all this while,' said Standfast, whose eyes were still full of her, 'you could not have set Madame Bubble more amply before me, nor have better described her features.' 'He that drew her picture was a good limner,' said Mr. Honest, 'and he that so wrote of her said true.' 'Oh,' said Standfast, 'what a mercy it is that I did resist her! for to what might she not have drawn me?'"

II. CHRIST AND HIS DISCIPLES HAVE A COMMON CONFLICT.—It is inevitable that there should be collision, and therefore conflict, and as a result tribulation. The world-spirit will not brook our disagreement with its plans and aims, and therefore they who persist in living godly lives in this present evil world must suffer persecution.

Conflict about the use of power and prerogative.—At His baptism our Lord was proclaimed to be the Son of the Highest, and anointed with the Holy Ghost and with power. Instantly the Prince of this world came to Him with the suggestion that He should use it for the purposes of

His own comfort and display. "Make these stones bread for thine hunger; cast Thyself down and attract the attention of the crowds." Here were the lust of the flesh, and the lust of the eyes. But our Lord refused to use for Himself the power which was entrusted to Him for the benediction and help of men.

Conflict as to the way of helping and saving men.—The world's way was to leap into the seat of power at any cost, and from the height of universal authority administer the affairs of the world. But Christ knew better. He saw that He must take the form of a servant, and humble Himself to the lowest. If He would save men, He cannot save Himself: if He would bring forth much fruit, He must fall into the ground to die: if He would ascend far above all heavens, bearing us with Him to the realms of eternal day, He must descend first into the lower parts of the earth.

Conflict in the estimate of poverty and suffering.—The world looked on these as the most terrible disasters that could befall. Christ, on the other hand, taught that blessedness lay most within reach of the poor in spirit, the mourners, the merciful, the forgiving, and the persecuted. But the Pharisees, who were lovers of money, when they heard all these things, scoffed at Him.

Conflict in their diverse notions of royalty.—The Jews looked for a Messiah who should revive the glories of the days of David and Solomon, driving the Gentiles from the land, and receiving the homage of the surrounding nations, whilst every son of Abraham enjoyed opulence and ease. Referring to this expectation, the Master said, "My kingdom is not of this world: if My kingdom were of this world, then would My servants fight." His conception of royalty was founded on service, which would wash the disciples' feet; on humility, which meekly bore the heavy yoke, on patience, which would not quench the smoking flax, on suffering, which flinched not from the cross; on the nobility and dignity of the inner life, which shone through the most humble circumstances, as the transfiguration glory through His robes. For this He died. The chief priests and scribes hunted Him to death, because He persisted in asserting that He was the true King of men. "And Pilate wrote a title also, and put it on the Cross, Jesus of Nazareth, the King of the Jews."

There was conflict in regard to religion.—The people of Christ's day were very religious. The world likes a flavor of religion. It makes a good background and screen, it serves to hide much that is unbecoming and questionable; it is respectable, and satisfies an instinctive longing of the soul. But the world manages its religion in such a way as not to interfere with its self-aggrandizement; but, in fact, to promote it. Christ, on the other hand, taught that religion was for the Father in secret; and consisted, not in the rigorous observance of outward rite, but in pity, mercy, forgiveness, solitary prayer, and purity of heart.

Thus the Lord's life was the reversal of everything that the world prized. Wherever He touched it there was conflict and collision, strong antagonism was evoked, and profound irritation on the part of the poor hollow appearance-loving world. So it must be with His followers. "These pilgrims must needs go through the fair. Well, so they did; but behold, even as they entered into the fair, all the people in the fair were moved, and the town itself, as it were, in a hubbub about them. They were clothed with such kind of raiment as was diverse from the raiment of any who traded in that fair; few could understand what they said; and the pilgrims set very light by all their wares. And they did not believe them to be any other than bedlams and mad. Therefore they took them and beat them, and besmeared them with dirt, and then put them in the cage, that they might be made a spectacle to all the men at the fair."

Child of God, your conflict may be altogether hidden from the eyes of those around you, lonely with the awful loneliness of one in a crowd of unsympathizing strangers, painful with the tribulation that Christ foretold. You have been ridiculed, sneered at, maligned; your tools hidden, your goods injured, violence threatened or executed. You have been as a speckled bird, pecked at by the birds around. But this is the way the Master went. By these marks you may be sure that you are in the way of His steps.

III. THE COMMON VICTORY.—"Be of good cheer, I have overcome the world."

In the midst of a battle, when the soldiers are weary with fatigue, galled with fire, and grimed with smoke, if the general rides into the midst to cheer them with a few hearty words, and tells them that the key to the position is in their hands, they cheer him enthusiastically, and take up new hope. So down the line our Leader and Commander sends the encouragement of these inspiring words. Let us drink their comfort and encouragement to the full, that, amid our tribulation, in Him we may have peace.

He conquered for Himself.—The Lord has shown that a great and blessed life is possible on conditions which the world pronounces simply unendurable. He would not accept the world's maxims, would not be ruled by the world's principles, did despite to the world's most favorite plans. He even tasted the dregs of reprobation that the world metes out to those who oppose her, enduring the cross, and despising the shame. But His life was blessed while it lasted, His name is the dearest and fairest treasure of our race, and He holds an empire such as none of the world's most favored conquerors ever won. Does not this show that the world is a lying temptress, that there is another and a better policy of life than hers, that the real sweets and prizes of this brief existence are, after all, not in her gift. Christ has overcome the world. Her prince came to Him, but found no response to any of His proposals. He disregarded her flatteries and threatenings; He would not have her help and despised her hate; He prosecuted His path in defiance of her, and has left an imperishable glory behind. Thus He overcame the world.

And he conquered as our representative and head.—What He did for Himself He is prepared to repeat in the life-story of His followers. Ah! lonely soul, thou shalt not be left unaided to withstand the seductions of the temptress world; Jesus is with thee, thy Great-heart and Champion. As the Father was with Him, so He is with thee; so thus thou mayest boldly say, "The Lord is my helper, I will not fear what man can do unto me."

He does more. Behind the light of this world's glory, Jesus reveals another; and it is as when the sun rises, while the yellow moon still lingers in the sky. The world has no glory by reason of that glory, which excelleth. We are content with this world until He reveals the glory of the unseen and eternal; then a holy discontent arises with us, such as the patriarchs felt toward Canaan, when by faith they beheld the city which hath foundations. I only say to you, get that vision, and it becomes as easy for you to refuse the passing and worthless attractions of the world as for an angel to ignore a wanton's beauty, or a child to make light of diamonds in the rough.

In Jesus you may have peace. It is not certainly ours, unless we follow the two conditions He lays down. First, of abiding in Him; and, secondly, of meditating on His words. But if these be observed we shall have in the midst of strife, just as there is an oratory in the heart of the castle keep; a hollow cone in the midst of the candle flame; and a centre of safety in the midst of the sweeping whirlwind. Oh, abide there, child of God!

And, in addition to peace, there shall one day be victory. We also shall overcome, and shall sit with Christ on His throne, as He overcame, and sits with the Father upon His. Then the fruit of the tree of life, immunity from the second death, the hidden manna, the white stone, the morning star, the confession before the angels of God, and the pillar in the temple of Eternity!

XXI

Consecrated to Consecrate

"For their sakes I sanctify Myself, that they themselves also may be sanctified in truth."—
JOHN xvii. 19.

"The most precious fragment of the past," is the unstinted eulogium which a thoughtful man
has passed on this transcendent prayer; transcending in its scope of view, its expressions, its
tender pathos, all other prayers of which we have record.

Its primary characteristic is timelessness. Though uttered within a few hours of Calvary, it
contains thoughts and expressions which must have been familiar to our Lord at any moment
during the centuries which have followed. As we study it, therefore, we are listening to words
which have been uttered many times on our behalf, and will be uttered until we are with Him,
where He is, beholding the glory of the Divine Son, superadded to that of the Perfect Servant.

The R. V. margin substitutes the word consecrate for sanctify, and it probably conveys a better
meaning, because devotion to the will of God is prominent, rather than the holiness of personal
character. Devotion to God's will is the primary thought suggested by the word; but of course it
involves a blameless and spotless character. Thus we might read the words, "For their sakes I
consecrate Myself, that they also may be consecrated in truth." Through the dim twilight the
Lord clearly foresaw what was awaiting Him—the agony and bloody sweat, the cross and
passion, the forsakenness and travail of His soul. The cross with out-stretched arms waited to
receive Him; the midnight darkness to engulf Him, the murderous band to wreak their hate on
the unresisting Lamb—and yet He flinched not, but went right forward, consecrating Himself.

I. THE SUBJECTS OF CHRIST'S SOLICITUDE.—In the earlier verses the Lord speaks of
Himself, of His finished work, of the glory which He had left, of that to which He went, asking
only that He might be able to glorify the Father in every movement of His coming sorrow (1-5).

Then He launches Himself on the full current of intercession, and pleads for those who had
been given to Him, as distinguished from the world of men out of which they had come.
Evidently the same thought was in His mind as inspired His words in John x., when He spoke of
the sheep whom the Father had given to Him, that He might give them eternal life (27-29). And
it may be that each of these two utterances was inspired by older words yet, that Zechariah had
addressed to the poor of the flock when he cut asunder his two slaves, Beauty and Bands (Zech.
xi. 7-14).

The underlying conception in all these passages seems to be that the Father has entrusted to the
special keeping of Jesus certain elect spirits having an affinity to His nature, and who should
stand in the inner circle to Him because associated with Him from high redemptive purpose. All
souls are God's by right of creation, and all are included in the redemption wrought on the cross;
but not all had been included in the Divine gift of which Jesus speaks, "Thine they were, and
Thou gavest them Me." We conclude that in the eternity of the past, as the Father beheld all
future things as though they were present, and surveyed the vast multitudes of the human family,
He discerned those who would be attracted by indissoluble union with His Son, manifest in the

flesh; and whom He did foreknow, these also He did predestinate to be His flock, His brethren and sisters, His chosen band of associates in His redemptive purpose. These were the subjects of His powerful solicitude, "I make request, not for the world, but for those whom Thou hast given Me."

What then? Did not God care for the world? Certainly. He so loved the world that He gave His only begotten Son.

How then can we reconcile the love of God to the world with the selection of some as the flock of the Lamb, whilst the great world seems expressly excluded from His prayer? That question is fitly put. The emphasis is on the word seems. It is only to the superficial view that the world is excluded. Are the planets excluded from the law of gravitation because suns are filled with fire and light? Are the lower orders of creation excluded from the circle of enjoyment because man with his high organization is more richly endowed than they? Are sufferers excluded from the healing virtues of nature because a comparative few are specially qualified as surgeons and physicians? Can a missionary be charged with neglecting a dark continent because he concentrates thought and care on a few elect spirits gathered around him? For instance, could Columba be held guilty of neglecting the Picts and Scots when on Iona's lone isle he focused his care upon the handful of followers who assembled around the ancient pile, whose ruins are his lasting memorial? There is but one answer to these questions. Election is not exclusive, but inclusive. Its purpose is not primarily the salvation or delectation of the few, but their equipment to become the apostles to the many. And if Jesus thought, cared, and prayed so much for those whom the Father had given Him, His ulterior thought was that the world might believe that the Father had sent Him (ver. 21). If then it should be proved that you, my reader, are not included in the band of the given ones, that would not necessarily involve you in the eternal condemnation and loss of the future; though it would exclude you from sharing with Christ in His lofty mission to the sons of men.

What are the marks then that we belong to the inner circle of the given ones? They are these—
1. That we have come to Him (John vi. 37).
2. That we hear His voice, listening for the slightest indication of His will (John x. 27).
3. That we follow His steps through the world.
4. That we receive His words and believe that the Father sent the Son to be our Saviour.
5. That the world hates us (ver. 14).

Wheresoever these marks are present, they indicate the hand of the Great Shepherd and Bishop of Souls, and though we be amongst the most timid and worthless of the flock, He is pledged to keep us, so that none shall snatch us from His hand, and conduct us through the valley of the shadow to those dewy upland lawns over which He will lead us forevermore.

II. WHAT HE SOUGHT FOR THEM—"that they might be consecrated in truth."

Christ does not ask that His own should be forgiven, comforted, supplied with the good things of life—all thought for these pales in the presence of His intense desire that they should be consecrated, i.e., inspired by the same consuming passion as was burning in His heart. He knew that He was no more in the world. High business connected with its interests summoned Him to the far country, whither He went to receive the kingdom and return. But He desired that the passion which filled His soul, His tears, His prayers, and, to an extent, His sufferings, might always be represented amongst the sons of men, embodied in human lives, finding utterance through human lips. He could not Himself perpetuate his corporeal visible ministry among men, and therefore desired with a great desire that those whom the Father had given Him should evermore show forth His death till He came. Not simply by gathering at His table, but by going forth to live His life, and fill up that which is behind of His sufferings.

Is this your life? We have sometimes heard consecration stated as though it were a matter of choice whether believers should bind themselves by its obligations or not. When a student enters the university there are certain subjects in which he must matriculate, but there are special ones which he may graduate in or not, as he pleases. Should he refuse them, he is not blamed. The matter was within his option. Now, let it be clearly understood from these words of Christ that consecration is not in the same sense optional, but obligatory. For all those whom the Father had given Him He pleaded with His dying breath that they should be consecrated; and if you are not consecrated, if there are extensive reserves in your life, if you are holding back part of the price, if you are saying of aught that you have, It is my own, I shall do as I choose, then understand that you are in direct conflict against Christ's purpose and prayer. He asked that you might be consecrated; and you have chosen to regard consecration as the craze of the fervid enthusiast.

III. CHRIST'S METHOD OF SECURING THE CONSECRATION OF HIS SERVANTS.—"For their sakes I consecrate Myself."

(1) There is the potency of example.—"He hath left us an example to follow in His steps." "He that saith he abideth in Him ought himself also to walk even as He walked." Once when He was praying in a certain place His disciples said, "Lord, teach us to pray." They had come within the powerful attraction of His Spirit. Like a swift current it had caught them, and they were eager to emulate Him. It is impossible for the saint to gaze long on the stigmata without becoming branded with the marks of Jesus; impossible to see Him hasting to the cross without being stirred to follow Him; impossible to behold the intensity of His purpose for a world's redemption without becoming imbued with it; impossible to see Him in love with the cross without feeling a similar infatuation; impossible to behold Him plunging into the dark floods of death that He might emerge in the sunlit ocean, without the consciousness of the uprising of an insatiable desire to be like Him, to drink of His cup, and be baptized with His baptism, to fall into the ground to die, that He may not abide alone, to know the fellowship of His sufferings, and conformity to His death, that He may appoint unto us a kingdom, as the Father hath appointed to Him.

(2) There is our implication in His mediatorial work.—"I have been crucified with Christ," the apostle said. And, again, "Ye died with Christ from the rudiments of the world." Of course, Christ died for us, presenting to the claims of a broken law a perfect satisfaction and oblation. It is also true that we died with Him, were in Him as our Representative, wrought through Him as our Forerunner; the first fruit-sheaf contained the promise of all its companions.

Consider for a moment a remarkable expression that casts light on this whole subject. In that memorable discussion with the Jews in Solomon's porch, which practically closed our Lord's public ministry, He said that the Father had sanctified and consecrated Him and sent Him into the world (John x. 36). In these sublime words He undoubtedly refers to a moment which preceded the Incarnation, when the Godhead designated the Second Person to redeem men? Was it the same moment, think you, as that in which Jesus said, "Sacrifice and offering thou wouldst not, but a body thou hast prepared for Me (or, Mine ears hast thou pierced). I delight to do Thy will, O My God." If so, what an august scene that must have been when, in the presence of the assembled hierarchies of heaven, the Father solemnly set apart the Son for His redemption work, consecrating Him to bring in everlasting salvation, to destroy the works of the devil, and to bring together in one the children of God that are scattered abroad!

In that solemn consecration of the head all the members were included. The King stood for His kingdom; the Shepherd for His flock. Any who refuse to be consecrated contravene and contradict that momentous decision.

When Christ approached His death, in these words He renewed His act of consecration, and again implicated those who belong to Him; bearing us with Him, He went to the cross, involving us by His actions, He yielded Himself up to death. In His holy purpose we were quickened together with Him, and raised up together, and made to sit together in the heavenly places; and by the same emphasis that we declare ourselves to be His, we confess that we are amongst those who are bound to a life of consecration. We are pledged to it by union with our Lord. We cannot draw back from the doorpost to which He was nailed without proving that we are deficient in appreciating the purpose which brought Him to our world, the surrender that withheld not His face from spitting, His soul from the shadow of death.

IV. OUR DUTY.—"Yield yourselves unto God." When Abraham Lincoln dedicated, for the purposes of a graveyard, the field of Gettysburg, where so many brave soldiers had lost their lives, he said: "We cannot dedicate, we cannot consecrate, we cannot hallow this ground. The brave men who struggled here have consecrated it far beyond our power to add or detract. It is for us, the living, rather to be dedicated to the unfinished work which they who fought here have thus far so nobly advanced. It is rather for us to be here dedicated to the great task remaining before us, that from these honored dead we take increased devotion to that cause for which they gave the last full measure of devotion; and that we here highly resolve that these dead shall not have died in vain."

These noble words, when we have made the needful alterations and adaptations, are most applicable to our present point. Let us dedicate ourselves to the great task before us, and to which Jesus has pledged us. Let us devote ourselves to this great cause for which Jesus died. Let us highly resolve that He shall not have died in vain. Let us offer and present ourselves, our souls and bodies, to be a reasonable, holy, and living sacrifice unto God, that His will might be done through us, as it is done in heaven.

XXII

The Lord's Prayer for His People's Oneness

"That they may all be one. . . . One in us. . . . That they may be one, even as we are one. . . . Perfect in one."—JOHN xvii. 21-23.

Thus our High Priest pleaded, and thus He pleads. In all the power of His endless life, He ever liveth to bear this great petition on His heart: and as the weight of the jewelled breast-plate lay heavy on the heart of the high priests of old, so does it press on Him, as the ages slowly pass by in their never-ceasing progress toward the consummation of all things. Listen to that voice, sweet and full as the distant rush of many waters, as it pleads in the midst of eternity that those which believe in Him may be one.

Nor is it true that this prayer awaits an answer indefinitely future. There seems good reason to believe, as we shall see, that in these words our Lord was making a request, which began to be fulfilled on the Day of Pentecost: and is being fulfilled continually, although the oneness which is being realized is still, like His kingdom, in mystery, and is waiting for the manifestation of the sons of God. Then, as the gauzy mists of time part before the breath of God, the accomplished oneness of the Church shall stand revealed.

I. THE ONENESS OF BELIEVERS IS A SPIRITUAL ONENESS.—Can there be any reasonable doubt of this when our Master asks so clearly that we may be one, as the Father and He are one? The model for Christian unity is evidently the unity between the Father and Son by the Holy Spirit; and since that unity, the unity of the blessed God, is not corporeal, nor physical, nor substantial to the eye of the flesh, may we not infer—nay, are we not compelled to infer— that the oneness of believers is to be after the same fashion, and to consist in so close an identity of nature, so absolute an interfusion of spirit, as that they shall be one in aim, and thought, and life, and spirit, spiritually one with each other, because spiritually one with Him?

The Church of Rome, which has ever travestied in gross material forms the most spiritual conceptions of God, sought to prove herself the true Church by achieving a oneness of her own. It was an outward and visible oneness. In the apostate church every one must utter the same formularies, worship in the same postures, and belong to the same ecclesiastical system. And its leaders did their best to realize their dream. They endeavored to exterminate heresy by fire, and sword, and torture. They spread their network through the world. And just before the dawn of the Reformation they seemed to have succeeded. At the beginning of the sixteenth century, Europe reposed in the monotony of almost universal uniformity, beneath the almost universal supremacy of the Papacy. Rome might indeed have adopted the insolent language of the Assyrian of prophecy: "As one gathereth eggs, so have I gathered all the earth, and there was none that moved the wing, or opened the mouth, or peeped." And what was the result? What but the deep sleep of spiritual death? And herein lay the most crushing condemnation of the Roman Catholic conception of the unity of the Church.

Many modern notions of Christian unity seem to proceed on the same line. The assent to a certain credal basis, the meeting in great Catholic conventions, the exchange of pulpits—these seem to exhaust the conceptions of large numbers, and to satisfy their ideal. But surely there is a bond of union deeper, holier, more vital and more blessed than any of these, which shyly reveals itself, now and again, in one or more of them, but is independent of all, and when all of them are wanting, still constitutes us one. And what is that bond of union but the possession of a common spiritual life, like that which unites the Father and the Son, and which pervades us also, making us one with each other, because we are already one with God?

You may not care to admit it; you may even be ignorant of the full meaning of this marvellous fact; you may live an exclusive life, never going beyond the walls of some small conventicle, or the barriers of some strict ecclesiastical system; you may bear yourself impatiently and brusquely toward those who differ from you; you may even brand them with your anathema: but if they are one with God, by His gracious indwelling Spirit of Life, and if you are also one with Him, you positively cannot help being one with them. Your creed may differ, or your mode of worship, or your views about the Church; but you cannot be otherwise than one with those who are one with God, in a union which is not material but spiritual.

II. THIS ONENESS ALSO ADMITS OF GREAT VARIETY.—"One, as Thou, Father, art in Me, and I in Thee." Now, of course, we all admit the unity of the Godhead. The first article of the Jew is also the first article of the Christian, that the Lord our God is one God, one in essence, one in purpose, one in action. The Son does nothing of Himself; the Father does nothing apart from the Son; the Holy Ghost proceedeth from the Father and the Son. We cannot, as yet, understand this mystery; but with reverence we accept it as the primary basis of our faith.

But though God is One, there is evidently a variety of function in the ever-blessed Trinity. The Father decrees, the Son executes. The Father sends, the Son is sent. The Father works in Creation, the Son in Redemption and Judgment. And the functions of both Father and Son differ from those of the Holy Spirit.

If, then, the unity of the Church is to resemble the unity of the Godhead, according to our Lord's request, we may expect that it will not be physical, nor mechanical, nor a uniformity; but it will be a variety in unity—a unity of Spirit and purpose, and yet a unity which admits of very diverse functions and operations. Diversities of gifts, but the same Spirit. Differences of administrations, but the same Lord. Diversities of operations, but the same God which worketh all in all.

(1) The very conception of unity involves variety.—You take me out into a piece of waste land, and pointing to a heap of bricks say, "There is a unity." I at once rebut your assertion; there is uniformity undoubtedly, but not unity. Unity requires that a variety of different things should be combined to form one structure and carry out one idea. A collection of bricks is not a unity, but a house is. A pole is not a unity, but a hop-plant is. A snow atom is not a unity, but a snow crystal is. And when our Lord spoke of His disciples as one, He not only expected that there would be varieties amongst them, in character, mind, and ecclesiastical preference; but by the very choice of His words He meant us to infer that it would be so. The unity on which He set His heart was not a uniformity.

(2) But with variety there may be the truest unity.—There is variety in the human body—from

eyelash to foot, from heart to blood-disc, from brain to quivering nerve-fibre; yet, in all this variety, each one is conscious of an indivisible unity. There is variety in the tree: the giant arms that wrestle with the storm, the far-spreading roots that moor it to the soil, the myriad leaves in which the wind makes music, the cones or nuts which it flings upon the forest floor; yet for all this it is one. There is a variety in the Bible: variety of authorship—king, prophet, priest, herdsman, and fisherman, scholar, sage, and saint; variety of style—prose, poetry, psalmody, argument, appeal; variety of age—from the days of Moses to those of John, the beloved apostle, writing amid the persecutions of the empire; yet for all this there is a oneness in the Bible which no mere binding could give. So with the Church of Christ: there may be, there must be infinite varieties and shades of thought and work. Some will prefer the methods of Wesley, others the freedom of Congregationalism. Some will pray most naturally through the venerable words of a Liturgy, others in the deep silence of a Friends' Meeting. Some will thrive best beneath the crozier of the Bishop, others in the plain barracks of the Salvation Army; but, notwithstanding all this variety, there may be a deep spiritual unity. Many folds, but one flock; many regiments, but one army; many stones, but one breast-plate. "There is one body, and one Spirit, even as ye are called in one hope of your calling; one Lord, one faith, one baptism, one God and Father of all, who is above all, and through all, and in you all."

III. THE BASIS OF CHRISTIAN UNITY IS THE UNION OF EACH BELIEVER TO CHRIST.—"I in them, that they may be made perfect in one." However much true believers in Christ differ, there are two points in which they agree.

(1) Each believer is in Christ: in Christ's heart, loved with an everlasting love, the beloved name engraven on its secret tables; in Christ's book, enrolled on those pages which are sealed so fast that He alone can break the seven-fold seal; in Christ's hand, which holds the ocean as a drop upon its palm, and which was pierced on Calvary, from which no power shall ever pluck the trembling soul; in Christ's grace, rooted as a tree in luxuriant soil, or a house in a foundation of rock; but above all in Christ's Person, for He is the Head, "from whom the whole body is fitly framed and knit together by that which every joint supplieth." There are innumerable texts which speak of the Church as the Body of Christ (Eph. i. 23; Col. i. 24); and directly a man believes in Christ, he becomes a member of that mystical body. "We are members of His body, of His flesh, and of His bones." You may be a very obscure member, or even a paralyzed member; but be sure of this, if you are a Christian you are in Christ, as the eye is in the eye-socket, the arm in the shoulder-joint, and the finger in the hand.

(2) Christ is in each believer.—The texts that teach Christ's real presence in the believer are as numerous as spring flowers. "Christ liveth in me." "Know ye not that Jesus Christ is in you, except ye be reprobates?" "Ye shall know that I am in My Father, and ye in Me, and I in you." The Lord Jesus is in the heart which makes Him welcome, as the steam is in the piston, as the sap is in the branch, as the blood is in the heart, as the life is in the body. It would be impossible for words to describe a more intense spiritual Oneness than that which is here presented to us. The Saviour is in each of us, as the Father is in Him, and we are in Him, and He in God. "Our life is hid with Christ in God." Therefore we are not only one with Jesus Christ, but through Him

we are one with God. "I in them, Thou in Me." The very life of God is pouring its glorious tides through us, and would do so more largely if only we were more receptive and obedient. He pours water out of the mouth of the Congo at the rate of 1,000,000 tons per second; and is willing to do marvels as mighty through each believer. And as this life permeates us all alike, it makes us not only one with the blessed God, but one with all who believe, as the blood makes all the members of the body one, and the sap the branches of the tree.

IV. THE MEANS OF THIS SPIRITUAL UNITY ARE THE INFLUENCES OF THE HOLY SPIRIT.—Influence means inflow. It was by the Holy Spirit that our Lord's human nature was made one with His Father's. And this same Holy Spirit He has bequeathed to us, that He may be the same bond of spiritual life between us and our Lord as He was between our Lord and His Father. May not this be the meaning of His words: "The glory which Thou gavest Me I have given them, that they may be one as we are one"? May not that glory have consisted in the oneness of His human nature with God the Father, by the Holy Spirit? And if so, it may be shared by us. The more that believers receive the indwelling of the Holy Spirit, the more clearly will they appreciate this great mystery, and the more closely will they be drawn to all other believers, hushing jealous thoughts and uncharitable words, and "endeavoring to keep the unity of the Spirit in the bond of peace."

It is abundantly clear, then, that this unity cannot be broken unless we break away from Christ. Men have used that word schism with terrible effect. If a man has broken away from some visible church, they have pointed to him as a schismatic. But what is schism? It is a breaking away from the Body of Christ. But what is the Body of Christ? The Roman Catholic will tell you that it is the Church of Rome; the Anglican will tell you that it is the Church of England; the High Churchman will tell you that it is the collection of churches which hold the doctrine of Apostolic Succession. What vestige of Scriptural proof is there for these assertions? What an absurdity it is to be told that we must submit to an outward rite, or we cannot belong to the Body of Christ! What then would become of all the saints and martyrs who died without membership with one of these visible organizations? No, the Body of Christ, as Scripture plainly teaches, is that great multitude which no man can number, of all nations, and kindreds, and peoples, and tongues, and sects, and eras, who are united by faith with the Saviour. The Church of Christ is not conterminous with any earthly or visible organization; it is long as the ages, wide as the poles, broad as the charity of God; it includes all in heaven and on earth who hold the Head. The only condition of membership in that Church is simple faith in Christ. And the only method of severance from that Church is through the severance of the soul's trust in Christ. He only is a schismatic who ceases to be Christ's.

The Papal Legate told Savonarola that he cut him off from the Church Militant and from the Church Triumphant. "From the Church Militant you may," was the martyr's reply; "but from the Church Triumphant, never." It was well spoken; but Savonarola might have gone further, and defied the scarlet-coated functionary even to cut him off from the Church Militant—nothing could do that but apostasy. A man may be excommunicated from our church systems, or he may never have belonged to one of them; but so long as he believes in Christ, he is a member of the

Holy Catholic Church. And schism is more likely to be charged against those who violate the spirit of Christian charity in making harsh and false statements against their fellow-members in the Body of Christ. Let us not retaliate, lest we also commit that sin. We can afford to wait. Five minutes in heaven, or less, will settle it all.

The object for which Christ prayed is already being partially accomplished. The world may not be as yet surrendering to the claims of Jesus Christ, but it is becoming increasingly impressed with His Divine mission: "that the world may believe that Thou hast sent Me." And in proportion as the Holy Spirit pervades and fills the hearts of the children of God, the manifestation of the Life of God in them, and through them, will have an ever-increasing effect, and will do what church systems and even the preachings of her thousand pulpits cannot effect in convincing and saving men.

Let us remember that Christ's own conception of the unity of His Church is that which is the result of the indwelling of the one Spirit. Such unity is already a fact in the eye of God, though undiscerned as yet in all its fullness by men. Let us thank God that this marvellous request has been already so largely realized, and let us dare to hold fellowship as Christians with all those who are indwelt by the Spirit of the Life, which is also in Christ Jesus.

XXIII

The Love that Bound Christ to the Cross

"Jesus, therefore, knowing all things that should come upon Him, went forth, and said unto them, Whom seek ye?"—JOHN xviii. 4.

The Cedron was never more than a mountain brook, and it is now dry. Its stony bed alone shows where it used to flow through the valley that separated Mount Zion from the Mount of Olives. The main road which led from the city gate, over the Mount of Olives to Bethany and Jericho, crossed it by an ancient bridge, from which, on this especial night, a fair scene must have presented itself.

Above, the Passover moon was shining in full-orbed splendor turning night into day. Beneath, the little stream was brawling down the valley, catching the moonlight on its wavelets. On the one slope dark, thick woods, above which rose the ancient walls and gates of the city, on the other, the swelling slopes of Olivet. Presently the Lord emerged out of the shadow, engaged in earnest converse with the apostles; crossed the bridge, but, instead of pursuing the path as it wound upward toward Bethany and Bethphage, they all turned into a large enclosure, well-known as the garden of the oil-press, and which we know best as Gethsemane. Somewhere, no doubt, within its enclosure stood the rock-hewn trough in which the rich juicy olives were trodden by naked feet. "When Jesus had spoken these words, He went forth with His disciples over the brook Cedron, where was a garden, into which He entered, and His disciples."

The sequel was so fully narrated by the other evangelists that there was no need for the writer of this narrative to tell of the awful anguish, the broken cries, the bloody sweat, the running to and fro of the disciples, the sleep of the chosen three, the strengthening angel. He confines himself almost entirely to the circumstances of the Lord's arrest.

Two hours only had passed since Judas left the supper-table; but that had given him all the time needed for the completion of his plan. Hastening to the authorities, he had told them that the favorable moment had arrived for his Master's arrest; that he knew the lonely spot to which He was wont to resort for meditation and prayer; and that he had need of an armed band to overpower all possible resistance on the part of Himself or His followers. This they were able to supply from the guards and custodians of the Temple. They were going against One who was deserted and defenceless; yet the soldiers were armed with sticks and staves. They were about to arrest One who would make no attempt at flight or concealment, and the moon was full; yet, lest He should make His escape to some limestone grotto, or amid the deep shadows, they carried torches and lanterns.

The Lord had just awoke His disciples for the third and last time, when probably His ear detected the tread of hurrying feet, the muffled clank of swords, the stifled murmur of an advancing crowd; perhaps He saw also the glancing lights, as they advanced through the garden shrubs, and began to encircle the place where He had prayed. By such signs, and especially by the inner intimation of the Holy Spirit, He knew all things that should come upon Him, and without waiting for His enemies to reach Him, with calm and dignified composure He went forth to meet the rabble band, stepping out into the moonlight and saluting them with the inquiry, "Whom seek ye?"

There are some deep and memorable suggestions here as to the

In order to His death having any value it must be free. If it could be shown that He had no choice than to die, because His own purpose was overmastered by the irresistible force of circumstances, His death could not have met the claims of a broken law, or inaugurated a new code of morals to His Church. But there are several points in this narrative which make it clear that He laid down His life of Himself, that none took it from Him, that He had power to lay it down, and power to take it again.

(1) When Jesus asked them the question, "Whom seek ye?" there were, no doubt, many in the band who knew Him well enough, and that He was the object of their midnight raid; but not one of them had the courage to answer, "Thee." A paralyzing awe had already commenced to cast its spell over their spirits. Those who knew Him shrank from identifying Him, and were content to answer generally, "Jesus of Nazareth." But when He answered, "I am He," what was it that so suddenly affected them? Did some stray beams of concealed glory burst forth from their confinement to indicate His majesty? Did they dread the putting-forth of that power which had been so often exerted to save and bless? Or, was there a direct miracle of Divine power, which secured their discomfiture? We cannot tell. But, whatever the cause, the crowd suddenly fell back in confusion, and were flung to the ground.

Here, for a moment, the would-be captors lay, as though pinioned to the dust by some unseen hand. The spell was soon withdrawn, and they were again on their feet, cursing themselves for their needless panic. But—and this is the point—the power that sent that rough hireling band reeling backward to the ground could easily have held them there, or plunged them as Korah, Dathan, and Abiram, into living graves. "One flash came forth to tell of the sleeping lightning which He would not use"; and then, having revealed the might, which could have delivered Him from their puny arms, He returned to His attitude of willing self-surrender. Who, then, shall say that our Saviour's death was not His own act and deed?

(2) When that rabble crew were again on their feet, confronting Jesus, He asked them a second time, Whom seek ye? Again they replied, "Jesus of Nazareth." Jesus answered, "I have told you that I am He; if, therefore, ye seek me, let these go their way." And, forthwith, He put forth such a power over His own as secured their freedom from arrest.

It is evident that it was no part of His foes' purpose beforehand to let them go; for, on their way back they arrested a young man, probably Mark himself, whom curiosity had drawn from his bed, and whom they took for one of His disciples. He escaped with great difficulty from their hands. It is hardly doubtful that if some special power had not been exerted over them, they would have treated the whole of the followers of Jesus as they sought to treat Him. Is it not evident, then, that the power which secured the safety of His disciples could have secured that of the Master Himself; or that He might have passed away through the midst of them, as He did through the infuriated crowd which proposed to cast Him headlong over the precipice near Nazareth at the commencement of His ministry? Every arm might have been struck nerveless, every foot paralyzed with lameness. Who, then, shall deny that Christ's death was His own act?

(3) But again, when Jesus had spoken thus there seemed some wavering among His captors, perhaps a hesitation as to who should first lay hand on Him. At this juncture, when the whole enterprise threatened to miscarry, Judas felt that he must, at all hazards, show how safe it was to touch the person of his Master; so, though the bold challenge of Jesus had made the preconcerted signal needless, he resolved still to give it, that the spell of that presence might be broken. The traitor, therefore, stepped up and kissed the Lord.

Encouraged by this sacrilegious act, His myrmidons now laid hands on Jesus, grasping His sacred person as they might have done Barabbas, or some other member of his gang. They then proceeded to bind Him after the merciless Roman fashion. Peter could not bear to see this. He sprang forth from the covert of the shadow, drew his sword, and cut at the nearest assailant's head. But the blade, glancing off the helmet, cut off the ear.

It was an unwelcome interference with the behavior of the meek and gentle Lord, whose hand was already bound. It could not be permitted. "Suffer ye thus far," He said to the rude soldier who was binding Him, and with His own finger touched the ear, stanched the flowing blood, and healed it. It has been remarked that this was the only act of healing wrought on one for whom it was neither asked of Him, and who had no faith in His beneficent power. But, surely, the hand that could work that miracle could have broken from the bonds that held it as easily as Samson from the two new cords which burned as flax in the flame. The power with which Jesus saved others might have saved Himself. Who, then, shall say that His death was not His own free act? Listen, moreover, to His own words. Then said Jesus unto Peter, "Put up thy sword into the sheath; the cup which My Father hath given Me, shall I not drink it?" "Thinkest thou that I cannot now pray to My Father, and He shall presently give Me more than twelve legions of angels; but how then shall the Scripture be fulfilled that thus it must be?"

As, then, we view the death of the Cross we must ever remember the voluntariness of that supreme act, which is all the more conspicuous as the agony of the Garden reminds us how greatly the Lord's spirit dreaded the awful pressure of the world's sin, which made Him cry: "My God, My God, why hast Thou forsaken Me?" How greatly He must have loved us! It was love, and only love, that kept Him standing at the bar of Pilate, bending beneath the scourge of the soldiers, hanging in apparent helplessness on the cross. Not the iron hand of relentless fate; not the overpowering numbers or closely-woven plots of His foes; not the nails that pierced His quivering flesh. No, it was none of these. It was not even the compulsion of the Divine purpose. It was His own choice, because of a love that would bear all things if only it might achieve redemption for those whom He loved more than Himself. "He loved me, and gave Himself for me."

Surely we may trust that love. If it moved Him to endure the Cross and despise the shame, is there anything that it will withhold, anything that it will not do? His love is stronger than death, and mightier than the grave. Strong waters cannot quench it, floods cannot drown it. It silences all praise, and beggars all recompense. To believe and accept it is eternal life. To dwell within its embrace is the foretaste of everlasting joy. To be filled by it is to be transfigured into the image of God Himself.

XXIV

Drinking the Cup

"The cup which My Father hath given Me, shall I not drink it?"—JOHN xviii. 1-14.

In our Master's arrest the one feature which stands out in unique splendor is its voluntariness. He went into the garden "knowing all things that should come upon Him." Even at the last moment He might have evaded the kiss of the traitor, and the binding thong with which Malchus sought to manacle His gracious hands. The spell of His intrinsic nobleness and glory, which had flung His captors to the ground, might have held them there; the power that could heal the wounded ear might have destroyed with equal ease the entire band.

The reason for all this hardly needs explaining. His life and death were not merely a sacrifice, but a self-sacrifice. He freely gave Himself up for us all. Each believer may dare to appropriate the words of the apostle: "He loved me, and gave Himself for me." It was through the Eternal Spirit that He offered Himself without spot to God. It was from His own invincible love that He gave Himself for the Church, His Bride. "From beginning to end the moving spring of all His actions was deliberate self-devotedness to the good of men, and the fulfillment of God's will, for these are equivalents. And His death as the crowning act of this career was to be conspicuously a death embodying and exhibiting the spirit of self-sacrifice." Let us learn:

I. THE SUPREME NOBILITY OF SURRENDER TO THE EVITABLE.—It is, of course, most noble, when the martyr goes to his death without a murmur of complaint; allowing his enemies to wreak their vengeance without recrimination or threatening; bowing the meek head to the block; extending the hand to the hungry flame. He has no alternative but to die; there are no legions waiting under arms to obey his summons; no John of Gaunt to stand beside him, as beside Wycliffe, to see him fairly tried and insist on his acquittal. Then, there is nothing for it but to evince the patience and gentleness of Christ in being led as a lamb to the slaughter.

But though this spectacle stirs the hearts of men, there is one still more illustrious—when the sufferer bends to a fate which he might easily avoid, but confronts for the sake of others. The former is submission to the inevitable, this to the evitable. That is bearing a yoke which is imposed by superior authority; this taking a yoke which might be evaded without blame, as judged by the tribunal of public opinion. And this is the sublimest spectacle on which the eye of man or angel can rest; for thus the sacrifice of Christ finds its noblest counterpart and fulfillment.

When a missionary, with ample means and loving friends, deliberately spends among squalid and repulsive conditions, the precious years which might have been passed among congenial society and luxurious comfort in the homeland; chooses a lot from which nature inevitably shrinks instead of that to which every conclusion but one points, and stays at his post, though his return, so far from being resented, would actually be favored by all whose opinion is of weight—this is a voluntary submission to the evitable.

When a home pastor stays by his poor flock because they need him so sorely, and sets his face toward grinding poverty and irksome toil when the city church invites him to a larger stipend and wealthier surroundings—this again is a voluntary surrender to the evitable.

When a wealthy bachelor is willing to forego the ease and quiet of his beautiful home in order to welcome the orphans of his deceased brother, who might have been sent to some charitable institution or cast on strangers, that they may be beneath his personal supervision, and have a better chance in life—this again is voluntary submission to the evitable.

In each such case, it is not inevitable that the cross should be borne, and the hands yielded to the binding thong. The tongue of scandal could hardly find cause for criticism if the easier path were chosen. Perhaps the soul hardly realizes the kindredness of its resolve with the loftiest that this world has seen. But it is superlatively beautiful, nevertheless. And let it never be forgotten, that nothing short of this will satisfy the standard of Christ. No Christian has a right to use all his rights. None can claim immunity from the duty of seeking the supreme good of others, though it involve the supreme cost to himself.

II. THE RECOGNITION OF GOD'S WILL IN HIS PERMISSIONS.—In the bitter anguish which had immediately preceded the arrest, our Lord had repeatedly referred to His cup. "If this cup," He said, "may not pass from Me, except I drink it, Thy will be done." The cup evidently referred to all the anguish caused to His holy nature in being numbered among the transgressors, and having to bear the sin of the world. Whether it was the anguish of the body, beneath which He feared He would succumb, as some think; or the dread of being made a sin-offering, a scape-goat laden with sin, as others, or the chill of the approaching eclipse, which extorted the cry of forsakenness, as seems to me the more likely—is not pertinent to our present consideration. It is enough to know that, whilst there was much that cried, "Back!" there was more that cried, "On!"—and that He chose from the profoundest depths of His nature, to do the Father's will, to execute His part in the compact into which they had entered before the worlds were made, and to drink to the dregs the cup which His Father had placed in His hands.

But here we note that to all appearances the cup was mingled, prepared, and presented by the malignity and hate of man. The High Priests had long resolved to put Him to death, because His success with the people, His fresh and living comments on the law, His opposition to their hypocrisies and pretensions had exasperated them to madness. Judas also seemed to have had a conspicuous share in his discovery and arrest. Had we been left to our unaided reasonings we might have supposed that the most bitter ingredients of His cup had been supplied by the ingratitude of His own, the implacable rancor of the priests, and the treachery of Judas; but, see, He recognizes none but the Father—it is always the Father, always the cup which the Father had given.

There had been times in our lives when we may have been tempted to distinguish between God's appointments and permissions, and to speak of the former as being manifestly His will for us, whilst we suspended our judgment about the latter, and questioned if we were authorized in accounting them as being equally from Heaven. But such distinctions are fatal to peace. Our souls were kept in constant perturbation, as we accounted ourselves the shuttlecock of rival powers, now God's, now man's. And we ended in ruling God out of more than half our life, and regarding ourselves as the hapless prey of strong and malicious forces to which we were sold, as Joseph to the Ishmaelites.

A deeper reading of Scripture has led us to a truer conclusion. There is no such distinction there. What God permits is as equally His will as what He appoints. Joseph tells his brethren that it was not they who sent him to Egypt, but God. David listens meekly to Shimei's shameful words, because he felt that God allowed them to be spoken. And here Jesus refuses to see the hand of His foes in His sufferings, but passes beyond the hand which bore the cup to His lips to the Father who was permitting it to be presented, and reposed absolutely in the choice of Him of One who loved Him with a love that was before the foundation of the world.

Oh, sufferer! whether by those strokes, which, like sickness or bereavement, seem to come direct from heaven, or by those which, like malicious speeches or oppressive acts, seem to emanate from man, look up into the face of God, and say, "My Father, this is Thy will for me; Thine angels would have delivered me had it been best. But since they have not interposed, I read Thy choice for Thy child, and I am satisfied. It is sweet to drink the cup which Thy hands have prepared."

III. THE DEEP LAW OF SUBSTITUTION.—Some of the rabble crowd had probably shown signs of a disposition to arrest some of Christ's followers. He, therefore, interfered, and reminded them of their own admission, that He was the object to their midnight raid, and bade them allow these to go their way. Is it surprising that the evangelist generalizes this act, finding in it an illustration of His Master's ceaseless interposition on behalf of His own—that of those whom the Father had given Him He should lose none.

In brief, this scene affords a conspicuous and striking illustration of the great doctrine of substitution. As the Good Shepherd steps to the front and sheathes the swords of His foes in His own breast, while He demands the release of the cowering flock, He is doing on a small scale what He did once and forever on Calvary; when, exposing Himself to the penalty due to sin, and braving the concentrated antagonism of a broken law, the drawn sword of inviolable justice, the sharpness of death, the shame of the cross, and the humiliation of the grave, He said, "If ye seek Me, let these go their way."

Christ sheltered us without reckoning the cost to Himself. He stood to the front, and bore the extreme brunt of all that was to be borne. He substituted His suffering for ours, His wounds for our pain, His death for our sins. If you are fearing the just recompense of your sins, like a band of arresting soldiers lurking in the dark shadows and threatening to drag you forth to pay the uttermost farthing, take heart; Jesus has met, and will meet, them for you. Listen to His majestic voice, saying, "Take Me, but let this soul, who clings to the skirts of My robe, go his way." He is arrested, and led away; thou art free—that in thy freedom thou shouldest give thyself to be His very slave.

XXV

The Hall of Annas

"They led Him away to Annas first, for he was father-in-law to
Caiaphas, which was the high priest that same year."—JOHN xviii. 13.

The band that had arrested Jesus led Him back across the Kedron bridge, up the steep ascent,
and through the ancient gateway, which at this season of the year stood always open, even at
night.

The passage of the armed men through the quiet streets must have aroused from their slumbers
many sleepers, who hurried to the windows to see them pass below in the clear moonlight. But
no one guessed who was being taken into custody, and most of them probably thought that the
soldiers had captured some more of the Barabbas gang, who, at that season of the year, would
make a rare harvest by plundering pilgrims to the feast.

Their destination, in the first place, was the mansion of Annas, the head of the reigning priestly
family, who was father-in-law of the actual high priest. He was now an old man; wealthy,
aristocratic, and laden with all the honors his nation could give. For many years he had worn the
high priest's robes, and though he had now nominally retired from that exalted office, he still
kept his hand upon the reins of government. Caiaphas, at the time of which we speak, had held
the priesthood for seventeen years under his tutelage; and he retained it for five years after. It is
easy therefore to understand why Annas is described as the high priest. He was still the most
powerful living bearer of that title. The whole family partook of his character, and was notorious
for unwearied plotting. The gliding, deadly, snake-like smoothness with which Annas and his
sons seized their prey is said to have won them the name of hissing vipers.

Annas and Caiaphas probably shared the same cluster of buildings, which was presumably the
official residence of the high priestly family. In the East the houses of the great are frequently a
group of buildings of unequal height standing near each other and surrounded by the same court,
but with passages between, independent entrances, and separate roofs. Sometimes they would
form a square or quadrangle with porticos and corridors around it, plants and fountains in the
midst, and a slight awning overhead to protect the open courtyard from the sun or rain, the
communication with the street being through a smaller courtyard and archway, called in the
Gospels "a porch." In some such cluster of splendid buildings Annas and Caiaphas and others of
their family would live, and the whole would be called the high priest's palace.

In one of the large reception halls Annas waited, impatient and feverish, to know the result of
the midnight expedition. He had a nervous dread of what Jesus might do when driven to bay;
and dreaded lest the secret should leak out, and the Galilean pilgrims rise in defence of their
favorite Prophet, whom four days before they had escorted into the city with shouts. What if
Judas should not prove true? All these disquieting thoughts chased each other like pursuing
phantoms through his mind, and it was an immense relief when the clank of weapons in the court
assured him of the safe return of Malchus' party, and answering voices told him that Jesus was at
last safe within his power.

The prisoner was at once brought before the old man, who eagerly scrutinized his features in the flickering light of lanterns and flambeaux, casting shadows which a Rembrandt would have loved to paint. One or two intimates may have stood around Him; but the main inquiry was left to Himself, as He put the Master through a preliminary and informal examination, in the hope of extracting from His replies materials on which the court, which was hastily summoned for an early hour in the morning, might proceed.

On the surface the inquiry seemed fair and innocent enough. The high priest, we learn from verse 19, asked Jesus of His disciples and His doctrine. But the lamb-skin hid a wolf. For the questions were so worded as to entangle, and to provide material on which to found the subsequent charge, which was even then being framed, that Jesus was a disturber of the public peace, and a teacher of revolutionary doctrine.

First, then, about His disciples.—Annas would like to be informed what this association of men meant. Why were they formed into a society? By what bond were they united? What secret instructions had they received? What hidden objects had they in view? If Jesus refused to answer these questions, might it not be made to appear that an attempt was on foot to organize a confederation throughout the entire country? If so, it would be easy to awaken the jealousy of the Roman authorities, and lead them to feel that they must take immediate steps to stamp out the plot by executing the ringleader.

And, next, as to His doctrine.—Had not Jesus repeatedly spoken about the Kingdom of Heaven? What did this mean? Was He contemplating the setting up of a kingdom? Did He intend it to be understood that He was the expected Messiah, and that He meditated revolt against Rome? Was the manifestation of force, which had accompanied His recent entrance into the city, at His instigation?

Our Lord at once penetrated the design of His crafty interrogator. And in His answer He took care not to mention His disciples, speaking only of Himself. He affirmed that He had nothing to say which He had not already said a hundred times in the synagogues and the Temple, before friends and foes. He had no secret doctrines for the initiated, but had declared all that was in His heart. Between His disciples and Himself there had been no connection other than was obvious on the surface. No meetings under cover of night; no discussions of revolutionary topics; nothing that could not bear the fullest scrutiny. "I spake openly to the world; I ever taught in the synagogue and in the temple, whither the Jews always resort; and in secret [that is, in the sense in which you use the word] I have said nothing. Why askest thou Me? Ask them which heard Me what I have said unto them: behold, they know what I have said."

Our Lord's reference to those who had heard Him is probably an allusion to the armies of spies whom Annas had set on His track, watching His actions, reporting His words. Was not this examination of the prisoner a confession that the close scrutiny to which He had been subjected for so long had failed to elicit aught on which a criminal charge could be based? Jesus knew that His most secret words had been tortured in vain to yield an accusation against Him. How great then was the hypocrisy which could feign ignorance! How evident it was that Annas was only intent on inveigling his prisoner to say something on which to base his after-accusation.

All this was implied in our Lord's noble and transparent words. We shall see that He adopted another tone when He was properly arraigned before the assembled Sanhedrim; but in this more private, injudicial, inquisitorial interview, with one scathing rebuke He tore away the cloak of assumed ignorance with which this crafty man veiled his sinister purpose, and laid His secret thoughts open to the gaze of all.

For the time Annas was silenced. He had made small headway in the informal examination of his prisoner, and he now gave it up. Whatever resentment he may have felt at our Lord's answer he carefully concealed, biding the hour when he might vent the vials of his hate without stint.

We must not suppose there was any anger in that long-suffering heart toward this judge. He was even then about to die for Him, and to bear the guilt of the very sin He so pitilessly exposed. But surely it was the part of love to show Annas what he was, and to utter words of rebuke in which, as in a mirror, his secret thoughts might be revealed. But if, in the moment of His humiliation, Jesus could thus search and reveal a man, what will He not do when He is no longer prisoner, but Judge? Oh, those awful eyes, which are as a flame of fire! Oh, those awful words, which pierce to the dividing asunder of the joints and marrow, and discern the thoughts and intents of the heart! What wonder that men shall at last call on the rocks to hide them from the wrath of the Lamb! Kiss the Son, lest ye perish from His presence, when His wrath is kindled but a little! Blessed are they who can stand before Him without blame!

Then followed one of the grossest indignities to which our Lord was at this time subjected. On speaking thus, one of the officers, in the spirit of that despicable flunkeyism which will sacrifice all nobility and self-respect to curry the flavor of a superior, smote our Lord with a rod, saying, "Answerest thou the high priest so?"

When afterward they came around Him to mock and smite, He answered nothing; but when this first stroke was inflicted the Master said quietly, "If I have spoken what is false or unbecoming, prove that I have done so; but if you cannot, why do you strike Me? No one has the right to take the law into his own hands, much less a servant of the court."

It is impossible not to recall the mighty utterances against the resistance of wrong, spoken from the Mount, in the Messiah's manifesto: "I say unto you that ye resist not evil; but whosoever shall smite thee on thy right cheek, turn to him the other also." Clearly our Lord did not literally do so in this instance, because He saw an opportunity of revealing to this man His true condition, and of bringing him to a better mind. Our bearing of wrong must always be determined by the state of mind of those who ill-use us. In the case of some we may best arrest them by the dignity of an unutterable patience, which will bear to the utmost without retaliation—this is to turn the other cheek. In the case of others we may best serve them by leading them calmly and quietly to take the true measure of their crime. In all cases our prime consideration should be, not what we may be suffering, nor the utter injustice which is meted out to us; but how best to save the evil-doer, who is injuring his own soul more fatally than he can possibly injure us, and who is sowing seeds of harvest of incredible torture to his own conscience, in the long future which lies behind the veil of sense.

If only we could drink in the pure love of Jesus, and view all wrong and wrong-doers, not in the light of our personal interest, but of their awful condition and certain penalty; if only we could grieve over the infinite horror of a warped and devil-possessed soul, drifting like a ship on fire before the breeze, straight to the rocks; if only we could see the wrong done to our Father God and His sorrow, we should understand Chrysostom's beautiful comment on this scene: "Think on Him who said these words; on him to whom they were said; and on the reason why they were said; and, with Divine power, they will cast down all wrath that may arise within thy soul."

XXVI

How it fared with Peter

"Peter stood at the door without. Then went out that other disciple, which was known unto the high priest, and spake unto her that kept the door, and brought in Peter."—John xviii. 16.

Remember that this very circumstantial account was given by one who was an eyewitness of the whole scene; and who, withal, was then and in after years the warm friend and companion of Peter. But his love did not lead him to conceal his brother's sins. Peter himself would not have wished him to do so, because where sin had abounded, grace had had the greater opportunity to super-abound.

At the moment of the Lord's arrest, all the disciples forsook Him and fled. "The Shepherd was smitten and the flock scattered." Two of them, however, speedily recovered their self-possession, and followed at a distance, eager to see what would befall. When the procession reached the palace gate John seems to have entered with the rest of the crowd, and the ponderous, massive doors closed behind him. On looking round for Peter he missed him, and concluding that he had been shut out and was still standing without, he went to the maid that kept the wicket-gate, opening in the main entrance doors for the admission of individuals, and asked her to admit his friend. She recognized him as being well known to the high priest, and readily assented to his request.

A fire of wood had been hastily lighted in the open courtyard, and cast its rays on the chilly April night; so that whilst Jesus was being examined by Annas the men who had taken part in the night adventure were grouped around the fire, discussing the exciting incident, with its moment of panic, the case of the arrest, the hurt and healing of the ear of Malchus, the seizure of the rich Eastern dress from the young man whom they had encountered on their homeward march. Peter did not wish to be recognized, and thought that the best way of preserving his incognito was to put on a bold face and take his place among the rest as though he, too, had been one of the capturing band, and had as much right to be there as any other of that mixed company. So he stood with them, and warmed himself.

Meanwhile, the doorkeeper, leaving her post, came to the fire, and in its kindling ray her eye fell upon Peter's face. She was surprised to see him there, feigning to be one of themselves. If, like John, he had gone quietly into some recess of the court, and waited unobtrusively in the shadow, she could have said nothing. In her kind-heartedness she would have respected them both; for she knew that they sympathized with the arrested Nazarene. But to find him there talking and acting as though he had no personal interest in the matter was so unseemly and unfit that she was provoked to expose him. She looked at him earnestly—as another evangelist tells us—to be quite sure that she was not mistaken; and feeling quite certain in her identification, said abruptly, "Art thou not one of this man's disciples?"

Peter was taken off his guard. If he had been arrested, and taken for trial, he would no doubt have played the hero—he had braced himself up for that; but he had not expected that the supreme trial of his life could come in the question of a servant-maid. It is so often thus. We lock and bolt the main door, and the thief breaks in at a tiny window which we had not thought of. We would burn at the stake; but in an hour of social intercourse with our friends, or a trivial business transaction, we say the word which fills our life with regret. Confused at the sudden pause in the conversation, and the turning of all eyes toward himself, Peter's first impulse was to allay suspicion, and he said bluntly, "I am not." Such was his first denial.

After this, as Matthew and Mark tell us, he went out into the outer porch or gateway, perhaps to avoid the glare of the light and the scrutiny of those prying eyes. He remembered afterward that, at the same moment, a cock was heralding the dawn—the dawn of the blackest, saddest day that ever broke upon Jerusalem, or the world. But its warning notes were just then lost on him; for there another maid, speaking to some male acquaintances, pointed him out as one of the Nazarene's friends. "This man also was with Jesus the Nazarene." Probably no harm was meant, but the words alarmed Peter greatly, and he denied, as Matthew says, with an oath, "I know not the man." This was the second denial.

An hour passed; Peter, as we learn from the twenty-fifth verse, was again at the fire, and it was hardly possible for him to talk in a large company without unconsciously, and by force of character, coming to the front and taking the lead. His perturbed spirit was perhaps the more vehement to drown conscience. But now he is challenged by many at once. They say unto him, "Art not thou also one of His disciples?" And another saith, "Of a truth, thou wast with Him"; and another, a kinsman to Malchus, and therefore specially likely to remember his relative's assailant, saith, "Did I not see thee in the garden with Him?" Beset and badgered thus, Peter begins to curse and to swear, saying, "I know not the man of whom ye speak." When men lose their temper, they drop naturally into their native speech; and so, as Peter's fear and passion vented themselves in the guttural patois of Galilee, he gave a final clue to his identification. "Thou art a Galilean, thy speech betrayeth thee." And again he denied with an oath, "I know not the man." This was his third denial. And immediately the cock crew.

It may have happened that, at this moment, Jesus was passing from Annas to Caiaphas, and cast on Peter that marvellous look of mingled sorrow and pity, of suffering more for His sake than his own, and of tender allusion to the scene and words of the previous evening, which broke Peter's heart, and sent him forth to weep bitterly.

The light was breaking over the hills of Moab, flushing with roseate hues the marble pinnacles of the temple, whilst the city and surrounding valleys were still shrouded in the grey gloom, as Peter went forth alone from the high priest's palace. Only those whose last words to the beloved dead were rude and thoughtless—not expecting that there would be no opportunity to unsay them and ask forgiveness, but that, ere they met again, death would have sealed in silence the only lips that could speak words of relief and peace—can realize just what Peter felt. Did he know Him? Of course he did, and ever since that memorable hour, when Andrew first brought him into His presence, he had been growing to a more perfect knowledge. Did he love Him? Of course he did; and Jesus, who knew all things, knew it too. But why had he acted thus? Ah, the reasons were not far to seek. He had boasted of his superiority to all his brethren; had relied on his own braggart resolutions; had counted himself strong because he could speak strongly and loudly when danger was not near; had thought that he could cope with Satan, though arrayed in no stronger armor than that which his red-hot impulse forged. He thought his resolutions wheat and his Master's cautions light as chaff; he had to learn his weakness and see his confidence winnowed away as clouds of chaff while Satan sifted him.

The resolutions of the evening are not strong enough to carry us victoriously through the morning conflict. We must learn to watch and pray, to lie low in humility and self-distrust, and to be strong in the grace which awaits all tempted ones in God.

And where could Peter go to weep his bitter tears but to Gethsemane! He would surely seek out the spot where his Master's form was still outlined in the crushed grass, and his tears would fall where the bloody sweat had fallen but a few hours before. But how different the cause of sorrow! The anguish of the blessed Lord had none of the ingredients that filled the cup of Peter to the brim! And all the while the memory of that sorrow, of those broken cries, of that coming and going for sympathy, of those remonstrances against his senseless sleep, and of that last tender, yearning, pitiful look of love, came back on him to arouse successive surges of grief. Contrast Christ's love with your ingratitude, Christ's constancy with your fickle devotion, Christ's meekness to take the yoke of His Father's will, and your unwillingness to bear His cross of shame, and ask if you, too, have no cause for tears like those that Peter shed.

It is remarkable that Peter should have fallen here. His open, ingenuous nature was not given to lying, his impetuous character was not prone to cowardice. Accustomed from boyhood to meet death in the wrestle with nature for daily sustenance, he was not subject to the apprehensions of a nervous dread. None of his fellow-disciples would have expected the rock-man to show that he was clay or sand after all. But this was permitted that we might learn that our noblest natural qualities as much need to be dealt with by the grace of God as our vices and defects. Many a fortress has been taken from a side which was deemed impregnable. No one expected that Wolfe would assail Quebec from the Heights of Abraham.

How often we have fallen into the same trap! We have, perhaps, been thrown into a company where it was fashionable to sneer at evangelical religion, and we have held our peace; where the ready sneer was passed on those who dared still to believe in miracle and inspiration, and we have been silent, where condemnation has been freely passed on some man of God whom we owned as friend, and knew to be innocent, and we have not tried to vindicate him; where some great religious movement in which we were interested was being discussed and condemned, whilst we have coolly joined in the conversation as if we had not made up our minds, or were totally indifferent. We have been unwilling to be unpopular, to stand alone, to bear the brunt of opposition, to seem eccentric and peculiar. Let those who are without sin cast their stones at Peter; but the most of us will take our place beside him, and realize that we, too, have given grief to Christ, and grave cause to His enemies to blaspheme.

But, be it remembered, the true quality of the soul is shown, not in the way in which it yields to temptation in some moment of weakness and unpreparedness, but in the way in which it repents afterward. Do we weep, not for the penalty we dread, but because we have sinned against Christ? Are we broken down before Him, waiting till He shall restore? Do we dare still to believe in His forgiving and renewing grace? Then this is a godly repentance, which needs not to be repented of. These are tears which His love shall transform to pearls. How different this to the attitude of a Judas! Each fell; but in their demeanor afterward the one was shown to be gold, silver, precious stones; the other wood, hay, and stubble.

How may we be kept from falling again?

(1) Let us not sleep through the precious moments which heaven affords before each hour of trial; but use them for putting on the whole armor of God, that we may be able to stand in the evil day.

(2) Let us not cast ourselves needlessly into situations where our most cherished convictions are likely to be assailed by wanton men; though if God should lead us there we need not fear, for it will be given us in the same hour what to answer. Take care of warming yourself at the world's fire.

(3) Let us keep within the environing presence of our Lord. It is always right to do right; always safe; always blessed. Satan can only hurt us when he allures us out of that safe hiding-place. Never forsake the things which are pure, and lovely, and of good report. You, in Jesus, shall yet overcome the world if you refuse to allow the world to come between Him and you.

XXVII

The Trial before Caiaphas

"Annas had sent Him bound unto Caiaphas the high priest."—JOHN xviii. 24.

It was as yet but two or three o'clock in the morning. Jerusalem was still asleep, and well it was for the foes of Jesus that no suspicion of what was on foot had breathed into the minds of the crowds of pilgrims; for, had the Galileans only known what was being done to their favorite prophet, they would have risen, and the plot must have miscarried before Jesus was handed over to the Romans. But, as the Lord said, "It was their hour and the power of darkness." The darkest hour before the dawn!

When Annas had completed his preliminary inquiry he gave orders that He should again be bound with the thongs of which He had been relieved, and led to that part of the palace specially used by Caiaphas, who was High Priest, but a mere puppet in the hands of the wily Annas. By this time the leading Pharisees, Sadducees, and priests, had been got together, summoned by special messengers; and though the formal meeting of the Council was probably not held till a little later (compare Matt. xxvi. 57 with xxvii. 1, 2), the trial was really conducted at that untimely hour, and the evidence procured on which final action was taken.

They awaited the Prisoner in one of the larger halls of the palace, sitting in Oriental fashion on cushions and pillows, in a half-circle, with turbaned heads, crossed legs, and bare feet; the High Priest in the centre, the others, on either side, according to age.

All the rules of justice were violated. The judge was chief inquisitor; witnesses against the prisoner were alone summoned; and the Court set itself from the first to get evidence to put the accused to death.

Ever since Jesus had commenced His ministry it had been certain that He would have to face some such tribunal as this. His soul was aflame for Righteousness and Truth; it was inevitable that He should come into conflict with these representatives of a traditional and external religiousness, which consisted in a number of formal rules and rites from which the life had long since fled.

This Gospel specially narrates the progress of the quarrel in the holy city. As far back as ch. ii. 18 we are told that there had been an altercation on the Lord's right to cleanse the Temple.

Ch. iv. 1-3.—He left Judaea because of the irritation of the Pharisees at the numerous baptisms which were taking place under His ministry.

Ch. v. 18.—He was only at the beginning of the second year of His ministry, and had just healed the impotent man at the pool of Bethesda, and we find the Jews consulting how they might kill Him, and He was compelled again to retire from Judaea.

Ch. vii. 19.—Such was the spirit of vindictiveness excited against our Lord that when twelve months afterward He came to Jerusalem at the Feast of Tabernacles, one of His first words was, "Why go ye about to kill Me?" The people were well acquainted with the designs of the rulers (vers. 25, 26); and ultimately officers were sent to arrest Him (vers. 30, 32).

Ch. viii. 59.—They were so exasperated with His words that they took up stones to stone Him.

Ch. ix. 34.—They excommunicated the blind man because their hated foe had cured him, and he in his favor had dared to protest.

Ch. x. 31.—The Jews (and the Apostle always uses that word of the Sanhedrim and their allies) took up stones to cast at Him; and in verse 39 we read that they sought again to take Him; but He escaped out of their land to Perea, where He remained until the message of the sisters called Him from His retreat.

Ch. xi. 47.—The raising of Lazarus produced such an effect that a special council was called to consider what should be done, with the result that from that day they took counsel to put Him to death.

Ch. xii. 10.—Their malignity was so great that they consulted whether they should not put Lazarus to death also; because by reason of him many of the Jews went away and believed in Jesus.

It was all this that made them fall in so eagerly with the proposal of Judas that he should betray Him unto them.

Now at last they had Him in their power, and their object was to convict Him of some crime which would justify the infliction of the severest sentence of the law. To preserve the appearance of justice, witnesses were called to testify to some action or speech which would involve blasphemy against their law, and, if possible, against the Roman law as well; and it was necessary that two of them should agree in some specific charge. The chief priests, and elders, and all the council, Matthew tells us, sought for witness against Jesus to put Him to death. They brought forward many, but either their charges did not reach the required degree of criminality, or the clumsy witnesses, brought hastily forward, undrilled beforehand, broke down so grossly in their story that for shame's sake they had to be dismissed.

At last two witnesses appeared who seemed likely to agree on a very momentous charge. They said they had heard Him utter, more than two years ago, words which seemed to threaten the very existence of the temple. But, when more closely questioned, their witness also broke down utterly. It seemed as though Jesus was not to die, except on His own testimony to His own supreme claims. All lesser counts failed.

All this time, as witness after witness was brought in, our Lord maintained an unbroken silence. He seemed as though He heard not, but was absorbed in some other scenes from those transpiring around. What need was there for Him to interpose, when all the charges proved abortive? He was, moreover, waiting till the Father gave Him the signal to open His lips.

At last Caiaphas could restrain his impatience no longer; he sprang to his feet, and with unconcealed fury fixed his eyes on Jesus and said: "Answerest Thou nothing? Hast Thou nothing to say, no question to put, no explanation to offer as to what these witnesses say?" Jesus quietly returned the look, but held His peace. There are times when it is treason to hold our peace, when God demands of us to raise our voice and cry like a trumpet. But when it is clear that high-handed wrong is bent on securing the condemnation of the innocent, and that the case is prejudged, it is the highest wisdom to be as a lamb dumb before its shearers, and not open the mouth.

There was a last alternative. Caiaphas might put Jesus on His oath, and extort from His own lips the charge on which to condemn Him; but he was evidently reluctant to do it, and only availed himself of this process as a last resource. It was well known to this astute and cunning priest that Jesus on more than one occasion had claimed, not only to be the long-expected Messiah, but to stand to God in the unique relationship of Son. Nearly two years before, He had called God His own Father, making Himself equal with God (John v. 18); and again, comparatively recently, at the Feast of Dedication, He had claimed that He and the Father were one; in consequence of which the bystanders threatened to take His life because that, being a man, He made Himself God (x. 31-33). Gathering, therefore, the two claims in one, and in the most solemn form, putting Jesus on His oath, the High Priest said unto Him, "I adjure Thee by the Living God, that Thou tell us whether Thou be the Christ, the Son of the Blessed?" (Matt. xxvi. 63; Mark xiv. 61). There was no need for further hesitation. Charged in this way, in the highest court of His nation, and by the representative of His people, He could not hold His peace without inconsistency with the whole tenor of His life and teaching. John, representing His disciples and friends, must be assured that his Master did not vacillate by a hair's-breadth at that supreme moment. Those high officials must understand, beyond the smallest possibility of doubt, that if they put Him to death He would die on the supreme count of His Messianic and Divine claims; and, therefore, amid the breathless silence of the court, without a falter in the calm, clear voice, Jesus said, "I AM." The Father that sent Him was with Him; He had not left Him in that awful moment alone, and it was a great pleasure to the Saviour to be able publicly to avow the relationship, which was shedding its radiance through His soul. Then, with evident allusion to the sublime vision of Daniel, he added, "Ye shall see the Son of Man sitting at the right hand of power, and coming with the clouds of Heaven." Though Son of God, He was not less the Son of Man; and though one with the Father, before the worlds were made, was yet prepared to exercise the functions of the expected Prince of the House of Israel. This is the force of nevertheless in Matt. xxvi. 64—"I am Son of God: nevertheless, ye shall see the Son of Man sitting on the right hand of power."

The words were very grateful to the ears of Caiaphas and his confederates, as they afforded ground for the double charge they needed. For a man to claim to be Son of God would make him guilty of blasphemy, and he must be put to death according to Jewish law; whilst if there was a prospect of his setting up a kingdom, the Romans' suspicions would be at once aroused. But in their glee at having entrapped their victim they must not forget to show a decorous horror of His crime. In well-assumed dismay the High Priest rent his clothes, saying, "He hath spoken blasphemy: what further need have we of witnesses? Behold, now ye have heard the blasphemy." And then came the decisive question which the judge was wont to put to his co-assessors, "What think ye? And they all condemned Him to be guilty of death."

Then ensued a brief interval, until the early formal session of the Sanhedrim could be held: and during this recess the disgraceful scenes were repeated which had already taken place in the hall of Annas. Luke tells us that the men that held Jesus mocked Him, beat Him, and asked Him to prophesy who it was that smote Him. Matthew adds that they spat in His face. But Mark lets in still more light on the horror of the scene, when he appears to distinguish between some who began to spit on Him, and to cover His face, and the officers who received Him with blows of their hands. And the expression some occurs so immediately after the record of their condemning Him, that the suggestion seems irresistible that several of these reverend dignitaries did not hesitate to disgrace their grey hairs in personally insulting the meek and holy sufferer, venting their spleen on one who gave no show of retaliation, though one word from those pale compressed lips would have laid them low in death, or withdrawn the veil of eternity, behind which legions of angels were waiting impatient to burst upon the impious scene. But do not condemn them as though they were sinners beyond all others; remember that we have all the same evil human heart.

At last the morning broke, and as soon as it was day the assembly of the elders of the people was gathered together, both chief priest and scribes; and they led Jesus away into their council (Luke xxii. 66). This scene had already been so well rehearsed that it probably did not take many minutes to run through the necessary stages, according to the precise formulae of Jewish procedure. The method that had already proved so valuable was quickly repeated. Questioning Him first as to His Messiahship, Caiaphas, as spokesman to the rest, said formally, "If Thou art Christ, tell us."

It was a sorry figure that stood before them. Dishevelled and in disarray, with disordered garments, the spittle still hanging about His face, and the marks of the awful storm and mental anguish stamped on every feature, the innate dignity and glory of Jesus shone out in His every movement, and notably in His majestic answer, "What do you ask Me? You have no real desire to know! If I tell you, ye are in no mood to believe! And if I ask you your warrant for refusing to believe, if I argue with you, if I adduce Scripture to support My claims, ye will not answer; but though I read the motive of your inquiry, I will give you all the evidence you desire. From henceforth shall the Son of Man be seated at the right hand of God."

As to the other charge, involving His Divine nature, the admission of which involved the crime of blasphemy, they were too eager to wait for Caiaphas; but with swollen faces, excited gestures, and loud cries, rising from their seats, and gesticulating with the fury of religious frenzy, they all said, "Art Thou then the Son of God?" And He said unto them, solemnly and emphatically, "Ye say that which I am."

Then they turned to one another and said, "What further need have we of witness? for we have heard from His own mouth." The inquiry was at an end so far as Jesus was concerned. But they held a further council against Him, how to construct the indictment which would compel Pilate to inflict death; for the execution of the sentence of death was kept resolutely by the Roman Procurator in his own hands.

Finally, as soon as they dared disturb him, they led Jesus from Caiaphas into the Praetorium, the palace of the Roman governor, who, in accordance with his custom, had come up from his usual residence at Caesarea to the Jewish capital, partly to keep order amid the vast crowds that gathered there at the feast, seething with religious fanaticism, and partly to try the cases which awaited his decision. The Jewish authorities anticipated no great difficulty in securing from him the necessary ratification of the death sentence. It surely would not matter to him to add another to the long tale of robbers and revolutionaries which are awaiting the cross, the more especially as they were able to prefer a charge of treason against the Roman power substantiated by the prisoner's own admissions made recently in their presence.

It is an awful spectacle, and one over which we would fain draw a veil; but let us dare to stay to watch the evolution of the diabolical plot to the end. This, at least, will become manifest— that Jesus died, because He claimed to be the Son of God, in the unique sense of oneness with the Father; that made Him equal with God, and constituted blasphemy in the eye of the Jewish law. And He who has taught the world Truth could neither have been a deceiver, nor deceived, in this high claim.

XXVIII

"Judas, which Betrayed Him"

"Judas, which betrayed Him."—JOHN xviii. 2.

On the Wednesday evening before our Lord died, He supped with His disciples in Bethany at the House of Simon. Lazarus was there, and his sisters—Martha, who served, and Mary, who anointed Him beforehand for His burying. The Master's reception of this act of love, and His rebuke of the parsimony which sought to check all such manifestations of devotion, exasperated Judas beyond all bounds; so, after supper, when Jesus and the rest had retired to their humble lodgment, he crossed the intervening valleys and returned by the moonlight to Jerusalem.

At that untimely hour the Sanhedrim may have been still in session, plotting to destroy Jesus. At any rate, the chief priests and captains were quickly summoned. Judas may have been in communication with some of them before; but, in any case, he met with a glad welcome. They were glad, and covenanted to give him money.

In the word, communed with them, used by the evangelist Luke, it is suggested that there was a certain amount of bargaining and haggling before the sum was fixed. Perhaps he wanted more, and they offered less, and at last he was induced to take less than he had hoped, but more than they had offered; and the price of betrayal was fixed at thirty pieces of silver, about 8 pounds, the price of a slave. From that moment he sought opportunity to betray Him unto them.

At the Passover Supper provided on the next day by Peter and John in the upper room, Judas must have reclined on the Lord's left, and John upon His right, so that the beloved disciple could lean back his head on the bosom of his Friend. When all were settled, Jesus exclaimed, with a sigh of innermost satisfaction, "With desire I have desired to eat this Passover with you before I suffer"; and as He uttered the words, Judas must have felt a thrill passing through his nature, as he realized more clearly than any around that table, what was approaching. Evidently, then, the Master had guessed what was being prepared for Him! Did He also know the share that he had had in preparing it? In any case, it was clear that, so far from resisting, He was prepared to suffer. Apparently, He would not take the opportunity of asserting His claims; but would allow events to take their course, yielding Himself to the will of His foes!

When He had given thanks, the Lord passed round the first cup; then followed the washing of the disciples' feet, in the midst of which He looked sorrowfully toward Judas, exclaiming, "Ye are clean, but not all"; for He knew from the first who would betray Him. It was with a strange blending of awe and wonder that the little group saw the dark cloud of anguish gather and rest on the beloved face when, on resuming His place, He was troubled in the spirit, and testified, and said, "Verily, verily, I say unto you, that one of you shall betray Me." The disciples looked at one another, doubting of whom He spoke, and Peter beckoned to John to ask. But Judas knew. And when He went on to say, "The Son of Man goeth, even as it is written of Him; but woe unto that man through whom the Son of Man is betrayed! good were it for that man if he had not been born"—again Judas' heart smote him. It may be that he asked himself whether he might not even now draw back.

For three years he had played his part so well that, in spite of his constant pilfering from the bag which held the slender resources of the little band, no one suspected him. His fellow-disciples might contend for the first places at the table, but all felt that Judas, at any rate, had a prescriptive right to sit near Jesus. All round, in sorrowful tones, the question passed, "Lord, is it I?" Each, conscious of the unfathomed evil of his own nature, thought himself more likely to be the traitor than that the admirable Judas should do the deed. It was terrible to know that the Shepherd should be smitten, and the flock scattered; but more, that the Master would be betrayed by the inner circle of His friends! But there seemed no reason for challenging His announcement, backed as it was by a quotation from a familiar Psalm, "He that dippeth his hand with Me in the dish, the same shall betray Me." From these words also it was evident that the traitor must be one of two or three; for only these could reach the common dish in which Jesus dipped His food.

It became, therefore, more and more clear to Judas, that the Master knew perfectly well all that had transpired, and he said to himself, "If He knows so much, it is almost certain that He knows all." Therefore, partly to disarm any suspicions that might be suggested to the others if he did not take up their question, partly because he felt that probably there was nothing to be gained by maintaining his disguise before Jesus, and being withal feverishly anxious to know how much of his plan was discovered, he asked, adopting the colder title Rabbi, rather than that of Lord, as employed by the others, "Rabbi, is it I?" Probably the question was asked under his breath, and that Jesus replied in the same tone, "Thou hast said."

Immediately the thoughts of Judas sprang back to the foot-washing, and all the other marks of extraordinary tenderness with which Jesus had treated him. At the time he had thought, "He would not act like this if He knew all." Now, however, he realized that Jesus had acted in the full knowledge of all that had passed, and was passing in his heart. It must have struck him as extraordinary that the Master should continue to treat him thus when He had read the whole dark secret. Why did He not unmask and expose him? Why not banish him from His company? Why count him still on speaking terms? Not till afterward was he aware of Jesus' motive, nor did he detect the loving purpose which was laying siege to his stony heart as though to turn him from his evil purpose before it was too late.

Once more the Lord made an effort to prove to him that though He knew all He loved him still, even to the end. It was the Jewish custom for one to dip a morsel in the common dish and pass it to another in token of special affection, so when He had dipped the sop, Jesus took and gave it to Judas, the son of Simon. He had previously answered John's whispered question, "Lord, who is it?" which had been suggested by a sign from Peter, by saying, "He it is to whom I shall give a sop when I have dipped it." But He did not give the token of love merely as a sign to John and Peter, but because He desired to assure Judas that, notwithstanding His perfect knowledge, His heart was full of tender affection.

But when the sun strikes on a foetid pond, its rays, beneath which all creation rejoices, bring out the repulsive odors that otherwise had slept undiscovered; so the love of God is ever a savor of life unto life or of death unto death, and the very fervor of Christ's love seems to have driven

Judas almost to madness. Shutting his heart against the Saviour, he opened it to Satan, who was waiting his opportunity. "After the sop, then Satan entered into him." Instantly the Master saw the change, and knew that He could do nothing more to save His disciple from the pit which he had digged for himself. Nothing could be gained by further delay. Jesus therefore said unto him, "That thou doest, do quickly."

So carefully had the Lord concealed His knowledge of Judas' real character that none of those who sat at table guessed the real significance and purport of His words. For some thought, because Judas had the bag, that Jesus said unto him, "Buy what things we have need of for the feast"; or that he should give something to the poor. Only John, and perhaps Peter, had the slightest suspicion of his possible errand. The sacred narrative adds significantly, "He then having received the sop, went out straightway, and it was night"; as though the black pall of darkness were a befitting symbol of the blackness of darkness that was enveloping his soul—a night broken only by one star, when Jesus once more in the garden sought to arrest him with the words, "Friend, to what a deed thou art come! Betrayest thou the Son of Man with a kiss?" But that lone star was soon obscured. The cloud-wreath hastened to conceal it. Head-long and precipitate over every obstacle, he rushed to his doom, until his career was consummated in the despairing act which the Evangelist so solemnly records.

The specified fee was no doubt paid to Judas, on his delivery of Jesus into the hands of the High Priest. As soon as the great doors closed behind the arresting band, Judas went to some inner pay-office, claimed his money, and then waited in the shadow to see what befell. Perhaps he met John; and if so, avoided him. Perhaps he heard Peter deny the Lord with oaths, and congratulated himself that there was not much to choose between them. But for the most part his mind was absorbed in what was transpiring. He beheld the shameful injustice and inhumanity of the trial. Though he had kissed his Master's face, his soul winced from the blows and spittle that befell it. Perhaps he had entertained some lingering hope and expectation that when the worst came to the worst the Master would use on His own behalf the power He had so often used for others. But if that thought had lodged in his mind, the dream was terribly dissipated. "He saw that He was condemned."

Then the full significance of his sin burst upon him. The veil fell from his eyes, and he stood face to face with his crime in all its naked horror. His ingratitude, his treachery, his petty pilfering, his resistence of a love which the strong waters of death could not extinguish. And the money scorched his hand. A wild and haggard man, he made his way into the presence of the chief priests and scribes, as they were congratulating themselves on the success of their plot. There was despair on his face, a piercing note in his voice, anguish in his soul; the flames of hell were already consuming him, the thirst of the bottomless pit already parching his lips; his hand convulsively clutched the thirty pieces of silver.

"I have sinned," he cried. "I have sinned. He whom you have condemned is innocent; take back your money, only let Him go free; and oh, relieve me, ye priests, accustomed to deal with burdened hearts, relieve me of this intolerable pain."

But they said, with a gleam as of cold steel, "What is that to us? That is your business. You made your bargain, and you must stand to it: see thou to it."

He knew that it was useless to parley with them. That icy sarcasm, that haughty indifference, told him how man must ever regard his miserable act. He had already refused the love of God, and dared not expect anything more from it. He foresaw how coming ages would spurn and abhor him. There seemed, therefore, nothing better than to leap into the awful abyss of suicide. It could bring nothing worse than he was suffering. Oh, if he had only dared to believe in the love of God, and had fallen even then at the feet of Jesus, he might have become a pillar in His temple, and an apostle of the Church. But he dared not think that there could be mercy for such as he was. He passes out into the morning air, the most wretched of men, shrinks away into some lonely spot, puts a rope around his neck, and dies.

We have been accustomed to think of Judas as one whose crime has put him far in front of all others in the enormity of his guilt. Dante draws an awful picture of him as alone even in hell, shunned by all other sinners, as Turkish prisoners will shun Christians, though sharing the same cell. But let us remember that he did not come to such a pitch of evil at a single bound. There was a time, no doubt, when, amid the cornfields, vineyards, and pastoral villages of his native Kerioth, he was regarded as a promising youth, quick at figures, the comfort of his parents, the pride of his instructors, the leader of his comrades.

During the early years of His manhood, Jesus came through that court country on a preaching tour, and there must have been a wonderful fascination in Him for young men, so many of whom left their friends and callings to join and follow Him. Judas felt the charm and joined himself to the Lord; perhaps Jesus even called him. At that time his life must have been fair, or the Master would never have committed Himself to him. He was practical, prompt, and businesslike, the very man to keep the bag. But the continual handling of the money at last awoke within him an appetite of the presence of which he had not been previously aware. He did not banish it, but dwelt on it, allowing it to lodge and expand within him, till, like a fungus in congenial soil, it ate out his heart and absorbed into itself all the qualities of his nobler nature, transmuting them into rank and noisome products. All love for Christ, all care for the poor, all thought of his fellow-disciples, were quenched before that remorseless passion; and at last he began to pilfer from those scant treasures, which were now and again replenished by those that loved to minister to the Master's comfort. At first, he must have been stung by keen remorse; but each time he sinned his conscience became more seared, until he finally reached the point when he could sell his Master for a bagatelle, and betray Him with a kiss.

Alas! Judas is not the only man of whom these particulars have been true. Change the name and you have an exact description of too many. Many a fair craft has come within the reach of the circling eddies of the same boiling whirlpool, and, after a struggle, has succumbed. The young man hails from his native village home, earnest and ingenuous. At first he stands firm against the worldly influences around; but gradually he becomes careless in his watch, and as money flows in he realizes the fascination of the idea of being a wealthy man. He becomes increasingly absorbed, until he begins to drift toward a goal from which in other days he would have shrunk in horror. If any reader of these words is conscious of such a passion beginning to lay hold of him, let him beware, lest, like Judas, he be lost in the divers hurtful lusts which drown men in perdition.

And if already you have been betrayed into sins which would bear comparison with that of Judas, do not despair—true, you have sinned against light and love, the eager, tender pleadings of God's love; but do not give up hope. Cast yourself on a love which wants to abound over sin, and glories in being able to save to the uttermost.

XXIX

The First Trial before Pilate

"Then led they Jesus from Caiaphas unto the hall of judgment: and it was early; and they themselves went not into the judgment hall, lest they should be denied; but that they might eat the Passover."—JOHN xviii. 28.

There is no doubt that had Pilate been absent from Jerusalem at the time of our Lord's trial before the Sanhedrim, they would have rushed Him to death, as afterward Stephen, and have risked the anger of the Governor. But they dared not attempt such a thing beneath the eyes of the dreaded Roman eagles. They must needs obtain Pilate's countersign to their death sentence, and, indeed, consign their victim to him for execution. The Lord was to die, not the Jewish death by stoning, but the terrible Roman death of crucifixion.

The day then breaking was that before the Passover. If the order for execution were not obtained that morning, the case could not come on for seven days, and it would have been highly impolitic, from their point of view, to keep Jesus so long in bonds. The national sentiment might have awoke and refused to sanction their treachery. For the same reason it was necessary to carry the sentence into effect with as little delay as possible, or the whole plot might miscarry. Then led they Jesus from Caiaphas to the official residence of Pilate, which had been the palace of the magnificent Herod—and it was early.

In the palace there was a hall where trials were usually conducted; but the Jewish dignitaries who had not scrupled shamelessly to condemn Jesus were too scrupulous to enter the house of a Gentile on the eve of the feast, for fear there might be a single grain of leaven there, and the mere suspicion of such a thing would have disqualified them from participating in the feast. Remember that these men had just broken every principle of justice in their treatment of Jesus, and now they palter over minute points of Rabbinical casuistry. So Philip of Spain abetted the massacres of Alva, but rigorously performed all the rites of the Church; and the Italian bandit will carefully honor priest, and host, and church. How well our Lord's sharp sword cut to the dividing of soul and spirit, in such cases as these: "Ye pay tithe of mint, and cummin, and anise, and have omitted the weightier matters of the law." It is an evil day when religion and morality are divorced.

Pilate knew too well the character of the men with whom he had to do, to attempt to force their scruples, and went out to them; so that for most of the time his intercourse with Jesus was apart from their interference and scrutiny. Without much interchange of formalities, the Governor asked, "What accusation bring ye against this man?"

It was not a little disappointing to their pride to be obliged to adduce and substantiate capital charges against Jesus, so they replied in general terms, and with the air of injured innocence, "If He were not a malefactor, we would not have delivered Him unto thee." It was as though they said, "There is no need for thee to enter into the details of this case; we have thoroughly investigated it, and are satisfied with the conclusive evidence of our prisoner's guilt; you may be sure that men like ourselves would never come to thee at such an hour, on such an errand, unless there were ample grounds for it."

But Pilate was in no mood to be talked with thus. He saw their eagerness to ward off inquiry, and this was quite enough to arouse his proud spirit to thwart and disappoint them. He knew well enough that they wanted him to pronounce the death sentence; but he pretended not to, and said, in effect, "If your judgment, and yours only, is to settle the case, take ye Him and judge Him according to your law, inflicting such penalty as it directs."

The Jewish notables at once saw that they must adopt a more conciliatory tone, or they would lose their case; they therefore explained that they wanted a severer sentence than they had the right to inflict. "It is not lawful," they said, "for us to put any man to death."

Pilate again asked for a statement of the crime of which Jesus was accused.

Now mark the baseness of their reply. The only crime on which they had condemned Jesus to death was His claim to Deity; but it would never have done to tell Pilate that. He would simply have laughed at them. They must find some charge which would bring Him within the range of the common law, and be of such a nature that Pilate must take cognizance of it, and award death. It was not easy to find ground for such a charge in the life of one who had so studiously threaded His way through the snares they had often laid for Him; who had bade them render Caesar's things to Caesar; and protested that He was neither a ruler nor judge. Their only hope was to rest their charge on His claim to be the Messiah, construing it as the Jews were wont to do, but as Jesus never did, into a claim to an outward and visible royalty. They said, therefore, as Luke informs us, "We found this man perverting the nation and forbidding to give tribute to Caesar, saying that He Himself is Christ a King."

This was quite enough to compel Pilate to institute further inquiry. There were thousands of Jews who questioned Caesar's right to tax them, and were willing to revolt under the lead of any man who showed himself capable. It was certainly suspicious that such a charge should be made by men who themselves abhorred the yoke of Rome. However, Pilate saw that he had no alternative but to investigate the case further. He therefore went within the palace to the inner judgment hall, summoned Jesus before him, and said, not without a touch of sarcasm in his tones, "Art Thou the King of the Jews?" Thou poor, worn, tear-stained outcast, forsaken by every friend in this Thy hour of need, so great a contrast to him who built these halls and aspired to the same title—art thou a king?

He probably expected that Jesus would at once disclaim any such title. But instead of doing so, instead of answering directly, our Lord answered his question by propounding another—"Sayest thou this thing of thyself, or did others tell it thee concerning Me?" The purport of this question seems to have been to probe Pilate's conscience, and make him aware of his own growing consciousness that this prisoner was too royal in mien to be an ordinary Jewish visionary. It was as though He said: "Dost thou use the term in the common sense, or as a soul confronted by a greater than thyself? Do you speak by hearsay or by conviction? Is it because the Jews have so taught thee, or because thou recognizest Me as able to bring order and peace into troubled hearts like thine?"

Whatever thoughts had instinctively made themselves felt were instantly beaten back by his strong Roman pride. Never before had he been catechised thus. And he answered haughtily, "Am I a Jew? Thine own nation and the chief priests have delivered Thee unto me: what hast Thou done?"

Our Lord did not answer that question by enumerating deeds which had filled Palestine with wonder; but contented Himself by saying that He had committed no political offence, and had no idea of setting Himself up as king, in the sense in which Pilate and the Jews used the word: "My kingdom is not of this world: if My kingdom were of this world, then would My servants fight, that I should not be delivered to the Jews: but now is My kingdom not from hence."

Never in the history of this world did the lips of man speak or his ears listen to a more pregnant or remarkable utterance. But it has been shamefully misunderstood. Men have misread the words, and said, See, the religion of Jesus is quite unworldly, has nothing to do with the institutions and arrangements of human life. It deals with the spiritual, and not with the secular. It treats of our spirits, not our hands or pockets. So long as we recognize Christ's authority in the Church, we may do as we like in the home, the counting-house, the factory, and the shop.

It was in no such sense that Jesus uttered these words, and the mistake has largely arisen through the misunderstanding of the word of as used by our translators. It has not the force of belonging to, or being the property of; but is the translation of a Greek preposition, meaning out of, springing from, originating in. We might freely translate the Master's words thus: "My kingdom does not originate from this world; it has come down from another, to bring the principles, methods, and inspirations of heaven to bear on all the provinces of human thought and activity." The Son of Man claims the whole of man and all that he does as a subject of His realm. He cannot spare one relationship of human life, one art, one industry, one interest, one joy, one hope from the domain of His empire. He has a word about the weight in the pedlar's bag, the dealings of the merchant on 'Change, the justice and injustice of wars that desolate continents.

The one conspicuous proof of the absolutely foreign origin of this heavenly kingdom is its refusal to employ force. Its servants do not fight. In the garden the King had repudiated the use of force, bidding His servant sheathe His sword. Whenever you encounter a system that cannot stand without the use of force, that appeals to the law court or bayonet, you are sure that, whatever else it is, it is not the Kingdom of Christ. Christ's kingdom distinctly and forever refuses to allow its subjects to fight. They who would surround Christianity with prestige, endow it with wealth, and guard it with the sword, expel its Divine Spirit, and leave only its semblance dead upon the field. But if the aid which might be deemed essential is withheld, whether of funds or force, it thrives and spreads until the hills are covered with its goodly shadow, and its products fill the earth with harvests of benediction. All the Gospel asks for is freedom—freedom to do what Jesus did, in the way He did it; freedom because of its belief that the power of truth is greater than all the power of the Adversary. Oh for a second Pentecost! Oh for the holy days of Apostolic trust and simplicity! Oh for one of the days of the Son of Man, who came to our world armed with no authority save that of truth, clothed with no power but that of love.

In Pilate's next question there seems a touch of awe and respect: "Art Thou a king then?" That moral nature which is in all men, however debased, seemed for a moment to assert itself, and a strange spell lay on his spirit.

With wondrous dignity our Lord immediately answered, "Thou sayest that I am—a king." But He hastens to show that it was a kingship not based upon material force like that of the Caesars, nor confined to one race of men: "To this end was I born, and for this cause came I into the world, that I should bear witness to the truth. Every one that is of the truth heareth My voice." There is no soul of man, in any clime or age, devoted to the truth, which does not recognize the royalty and supremacy of Jesus Christ. There is an accent in His words which all the children of the truth instantly recognize. The idea here given of Jesus gazing ever into the depths of eternal truth, and bearing witness of what He saw, not in His words alone, but in His life and death; and of the assent given to His witness by all who have looked upon the sublime outlines of truth, is one of those majestic conceptions which cannot be accounted for on any hypothesis than that the speaker was Divine.

When Pilate heard these words, he probably thought of the Epicureans, and Stoics, and other philosophers, who were perpetually wrangling about the truth, and demanding men's allegiance. "Oh," said he to himself, "here is another enthusiast, touched with the same madness, though He does seem nobler than many of His craft. One thing is clear, that my lord has nothing to fear from His pretensions. He may sit as long as He likes on His ideal throne without detriment to the empire of the Caesars." With mingled bitterness and cynicism, he answered, "What is truth?" and, without waiting for an answer, went out to the group of Jewish rabbis waiting in the opening daylight, and threw them into convulsions of excitement by saying, "I find in Him no fault at all."

They were the more urgent, saying, "He stirreth up the people, teaching throughout all Judaea, and beginning from Galilee even unto this place."

The mention of Galilee came as a gleam of light to Pilate. He was sincerely desirous not to be an accomplice in the death of Jesus, by falling into the plot which he had been astute enough to detect. But not daring to take the only honorable and safe way of declaring His innocence, and summoning a cohort of soldiers to clear the court, he endeavored to exculpate himself by throwing the responsibility on Herod. He congratulated himself on the ingenuity of a plan which should relieve him of the necessity of grieving his conscience on the one hand, or of irritating the Jews on the other, and which would conciliate Herod, with whom he was at this time on unfriendly terms. When he knew therefore that He was of Herod's jurisdiction he sent Him unto Herod, who himself was at Jerusalem in those days.

Herod was glad to see the wonderful miracle-worker of whom he had heard so much, and hoped that He might do some wonder in his presence; and, in the hope of extorting it, set Him at nought, and mocked Him, with his mighty men. But the Lord remained absolutely silent in his presence, as though the love of God could say nothing to the murderer of the Baptist, who had not repented of his deed. Finally, therefore, disappointed and chagrined, Herod sent Jesus back to Pilate, admitting that he had found in Him no cause of death.

XXX

The Second Trial before Pilate

"Ye have a custom, that I should release unto you one at the passover: will ye therefore that I release unto you the King of the Jews?"—JOHN xviii. 39.

Pilate must have felt mortified when he heard that Herod had sent Jesus back to his tribunal. He had hoped that the Jewish monarch would so settle the matter that there would be no need for him to choose between his conscience and his fear of the Jewish leaders. But it was not to be. It was decreed that he should pronounce the judicial sentence on our Lord, and so on himself.

Now was the time for him to act decisively, and to say clearly that he would be no party to the unrighteous deed to which these priests were urging him. To have done so firmly and decisively, and before they could further inflame popular passion, the whole matter would have come to an end. Alas! he let the golden moment slip past him unused, and every succeeding moment made it more impossible for him to retrieve it.

Pilate is one of the most notable instances in history of the fatal error of preferring expediency to principle. He wished to do right, but not to do it avowedly because it was right. He wished to do right without seeming to do it, or making a positive stand for it. And in consequence he was finally entrapped into doing the very deed which he had taken the greatest trouble to avoid. Therefore, on the plains of time he stands as a beacon and warning; and to all who do not dare to oppose the stream of public passion and practice with the single affirmation of inflexible adherence to righteousness, the voice of inspiration cries aloud, "Remember Pilate!" However promising a tortuous course may look, it will certainly end in disaster. However discouraging a righteous one may appear, it will at last lead out into the open. And in doing the right thing, be sure to speak out firmly at once. It may be harder for the moment, but it will be always easier afterward. One brave word will put you into a position of moral advantage, from which no power shall avail to shake or dislodge you.

Such a word, however, Pilate failed to speak; and when Jesus was again brought before him, he began to think of some way by which he might do as conscience prompted, without running counter to the Jewish leaders. He, therefore, summoned around him the chief priests and rulers of the people. The latter are particularly mentioned, as though Pilate thought that his best method of saving Jesus would be by appealing over the heads of the priests to the humanity of the common people. When all were again assembled he made, as Luke tells us, a short speech to them, reiterating his conviction of His innocence, corroborating his own opinion by Herod's, and closing by a proposal which he hoped would meet the whole case. "I will therefore chastise Him and release Him." Was there ever such a compromise? A little before he had solemnly affirmed that he could find in Him no fault at all, but if that were the case, why chastise Him? And if He were guilty of the charges brought against Him, as chastisement might seem to suggest, surely He should not be released. Pilate meant to do the best. The chastisement was intended as a sop to the priests, and to win their acquiescence to their victim's release. But it was not straightforward, or strong, or right. And, like all compromises, it miserably failed.

Those keen Jewish eyes saw in a moment that Pilate had left the ground of simple justice. He had shifted from the principle on which Roman law was generally administered, and they saw that it was only a question of bringing sufficient pressure to bear on him, and they could make him a tool for the accomplishment of the fell purpose on which their heart was set. The proposal, therefore, was swept ignominiously away, and Pilate could never regain the position he had renounced.

Pilate then resorted to another expedient for saving Jesus. It was the custom to carry out capital sentences at feast times, which were the occasions of great popular convocations; but it was also customary for the governor to release any one prisoner, condemned to death, whom the multitude, on the Passover week, might agree to name. Pilate recollected this, and also that there was a notorious criminal awaiting execution, who for sedition and murder had been arrested and condemned to die. It occurred to him that, instead of asking the people generally whom they wished him to release, he should narrow the choice and present the alternative between Barabbas and Jesus. They would hardly fail, he thought, to choose the release of this pale Prisoner, who was innocent of crime, and, indeed, had lived a life notable for its benevolence.

Pilate took care to announce his proposal with the greatest effect. The vast space before his palace was rapidly filling with excited crowds, who guessed that something unusual was astir, and were pouring in surging volumes into the piazza, although it was still early. That he might be the better seen and heard he ascended a movable rostrum, or judgment-seat, which was placed on the tessellated pavement that ran from end to end of the palace. "Whom will ye," he asked, "that I release unto you—Barabbas, or Jesus which is called the Christ?" And then he suggested the answer: "Will ye that I release unto you the King of Jews?"

At this moment, and perhaps whilst waiting for their answer, a messenger hurried to speak to him from his wife. It must have been most unusual for her to interfere with his judicial acts; but she had been so impressed by a dream about her husband's connection with Jesus, the unwonted Prisoner who stood before him, that she was impelled to urge him to have nothing to do with Him. It was a remarkable episode, and must have made Pilate more than ever anxious to extricate himself from his dilemma.

It was still not absolutely too late to set himself free by the resolute expression of his will. But his temporizing policy was making it immensely difficult, and he was becoming every moment more entangled in the meshes of the merciless priests.

He had hoped much from his last proposal, but was destined to be bitterly disappointed. The chief priests and elders had been busy amongst the crowds, persuading and moving them. We do not know the arguments they would employ; but we all know how inflammable a mob is, and presently the name of Barabbas began to sound ominously from amid the hubbub and murmur of that sea of human beings. Presently the isolated cries spread into a tumultuous clamor, which rang out in the morning air, "Not this man, but Barabbas!"

Pilate seems to have been dumbfoundered at this unexpected demand; and said, almost pitifully, "What then shall I do with Jesus, which is called Christ?" As though he had said, "You surely cannot mean that He should suffer the fate prepared for a murderer!" Then they cried out for the first time, To the cross, to the cross! "Crucify Him! crucify Him!"

Pilate had failed twice; he felt that he was being swept away by a current which already he could not stem, and which was becoming at every moment deeper and swifter. But he was very anxious to release Jesus; and so he tried to reason with them, and said, "Why, what evil hath He done?" But he might as hopefully have tried to argue with an angry sea, or with a pack of wolves. He felt this, and, mustering a little show of authority, said: "I have found no cause of death in Him; I will, therefore, chastise Him, and release Him." But this announcement was met by an infuriated shout of disapproval. "They were instant with loud voices, requiring that He might be crucified." "They cried out the more exceedingly, Crucify Him." A little before this Pilate had been besieged for six days in his palace at Caesarea by similar crowds, whose persistent fury at last compelled him to give in to them. He dared not provoke similar scenes, lest they should result in a revolution. When he saw that he could prevail nothing, but that rather a tumult was made, he called for water. He said to himself, "I am very sorry, this Man is innocent, and I should like to save Him. But I have done my best, and can do no more. I will, at least, relieve myself of the responsibility of His blood. 'Slave, bring me water!'"

As he washed his hands he said, "I am innocent of the blood of this righteous Man; see ye to it." "Yes, yes," cried those bloodthirsty voices, "His blood be on us, and on our children." See how God sometimes takes men at their word. The blood of Jesus was required of that generation at the sack of Jerusalem, forty years after; and it has been required of their children through all the ages. Why that wandering foot, found in every land, yet homeless in all? Why the hideous tortures, plunderings, and massacres of the Middle Ages? Why the modern Jew-hate, disguised under the more refined term anti-Semitism? Why the banishment from their holy places for eighteen centuries? All is attributable to that terrible imprecation which attracted to the race the blood of an innocent Victim. It does not exculpate them to say that they did not realize who Jesus was, and that they would not have crucified Him if they had realized His Divine dignity. They are being punished to-day, not because they crucified the Son of God, knowing Him to be such, but because they crucified One against whom they could allege no crime, and whose life had been full of truth and grace.

After he had washed his hands "Pilate gave sentence that it should be as they required, and released unto them him that for sedition and murder had been cast into prison, whom they desired; but he delivered Jesus to their will."

Those condemned to die by crucifixion first underwent the hideous torture of the scourge. This, then, was inflicted on Jesus, and it was carried out in the inner courtyard by the Roman soldiery, under Pilate's direction. "Then Pilate therefore took Jesus, and scourged Him." Stripped to the waist, and bound in a stooping posture to a low pillar, He was beaten till the officer in charge gave the signal to stop. The plaited leathern thongs, armed at the ends with lead and sharp-pointed bone, cut the back open in all directions, and inflicted such torture that the sufferers generally fainted, and often died.

But the scourging in this case did not satisfy the soldiers, whom scenes of this nature had brutalized. They had been told by their comrades of the mockery of Herod's palace, and they would not lag behind. Had He been robed in mockery as King of the Jews, then He shall pose as mock emperor. They found a purple robe, wove some tough thorns into a mimic crown, placed a long reed in His hand as sceptre, then bowed the knee, as in the imperial court, and cried, "Hail, King of the Jews!" Finally, tiring of their brutal jests, they tore the reed from His hands, smote Him with it on His thorn-girt brow, and struck Him with their fists. We cannot tell how long it lasted, but Jesus bore it all—silent, uncomplaining, noble. There was a majesty about Him which these indignities could not suppress or disturb.

Pilate had never seen such elevation of demeanor, and was greatly struck by it. He was more than ever desirous to save Him, and it suddenly occurred to him that perhaps that spectacle of sorrow and majesty might arrest the fury of the rabble. He therefore led Jesus forth wearing the crown of thorns and the purple robe, and, stationing Him where all could see, said, "Behold the Man! Behold Him and admire! Behold Him and pity! Behold Him and be content!" But the priests were obdurate. There is no hate so virulent as religious hate, and they raised again the cry, "Crucify Him, crucify Him!" Pilate was not only annoyed, but provoked. "Take ye Him," he said, in surly tones, "crucify Him as best ye can, my soldiers and I will have nothing to do with the foul deed."

Then it was that the Jewish leaders, in their eagerness not to lose their prey, brought forward a weapon which they had been reluctant to use. "We have a law," they said, "and by our law He ought to die, because He made Himself the Son of God." We hardly know how much those words meant to Pilate, but they awakened a strange awe. "He was the more afraid." He had some knowledge of the old stories of mythology, in which the gods walked the world in the semblance of men. Could this be the explanation of the strange majesty in the wonderful Sufferer, whose presence raised such extraordinary passion and ferment? So he took Jesus apart, and said to Him, "Whence art Thou?" "Art Thou of human birth, or more?" But Jesus gave him no answer. This is the fifth time that He had answered nothing; but we can detect the reason. It would have been useless to explain all to Pilate then. It would not have arrested his action, for he had lost control, but would have increased His condemnation. Yet His silence was itself an answer; for if He had been only of earth, He could never have allowed Pilate to entertain the faintest suspicion that He might be of heaven.

Pilate's pride was touched by that silence. It was at least possible to assert a power over this defenceless Prisoner, which had been defied by those vindictive Jews. "Speakest Thou not unto me? Knowest Thou not that I have power to release or to crucify Thee?" And Jesus answered, "Thou wouldst have no power against Me, except it were given thee from above; therefore, he that delivered Me unto thee hath the greater sin." In these words our Lord seems to refer to the mystery of evil, and specially the power of the prince of this world, who was now venting on Him all his malice. At this moment the serpent was bruising the heel of the Son of Man, who shortly would bruise His head. It would appear as though our Lord were addressing kind and compassionate words to Pilate. "Great as your sin is, in abusing your prerogative, given to you from above, it is less than the sin of that Evil Spirit who has cast Me into your power, and is urging you to extreme measures against Me. The devil sinneth from the beginning." Even in His sore travail, the Lord was tender and pitiful to this weak and craven soul, and spoke to it as though Pilate and not He were arraigned at the bar.

Pilate was now more than ever set on His deliverance. "He sought to release Him." And then the Jews brought out their last crushing and conclusive argument, "If thou release this Man, thou art not Caesar's friend; every one that maketh himself a king, speaketh against Caesar." Pilate knew what that meant, and that if he did not let them have their way, they would lodge an accusation against him for complicity with treason before his imperial master. Already strong representations had been made in the same quarter against his maladministration of his province, and he positively dare not risk another. "When, therefore, he heard these words, he brought Jesus out, and sat down in the judgment-seat at a place called the Pavement, and it was about the sixth hour."

With ill-concealed irritation, and adopting the recent phraseology of the priests, he said, "Behold your King!" At which they cried, "We have no king but Caesar. Away with Him; away with Him; crucify Him." It gave Pilate savage pleasure to put the cup of humiliation to their lips, and make them drain it to its dregs. "What!" said he; "shall I crucify your King?" Then they touched the lowest depth of degradation, as, abandoning all their Messianic hopes, and trampling under foot their national pride, they answered, "We have no king but Caesar."

At last, therefore, he delivered Jesus to them to be crucified, signed the usual documents, gave the customary order, and retired into his palace, as one who had heard his own sentence pronounced, and carried in his soul the presage of his doom.

Long years after, when, stripped of his Procuratorship, which he had sacrificed Christ to save, worn out by his misfortunes, and universally execrated, he was an exile in a foreign land, with his faithful wife, how often must they have spoken together of the events of that morning, which had so strangely affected their lives!

XXXI

The Seven Sayings of the Cross

"Then delivered he Him therefore unto them to be crucified. And they took Jesus and led Him away."—JOHN xix. 16.

Driven from one position after another by the Jewish notables and rabble, Pilate at last, much against his will, gave directions for the Lord's crucifixion. The purple robe flung over His shoulders was replaced by His own simple clothes, though the crown of thorns was not improbably left upon His head.

Two others were led out to suffer with Him—highwaymen lately captured in some red-handed deed. Barabbas, their chief, for whom the central cross had been designed, had escaped it by a miracle; but they were to suffer the just reward of their deeds. A detachment of soldiers was told off under a centurion, to see to the execution of the sentence, and the heavy crosses were placed upon the shoulders of the sufferers, that they might bear them to the place of execution.

It was probably about ten A. M. when the sad procession started on its way. Two incidents took place as it passed through the crowded streets, which surely had never witnessed such a spectacle: no, not even in the days when David traversed them in flight from Absalom.

The beams laid on our Lord proved too heavy in the steeper ascents for His exhausted strength, and His slow advance so delayed the procession that the guard became impatient. Here comes a foreigner! A Jew of Cyrene! Harmless and inoffensive, gladly would he make way for the crowd. Why should he not bear this burden under which Jesus of Nazareth is falling to the ground? The insolent soldiers, with oath and jest, constrain him, and he dares not resist. Probably Simon had no previous knowledge of Him for whom he bore this load, and loathed the service he was compelled to render; but that compulsory companionship with Jesus carried him to Calvary. He beheld the wondrous tragedy, heard the words which we are to recite; from that day became, with his family, a humble follower of Jesus. We at least infer this from Mark's emphatic mention of the fact that he was father of Alexander and Rufus; whilst the Apostle Paul, in the Epistle to the Romans, tenderly refers to Rufus and his mother. This is not the only instance in the history of Christianity, when the compulsion of an apparent accident has led a man to Christ. Many a time has compulsory cross-carrying led men to the Crucified.

Of the vast multitude who followed Jesus, a large contingent consisted of women. From the men, in that moving crowd, He does not appear to have received one word of sympathy. Timidity, or questioning with their own hearts, or inveterate hatred closed their lips. But the women expressed their sorrow with all the outcry of Oriental grief, rending the air with piercing cries. "Weep not for Me," the Saviour said, ever more thoughtful for others than Himself; "but for yourselves and your children." And He who had been mocked because of His claim to be a King, and who would shortly from the cross begin to minister as a Priest, then as Prophet foretold the approaching fate of that fair city, asking significantly, since the Romans dealt thus with Himself an innocent sufferer, what would they not do when exasperated by the pertinacious resistance of the Jewish people in the protracted siege.

Just outside the city gates, by the side of the main road, was a little conical eminence which, from its likeness to the shape of a skull, was called in the Aramaic Golgotha, in the Greek Cranion, in the Latin Calvary. As we speak of the brow of a hill, they called the bald eminence a skull. There the procession stayed, and what transpired may be best followed as we touch on the seven sentences our Lord uttered on the Cross, as we collate them and set them in order from the four Gospels.

I. "Father, forgive them; for they know not what they do."—Arrived at the place of execution, Jesus would be stripped once more, a linen cloth at most being left about His loins. He would then be laid upon the cross, as it rested on the ground, His arms stretched along the crossbeams, His body resting on a projecting piece of rough wood, misnamed a seat. Huge nails would then be driven through the tender palm of each hand, and the shrinking centre of each foot. The cross would then be lifted up and planted in a hole previously dug to receive it, with a rude shock causing indescribable anguish. "So they crucified Him, and two others with Him, on either side one, and Jesus in the midst."

Pilate had written a title to be nailed to the head-piece of the cross, according to the usual custom, with the name and designation of the crucified, "This is Jesus, the King of the Jews." It was written in Greek, the language of science; Latin, the language of government; and Hebrew, the language of religion. It is this fact that accounts for the differences in the Gospels. One evangelist translates from one language, another from another. The inscription was meant to insult the Jews. It was equivalent to saying, "This nation cannot produce a better monarch than this; and this is the fate which will be meted out to all such pretenders." The authorities were indignant, and did their utmost to induce Pilate to alter it. But in vain. He would be master this time, and dismissed them with the curt reply, "What I have written I have written." Each man is writing his conception of the nature and claims of Christ by the way in which he treats Him, either acknowledging His Divine glory as he enthrones Him, or repudiating His claims as he tramples Him under foot, and turns away to his sin.

The criminal's clothes fell as a perquisite to the soldiers specially charged with the execution of the sentence. With our Lord's outer clothes they had no difficulty; they were too poor to be worth keeping entire, so they tore them up into equal pieces. But the inner tunic was of unusual texture; perhaps it had been woven for Him by His mother's hands, or by one of the women who so carefully administered to Him. In any case it was too good to tear. The dice were ready in the pocket, one of the helmets would serve as dice-box; and so "they parted His raiment among them, and for His vesture they did cast lots. These things therefore the soldiers did."

It was probably during this byplay that our Lord uttered the first cry of the cross, and entered on that work of intercession, which He ever lives to perpetuate and crown. He thinks, not of Himself, but of others; is occupied, not with His own pains, but with their sins. Not a threat, nor a menace; but the purest, tenderest accents of pleading intercession.

When was that prayer answered? Seven weeks after this, on the day of Pentecost, three thousand of these people, whom Peter described as the murderers of Christ, repented and believed, and in the days that followed thousands more, and a great company of the priests. That was the answer to this intercession. When we see our brethren sinning a sin not unto death, without realizing its full significance and enormity, if we ask God, as Jesus did, He will give us life for those that sin not unto death. There is a sin unto death, and concerning that we are not encouraged to pray. "I obtained mercy," said the great apostle, "because I did it ignorantly in unbelief."

II. "Woman, behold thy Son; son behold thy mother."—The second saying was about His mother. His cross was the centre of bitter mockery. The chief priests, and scribes, and elders challenged Him to descend from the cross, pledging themselves to believe if He did. The crowd caught their spirit with contemptible servility, and repeated their words, "Son of God, come down from the cross, that we may believe." A passer-by called out derisively, "Where is now the boast that He could raise the temple in three days? Let Him do it if He can." The soldiers even caught up the abuse, and vented their coarse jokes on one whose innocence and gentleness appeared to exasperate them. And the malefactors who were hanged cast the same in His teeth.

Were there no sympathizers in all that crowd to exchange glances of love and faith? Yes, there was one little group. When Peter left the Hall of Caiaphas John probably lingered there still, followed to the bar of Pilate, waited long enough to know how the matter would fall, and then hastened to the humble lodgings where Mary and a few other women, in awful suspense, were awaiting tidings. As soon as the mother knew all, she resolved to see her beloved Son once more. "It is no place for women," John would say. But she answered, "I must see Him yet again." Then said John, "If you will indeed go, I will take you." "I too will go," sadly said Mary, her sister, the wife of Cleophas; "and I also," said Mary of Magdala. What a sight for those loving hearts, when they saw the crosses in the distance, and knew that on one of them was hanging the dearest to them of all on earth! But the love that makes the timid deer turn to fight valiantly for its young made them oblivious to everything except to get near Him. But how little had the young mother realized that Simeon meant this, when he told her that a sword would one day pierce her soul!

Jesus knew how much she was suffering, and how lonely she would be when He was gone. He had neither silver nor gold to leave, but would at least provide a home and tender care as long as she required them. Elevated but very little above the ground, He could easily speak to the little group. "Woman," He said, not calling her "mother," lest identification with Himself might expose her to insult, "behold thy Son." Then, looking tenderly toward John, He consigned her to his care.

Did He give a further look, which John interpreted to mean that he should lead her away? It may have been so, for from that hour he took her to his home; and so she passes from the page of Scripture, except for the one glimpse we have of her, in the upper room, awaiting the baptism of the Holy Spirit.

III. "To-day thou shalt be with Me in Paradise."—We cannot explore all the causes which brought about so great a change in this man, and produced so lofty an ideal of his Fellow-sufferer. We have to deal rather with the response of Jesus. Lost by the first Adam, Paradise was being regained by the last; and it is now not far away. A dying man may see the sun leave the zenith, but ere it set in the western wave he may be in the land of Paradise. Absent from the body, present with the Lord. There is no State of unconsciousness between the two. We close our eyes on the dimming spectacles of this world at one moment, to behold the King in His beauty the next.

Men may strip Jesus of everything, but they cannot touch His power to save. In a moment of His greatest weakness He was able to rescue a man from the very brink of perdition, and take him as a trophy of His power to Heaven. What will He not be able to do now that the mortal weakness is passed, and that He is exalted to be a Prince and a Saviour!

IV. "My God, My God, why hast Thou forsaken Me?"—It would be between eleven o'clock and noon that these incidents took place; but from noon till three in the afternoon a pall of darkness hung over the cross and city. We know not how it came, but it appears to have silenced all the uproar which had surged around the cross, and to have filled the minds of all with awe. Men might have gazed rudely on His dying agony; Nature refused to behold it. Men had stripped Him, but an unseen hand drew drapery about Him. For three hours it lasted, and was a befitting emblem of the darkness that enveloped His soul, when He who knew no sin was made to be sin for us, "that we might be made the righteousness of God in Him."

Do you wonder that He felt thus, and question how such a forsaking had been possible at such an hour? There is but one explanation. This was not a normal human experience. Only once in the history of the race has all iniquity been laid on one head; only once has the curse of the sin of the world been borne by one heart; only once has it been possible, in drinking the cup of death, to taste death for every man. "He who knew no sin was made sin for us. He was wounded for our transgressions, bruised for our iniquities." On no other hypothesis than that Jesus was the Lamb of God, bearing away the sin of the world, can you account for the darkness of that midday midnight which obscured His soul. I cannot tell what transpired; I have no philosophy of the Atonement to offer; I only believe that the whole nature of God was in Christ, reconciling the world unto Himself; and that, in virtue of what was done there, we may apply for forgiveness to the faithfulness and justice of God.

V. "I thirst."—During the hours of spiritual anguish, our Lord was largely oblivious to His physical needs; now, as the long hours passed, these latter began to assert themselves. Inflammation, spreading from hands and feet, had resulted in a fever of thirst. He had refused the medicated drink offered at the beginning of His sufferings, because He had no desire to avoid one throb of anguish which lay in His path; but there was no reason why He should not drink of the sour wine which stood hard by the cross, now that He had drunk the cup which God had placed to His lips.

As He looked through the long line of predictions that bore on His passion. He could see that they had all been fulfilled save one; and, that this Scripture might be fulfilled, He said, "I thirst." Some, who stood near the cross, and, in the growing light, began to regain their confidence, tried to make ridicule of this plaintive ejaculation; but one who noticed His pale and parched lips was touched with pity, and took a stalk of hyssop, which was just long enough to reach the mouth of the Sufferer, and elevating a sponge dipped in vinegar, fulfilled thus unwittingly the ancient prediction, "They gave Me also gall for My meat, and in My thirst they gave Me vinegar to drink."

VI. "It is finished."—As we compare the Gospels, we find that these words were spoken with a loud voice. It was, in fact, the shout of a conqueror. Finished the long list of prophecies, which closed, like gates, behind Him. Finished the types and shadows of the Jewish ritual. Finished the work which the Father had given Him to do. Finished the matchless beauty of a perfect life. Finished the work of man's redemption. Through the eternal Spirit, He had offered Himself without spot to God; and by that one sacrifice for sin, once for all and forever. He had perfected them that are being sanctified. He had done all that was required to reconcile the world unto God, and to make an end of sin.

Finished! Let the words roll in volumes of melody through all the spheres! There is nothing now left for man to do but enter on the results of Christ's finished work. As the Creator finished on the evening of the sixth day all the work which He had made, so did the Redeemer cease on the sixth day from the work of Atonement, and, lo! it was very good.

VII. "Father, into Thy hands I commend My spirit."—The words were quoted from the Book of Psalms, which He so dearly loved. He only prefixed the name of Father; for the cloud which had extorted the cry, My God, My God, had broken, and under a blue heaven of conscious fellowship He exchanged it for Father.

If the words, "It is finished," be taken as our Lord's farewell to the world He was leaving, these words are surely His greeting to that on whose confines He was standing. It seems as though the spirit of Christ were poising itself before it departed to the Father, and it saw before no dismal abyss, no gulf of darkness, no footless chaos, but hands, even the hands of the Father, and to these He committed Himself.

The first martyr, who died after Christ, passed away with words of the same import upon his lips, with a significant alteration, "Lord Jesus, receive My spirit." We may use them as they have been used by countless thousands in all ages; and we know Him whom we have believed, and are persuaded that He is able to keep that which we have committed unto Him.

And when Jesus had said these words, He bowed His head upon His breast, and breathed out His spirit. No one took His life from Him: He laid it down of Himself: He had power to lay it down.

So ended that marvellous scene. The expectation of all the ages was more than realized. If it be true that on that day a tidal wave of immense volume swept around the world, and rose high up in all rivers and estuaries, this may be taken as an emblem of the much more abounding grace, which on that day rose high above the mighty obstacles of human sin, and is destined to lift the entire universe nearer God. For by it God will reconcile all things to Himself, whether in heaven or on earth.

Three items remain to be noticed.

At the moment that Jesus died there was a great earthquake, which made the earth tremble and the rocks rend, so that the ancient graves were opened, preparatory to the rising of the bodies of the saints on the Resurrection morning, following the Lord from the power of Death. And when the centurion, and they that were with him, watching Jesus, charged to see the sentence executed, saw the earthquake and the things that were done, they feared exceedingly, saying, "Truly this was the Son of God."

The vail of the Temple, also, was rent in twain from the top to the bottom, at the moment that the Great High Priest Jesus was entering the Temple not made with hands, with the blood of His propitiation. Is it to be wondered at that afterward many priests, who had been in close contiguity to that marvellous type, became obedient to the faith?

Finally, from the pierced side of Christ came out blood and water, as John solemnly attests. "He knoweth that he saith true." This was a symptom that there had been heart-rupture, and that the Lord had literally died of a broken heart. But it was also a symbol of "the double cure" which Jesus has effected. Blood to atone; water to cleanse. "This is He that came by water and blood, not with the water only."

XXXII

Christ's Burial

"Then took they the body of Jesus, and wound it in linen clothes with the spices, as the manner of the Jews is to bury."—JOHN xix. 40.

"Against the day of My burying hath she kept this!" so had Jesus spoken when Mary anointed His feet with the very precious spikenard. I do not suppose that any in the room save herself and her Lord understood His reference; not one of them believed that He would really die, and His body be carried to the tomb; but Mary knew better. She had sat at His feet, and drunk in His very spirit. In the glow of the evening twilight, when Martha was busy in the house, and Lazarus was away in the field, they two had sat together, and Jesus, in words similar to those He had so often used to His apostles, had told her of what was coming upon Him. Mary believed it all. She knew that she would not be present at that scene. She did not think that any would be able to perform the last loving rites for that beloved form. She feared that it might be utterly dishonored; but she did what she could, she came beforehand to anoint the Lord's body for His burying.

It was a beautiful act of tender foresight. But in the sense of being absolutely necessary, as the only act of care and love bestowed on the Lord's dead body, it was not required; for He who at birth had prepared the body for His Son, took care that in death it should receive due honor. When Jesus expired, Luke tells us that many of His acquaintances, and the women that had followed Him from Galilee were standing afar off, beholding all that was done; John too was there, and others who had loved Him and were the grateful monuments of His healing power: they must have wondered greatly what would be done with that loved form. Yet what could they do?—they were poor and unimportant; they had no influence with the capricious and terrible Pilate; they seemed helpless to do more than wait with choking sobs until some possible chance should allow them to intervene.

Meanwhile God was preparing a solution of the difficulty. Amongst the crowd around the cross there stood a very wealthy man named Joseph. He was a native of the little town of Arimathea, that lay among the fruitful hills of Ephraim; but was resident in Jerusalem, where he had considerable property. Some of this lay in the close neighborhood of the highway by which the cross of our Lord had been erected. He was also a member of the Jewish Sanhedrim, but it is expressly stated that he had not consented to the counsel or deed of them; if indeed he was summoned to that secret midnight meeting in the palace of Caiaphas, he certainly did not go; he was therefore innocent of any complicity in our Lord's condemnation and death. He was a good man and a just; and like Nathanael, and Simeon, and many more, he waited for the kingdom of God. More than this, he was a disciple of Jesus, though secretly.

Whatever our judgment may be about his action during the lifetime of our Lord, we have nothing but admiration for the way in which he acted when He died. What he had seen had more than decided him. Christ's meekness and majestic silence under all reproaches and indignities; the veiled sky and trembling earth; the cry of the Forsaken which ended in the trustful committal of the soul to the Father; the loud shriek and the sudden death—all these had convinced him and awed his soul, and lifted him far above the fear of man. He had been waiting for the kingdom, he would now identify himself with the King.

By his side there would seem to have stood an old friend of ours, Nicodemus. Our evangelist identifies him as having at the first come to Jesus by night. The very opening of the Lord's ministry in Jerusalem seems to have made a deep impression on his mind; but he was very timid. He was an old man, a very rich man, a member of the Sanhedrim, and he did not like to risk his position or prestige. It was much therefore for him to come to Jesus at all, and especially to come to Him in the spirit of deep respect and inquiry. There must have been something very engaging in him; for our Lord, who did not commit Himself to men in general, made very clear unfoldings of His great work to this inquiring Rabbi. From that night, even if not a real disciple, Nicodemus was strongly prejudiced in favor of Jesus; and on one occasion, at least, brought on himself reproach for attempting indirectly to shield Him. He had not dared, however, to go beyond his first nervous question. Then, like Joseph, he was decided by what he had seen: come what may, he will now avow the thoughts which have long been in his heart.

The two men exchange a few hurried sentences. "What will be done with His body?"

"At least it must not suffer the fate of common malefactors. Yet how shall it be prevented?"

"Look you," says Joseph, "in my garden close at hand there is a new tomb, hewn out in the rock, wherein was man never yet laid, I had prepared it for myself; but I will gladly use it for Him, if I can but get Pilate to yield me His body. I will go at once and ask for it."

"Well," says Nicodemus, "if you can succeed in getting the body, I will see to it that there are not wanting the garments and spices of death."

Without a moment's delay, for the sun is fast sinking toward the west, Joseph hastens to Pilate, and asks that he may take away the body of Jesus; and not unlikely he quickens Pilate's response by an offer of a liberal bribe if he will but accede to his request. Pilate, who had just given orders to the soldiers to hasten the death of the crucified, marvelled that Jesus was really dead; nor was he reassured until he had asked the centurion; and when he knew it of him, he gave to Joseph the necessary leave, with which he hastened back to the cross.

The sun would be very low on the horizon, flinging its last beams upon the scene, as he reached Calvary. The crowds would for the most part have dispersed. The soldiers might be engaged in taking down the bodies of the thieves. The body of Jesus was however still on the cross; and not far off would be the little band of attached friends of whom we have already spoken, and who would be the sole remnants of the vast crowds who had now ebbed away to their homes. What wonder, what joy, as they see Joseph reverently and lovingly begin to take Him down; with evident authority from the Governor, with manifest preparations for His careful burial; they had never before known him to be interested in their Master. And who is this that waits beneath the cross with the clean linen shroud, and the wealth of spices? Ah! that is Nicodemus; but who would have thought that he would help to perform these last offices!

Oh to be a painter, and depict that scene! The discolored corpse stained with blood, muscles flaccid, eyes closed, head helpless; Joseph, and Nicodemus, and John, and other strong men busy. The women weeping as if their hearts must break, but ready at any moment to give the needed aid. Between them they carry the body into Joseph's garden, and to the mouth of his new sepulchre. There on some grassy bank they rest it for a moment, that it may be tenderly washed and wrapped in the white linen cloth on which powdered myrrh and aloes had been thickly strewn. A white cloth would then be wrapped about the head and face, after long farewell looks, and reverent kisses. Then lifted once again, the precious burden was born into the sepulchre, and laid in a rocky niche. There was no door; but a great stone, probably circular, prepared for the purpose, was rolled with united and strenuous efforts against the aperture, to prevent the entrance of wild beasts and unkindly foe. And then as the chill twilight was flinging its shadows over the world, they reverently withdrew.

Joseph and Nicodemus had done their work and had gone to their homes, and yet there were some who lingered as if unable to leave the spot. There were Mary Magdalene, and the other Mary, sitting over against the sepulchre, gazing through their tears at the place where Jesus was laid. How keen was their mental anguish! There was bereaved love; with all purity the strongest love had grown up around Christ; and now that He was gone, it seemed as if there was nothing more to live for. The prop had been rudely taken away, and the tendrils of their hearts' affection were torn and wrenched. Then there would come a rush of hot tears, indignant passion with those who had pursued Him, with such unrelenting torture, to His bitter end. Then again, broken-hearted grief at the remembrance of His anguish, and gentle patience, and shame. And, mingling sadly with all these, were disappointed hopes. Was this the end? He who died thus could not have been the Messiah! He had taught them to believe He was! He must have been self-deceived! For this life only they had hope in Christ, and they were of all most miserable! That gravestone hid not only the body of Christ, but the structure of the brightest, fairest hopes that had ever filled the hearts of mortals!

In spite of all, they love. This is the love of women: the object of their fond attachment may be misrepresented and abused, the life may seem to be an entire failure; they may themselves be suffering greatly from the results of the beloved one's mistakes and follies—yet will they love still! And so through the gathering gloom and evening stillness they lingered on, until the increasing darkness told them that the Sabbath had come. Then they returned and rested the Sabbath day, according to the commandment; but neither they, nor Joseph, nor Nicodemus, nor John, would be able to partake of the Paschal festivities. To take part in a burial at any time would defile them for seven days, and make everything which they touched unclean; to do so at that time involved seclusion through the whole of the Passover week, with all its holy observances and rejoicings.

As we peruse this narrative, many thoughts are suggested.

We see the minute fulfillment of prophetic Scriptures.—It had been written by Isaiah on the page of inspiration, that the Messiah would make His grave with the rich. When Jesus died that prophecy seemed most unlikely of accomplishment; but it was literally fulfilled. There is not a prophecy, however minute, concerning our Lord's life and death, which did not have an actual fulfillment; and does not this show us how we are to treat the prophecies which foretell His future glory and second advent? They too shall have a literal and exact fulfillment.

We learn, too, that there are more friends of Christ in the world than we know.—They sit in our legislature, in our councils, in our pews; we meet them day after day: they give little or no sign of their discipleship: the most large-hearted friend would be surprised to hear that they were Christians. But they are Christ's. Christ knows and owns them. But if they are secret disciples now, they will not be secret disciples always. A time will come when the fire of their love will burn the bushel that hides it, and they will avow themselves on the Lord's side.

We gather, too, that God can always find instruments to carry out His purposes.—The immediate followers of Christ could not see how to preserve the beloved corpse from defilement, but God had His place and His servants ready; and at the very crisis of need He brought them to the point. So has it been again and again: when influence and money and men have been really required for the work of God, they have been all at once forthcoming. He says to men like Joseph, Go, and he goeth; and to men like Nicodemus, Come, and he cometh; and to His servants, Do this, and it is done. Even the king's heart is in the hand of the Lord; as the rivers of water, He turneth it wheresoever He will.

There is also a very significant meaning contained in verse 41: "In the place where He was crucified there was a garden; and in the garden a new sepulchre." There is something startling in the association—the cross, the garden. The one—the symbol of shame and suffering, the most awful witness to the destructive power of that sin which has laid waste our world; the other—where flowers, Eden's brightest relics, were guarded for man's enjoyment. Flowers, blooming in all the luxuriance of an Oriental spring, shed their fragrance around our Saviour when He died; one loves to dwell upon the thought that Golgotha was part of the garden—that earth's fairest, brightest, gentlest nurslings were there, mingling their smiles and balm with the trampling angry footsteps and the cursings of malignant foes. They had been very dear to Him in His life-course; it was only meet that they should be near Him when He died. Was it not symbolical? In a garden man fell; in a garden he was redeemed! And that death of Christ has sown our world with the flowers of peace and joy and blessedness, so that many a wilderness has begun to rejoice and to blossom as the rose.

Whilst the burial of Christ was proceeding, the chief priests and their party were holding a meeting in all haste before the Sabbath began. The success of their scheme was no doubt the theme of hearty congratulation. But they dreaded Him still; they feared that all might not be over; they could not forget that He had spoken of rising the third day; and at the least, might not the disciples steal away the body, and spread abroad the report that He had risen, and so the last error would be worse than the first? A deputation was therefore appointed to wait on Pilate representing their fears. Tired of them and the whole case, he was in no humor to please them. "Ye have a guard," said he, brusquely, "go, make it as sure as you can!" This they did. They passed a strong cord across the stone, and sealed its ends, and then placed soldiers to keep due watch and ward that none should lay hands upon the body that lay within.

So Christ lay entombed; but He was not there. He was in the world of spirits. The place of disembodied spirits was called, by the Jews, Sheol. It had two divisions, Paradise and Gehenna. Christ, we know from His own words, went to the former; and from Peter we gather that He also went through the realms of Gehenna, proclaiming His victory.

The practical conclusion of the whole is, however, contained in Romans vi. Just as the body of Christ after crucifixion was buried in the grave, so our sinful, sensual, selfish selves must be done away in the grave of forgetfulness and oblivion and disuse—buried with Christ, "that like as Christ was raised from the dead, through the glory of the Father, so we also should walk in newness of life."

XXXIII

The Day of Resurrection
"The first day of the week."—JOHN xx. 1.

It may be helpful if we tabulate in a brief and concise form the various appearances of our Lord on the great day, when He was declared to be the Son of God with power by the resurrection from the dead.

Mary of Magdala—a squalid Arab village on the south of the plain of Gennesaret still bears that name—with another Mary had remained beside the tomb, till the trumpet of the Passover Sabbath and the gathering darkness had warned them to retire. They rested the Sabbath day, according to the commandment, in the saddest, darkest grief that ever oppressed the human heart; for they had not only lost the dearest object of their affection, under the most harrowing circumstances, but their hopes that this was the Messiah seemed to have been rudely shattered. But how tenacious is human love, especially the love of women! How it will cling around the ruins of the temple, even when some rude shock of earthquake has shattered it to the ground! So, when the Sabbath was over (after sundown on Saturday), they stole out to purchase additional sweet spices, which they prepared that night in order to complete the embalming of the body, which had been left incomplete on the day of crucifixion. They would probably sleep outside the city gates, which only opened at daybreak, because they were resolved to reach the sepulchre while it was yet dark.

But before they could arrive the sublime event had occurred, which has filled the world with light and joy in all succeeding years. For behold, whilst the Roman sentries were pacing to and fro before the sepulchre, there had been a great earthquake, and the angel of the Lord had descended from heaven, rolled back the stone from the door, and sat upon it. Then from that opened door the Lord had come forth unperceived by the eye of man (for the watchers were dazed and dazzled by the appearance of the angel and the terror of the earthquake), and in sublime majesty had become the Firstborn from among the dead, and the First-fruits of them that sleep.

The women, meanwhile, were hurrying to the grave, debating as they did so, how they would be able to roll away the stone from its mouth. Probably they had heard nothing of the seals and sentries with which the Sanhedrim had endeavored to guard against all eventualities; for, had they known, they would hardly have ventured to come at all. They were greatly startled, however, when, on approaching the grave, they saw that the stone was rolled away. Mary of Magdala apparently detected this first; and without staying to see further, and with the conviction that it must have been rifled of its precious contents, started off to apprise Simon Peter and the disciple whom Jesus loved. What a shock, as she broke in on their grief, with the tidings, "They have taken away the Lord out of the sepulchre, and we know not where they have laid Him."

What a series of mistakes was hers! She had gone to anoint the dead while the morning light still lingered over the hills of Moab; she did not realize that He could not be holden by the bands of death, and had passed out into the richer, fuller life, of which death is the portal.

She came with aromatic spices that her means had bought, and her hands prepared; she did not know that all His garments were already smelling of aloes and cassia, of the perfume of heaven with which His Father had made Him glad.

She came to a Victim, so she thought, who had fallen beneath the knife of His foes as a Lamb led to slaughter, she was not aware that He was a Priest on the point of entering the most Holy Place on her behalf.

She came for the Vanquished; but failed to understand that He was a
Victor over the principalities and powers of hell; and that the keys of
Hades and the grave were hanging at His girdle, whilst the serpent was
bruised beneath His feet.

She thought that she had come to put a final touch, such as only a woman can, to a life of sad and irremediable failure; but had no conception that on that morning a career had been inaugurated which was not only endless and indissoluble in itself, but was destined to vitalize uncounted myriads.

She thought that the empty tomb could only be accounted for by the rifling hands that had taken away the precious body, but could not guess that the Rifler of the perquisites of death was none other than the Lord Himself.

We all make mistakes like this. Our treasures, whether of things or people, which had been our pride and joy, pass from us; and we stand beside the grave, gazing in on vacancy and emptiness; we think that we can never be happy again: we suppose that God's mercies are clean gone forever, and that His mercies have failed forevermore. But, all the while, near at hand, the radiant vision of a transfigured blessing waits to greet us, and to fill us with an ecstasy that shall never pall upon us, but make our after-life one long summer day.

In the meanwhile, the other women had pursued their way to the grave. The guard had already fled in terror, so there was none to intercept or frighten them; and entering the sepulchre they saw a young man, emblem of the immortal youth of God's angels, sitting on the right side, clothed in a long white garment, and they were affrighted. Presently, as they were much perplexed, behold, two men stood by them in shining garments; and as they were afraid and bowed down their faces to the earth, they said unto them, "Be not affrighted, ye seek Jesus, which was crucified. He is not here; for He is risen, as He said. Remember how He said into you when He was yet in Galilee, that He would rise again. Come, see the place where they laid Him. And go quickly, tell His disciples, and Peter, that He goeth before you into Galilee; there shall ye see Him, as He said unto you." And they departed quickly from the sepulchre with fear and great joy; and did run to bring His disciples word.

In the meanwhile, Peter and John were hurrying to the sepulchre by another route, and probably reached it just after the women had left. John, younger than Peter, had outrun him, but was withheld by reverential awe from doing more than peering into the empty grave. The linen clothes, lying orderly disposed, seem to have specially arrested his notice, yet went he not in. Peter, however, went at once into the sepulchre; he also saw the linen clothes, and especially that the cloth which had covered the face of the dead was wrapped together in a place by itself. Then

John also went in; he saw and believed. It was evident to them both that the tomb had not been rifled, nor the body stolen by violent hands; for these garments and the spices would have been of more value to thieves than a naked corpse. In any case, thieves would not have been at the pains to fold the garments up so carefully. Whilst the same indications proved that the body had not been removed by friends; for they would not have left the grave-clothes behind.

When the disciples had gone back to their own home, Mary stood without at the door of the sepulchre weeping; and as she wept she stooped down, and looked into the sepulchre. What earnest heart is there, that has not at some time stood there with her, looking down into the grave of ordinances, of spent emotions, of old and sacred memories, seeking everywhere for the Redeemer, who had been once the dearest reality, the one object of love and life? The two sentry-angels, who sat, the one at the head and the other at the feet, where the body of Jesus had lain, sought in vain to comfort her. "Woman," they said, in effect, "there is no need for tears; didst thou but know, couldst thou but understand, thy heart would overflow with supreme joy, and thy tears become smiles." "They have taken away my Lord," she said, "and I know not where they have laid Him." What could angel voices do for her, who longed to hear one voice only? What were the griefs of others in comparison with hers? In an especial sense Jesus was hers! my Lord! Had He not cast out from her seven devils?

Some slight movement behind, or perhaps, as Chrysostom finely supposes, because of an expression of love and awe which passed over the angel faces, led her to turn herself back, and she saw Jesus standing, but she knew not that it was Jesus. Supposing him, in her grief and confusion, to be the gardener, she said that if he knew the whereabouts of the body she sought, she would gladly have it removed at her expense: nay, she even volunteered to bear it off herself. Then He spoke the old familiar name with the old intonation and emphasis, and she answered in the country tongue they both knew and loved so well, "Rabboni!" In her rapture she sought to embrace Him, but this must not be; and there was need for Christ to work in her love, with His high art, as the artificer may carve the stone, or engrave some legend on the intaglio. He therefore withdrew Himself, saying, "Touch Me not." To Thomas afterward He said, "Behold My hands and My side; reach hither thy finger": because there was no danger of his abusing the permission, or leaning unduly on the sensuous and physical. But Mary must learn to exchange the outward for the inward, the transient for the eternal, and to pass from the old fellowship with Jesus as friend and companion into a spiritual relationship which would subsist to all eternity. Therefore Jesus spoke of His ascension, and bade her look upward, and see, gleaming on high, diviner things. So she was prepared for the time, when, in the upper room, she should continue steadfastly in prayer, and come nearer to Him whom she loved than ever previously.

Did you ever realize that the intonations of the voice of Jesus, which had passed unimpaired through death, suggest that in that new life, which lies on the other side of death, we shall hear the voices speak again which have been familiar to us from childhood? As is the heavenly, so are they who are heavenly; and as we have borne the image of the earthy, we shall bear that of the heavenly, and shall speak again with those whom we have lost awhile, and they with us.

Mary Magdalene went and told them that had been with Him, as they mourned and wept, that she had seen the Lord, and that He had spoken these things unto her. But they, when they had heard that He was alive, and had been seen of her, believed not.

In close succession, the Lord appeared to others of the little group. To the women, as they did run to bring His disciples word. To Peter, whom He encountered on His way back, in lonely astonishment and awe, and restored with gracious words of forgiveness. To the two that walked to Emmaus, in the afternoon, and talked of all that had happened. Finally He appeared to the whole company of the apostles, as they sat at meat. They had carefully shut their doors, since there was every reason to fear that the rumors of the events of the morning would arouse against them the strong hate and fear of the Pharisees. It may be that they were startled by every passing footfall, and every movement on the stair, as when the two returned from Emmaus to tell how Jesus had been made known unto them in the breaking of bread. Then, suddenly, without announcement or preparation, the figure of their beloved Master stood in the midst of them, with the familiar greeting of peace! And, as the sacred historian naïvely puts it, they were terrified and affrighted, and supposed that they were gazing on a spirit. But the Lord allayed their fears, first by showing them His hands and His feet; and next, by partaking of a piece of broiled fish and of an honeycomb.

Evidently He was clothed in the resurrection or spiritual body of which the Apostle Paul speaks. He was not subject to all the laws that govern our physical life. He could pass freely through unopened doors, and at will He could manifest Himself, speak, stand, and walk, or subject Himself to physical sense.

His words were very significant. He began by upbraiding them for their reluctance to believe that He had risen. Again He said, "Peace be unto you"; and accompanied His words with the indication of His wounds—"He showed them His hands and side." This was the peace of forgiveness, which falls on our conscience-stricken hearts, as the dew distils on the parched heritage. "Look at the wounds of Jesus," cried Staupitz to Luther; and there is no other sign that will give rest to the penitent.

After this He opened their understandings, that they might understand the Scriptures, and showed them that a suffering Messiah was the thought which pervaded the entire Hebrew Scriptures. "Thus it is written, and thus it behoved the Messiah to suffer, and to rise from the dead the third day." What would we not give to have some transcript of that wonderful conversation! With what new eyes should we read the Bible, if only we could know what Jesus said on that occasion!

Next He repeated the "Peace be unto you," and told them that He was sending them forth as the Father had sent Him—"Go ye unto all the world, and preach the Gospel to every creature." But He added, "Behold, I send the promise of My Father upon you; but tarry ye in the city of Jerusalem, until ye be endued with power from on high." "And these signs shall follow them that believe. In My name shall they cast out demons; they shall speak with new tongues; they shall take up serpents; and if they drink any deadly thing, it shall not hurt them; they shall lay hands on the sick, and they shall recover."

Then, to fit them for this time of waiting, and that the Holy Spirit might prepare them to receive His fuller inflow, the Lord breathed on them and said, "Receive ye the Holy Ghost: Whose soever sins ye remit, they are remitted unto them; whose soever sins ye retain, they are retained." By which He surely meant that there was no other way by which sins would be forgiven and put away than by the preaching of the Gospel, which He now committed to their trust. They are therefore parallel with Peter's statement in after days, "Neither is there salvation in any other, for there is none other name given under heaven, among men, by which we must be saved." The Church of God alone can proclaim to men the conditions of evangelical repentance,—and those who refuse her testimony, and disbelieve her Gospel, expose themselves to unspeakable condemnation and loss. "There remaineth no other sacrifice for sin; but a certain looking for of judgment, and fiery indignation." Refuse Christ, and there is no alternative way of salvation. Whatever else is contained in these words, it is quite clear that there was nothing exclusively reserved to the apostles and their successors, which is not equally the possession of all who believe; for we know that the Lord's words were spoken not to the apostles only, but to the two that had come from Emmaus with burning hearts, and to those who were in the habit of commingling with the immediate followers of Christ. "Them that were with them" (Luke xxiv. 33, 35, 36). All had been witnesses of these things, and all were now to proclaim in His name repentance and remission of sins among all nations, beginning at Jerusalem.

Thomas was not there on that memorable occasion. He was always accustomed to look on the dark side of things. When Jesus proposed to go into Judaea to raise Lazarus, he made sure that there was no alternative but to die with Him; and when the Master spoke of His impending absence, he said gloomily, "Lord, we know not whither Thou goest, and how can we know the way?" He was doubtless at this time wandering alone over the scenes of that awful tragedy, which had so deeply imprinted itself on his imagination that he could not forget the print of the nails, and the wound in His side, and the unlikelihood of any surviving such treatment as He had received.

When he heard the story of the others, he seemed inclined to treat them as too credulous; and with the air of superior caution said, that he must not only see the wounds which death had made, but touch them with his fingers and hand. Yet we may be grateful for this story. First, because it wears the aspect of truth. What weaver of an imaginary history would ever have dared to suggest that the resurrection was impugned by some of Christ's close followers? And, next, because it shows us that the resurrection was subjected to the severest tests, just those which we would ourselves apply.

Thomas was left for a whole week. Day after day he heard the repeated story of Christ's appearances; and waited for Him to come again; and became more and more confirmed in his sad presentment that the whole story was a myth. How great must have been his anguish during those days, as he tossed between hope and fear, saw on other faces the light which he might not share, and thought that the Master, if really living, was neglectful of His friend!

At last Jesus came, not to anathematize or exclude him, not to break the bruised reed or quench the smoking flax, but to restore him, and to lift on him the light of His countenance.

He suited himself to his needs. He stooped to comply with the conditions that his poor faith had laid down. He was willing to give proofs, over and above those which were absolutely necessary, to win faith. So eager was He to win one poor soul to Himself and blessedness, that He said unto Thomas, "Reach hither thy finger, and behold My hands; and reach hither thy hand, and thrust it into My side; and be not faithless but believing."

I do not suppose that Thomas availed himself of the invitation. It was sufficient to see. Such an act of cold scrutiny would hardly have been compatible with his joyous shout, "My Lord and my God." Christ's voice and form, omniscience and humility, in taking such trouble to win one to Himself—these were sufficient to convince him, and dispel all doubt.

Ah, Thomas, in that glad outburst of thine, thou reachedst a higher level than all the rest; and thou art not the last man, who has seemed a hopeless and helpless wreck, unable to exercise the faith that seemed so natural to others; but who, after a time, under the teaching of Jesus, has been enabled to assume a position to which none of his associates could aspire!

Because he saw, he believed. Too many wait for signs and manifestations, for sensible emotion and conviction: but there is a more excellent way—when we do not see, and yet believe. When there is no star on the bosom of night, no chart on the unknown sea, no lover or friend or interpreter of the ways of God; and when, in spite of all, the soul knows Him whom it has believed, and clings to Him though unseen, and reckons that neither life, nor death, nor principalities, nor powers, can shut out the love of God in Christ. "Blessed are they who have not seen, and yet have believed."

XXXIV

The Lake of Galilee
"Jesus showed Himself again to the disciples at the Sea of
Tiberias."—JOHN xxi. 1.

"All ye shall be offended because of Me this night; for it is written, I will smite the Shepherd, and the sheep shall be scattered. But after that I am risen, I will go before you into Galilee." So had the Chief Shepherd spoken to His sad and anxious followers on the night of His betrayal. They little understood His meaning, and would perhaps have even forgotten the appointment of the rendezvous, unless it had been recalled again and yet again to their minds. But they were not allowed to forget. On the resurrection morn, the angel said to the first visitants at the empty grave: "Go your way, tell His disciples, and Peter, that He goeth before you into Galilee; there shall ye see Him as He said unto you." And as they went to execute this bidding, Jesus Himself met them and said: "Be not afraid; go tell My brethren, that they go into Galilee; there shall they see Me." The customs of the Passover Feast forbade their instant compliance with this command, and the Master sanctioned their delay by appearing to them twice whilst they yet lingered in the metropolis. But as soon as it was possible they hastened back to the familiar scenes of their early life and of the Master's ministry.

We cannot fathom all the reasons that led our Lord to make such special arrangements for meeting with them in Galilee; but it was natural that He should wish to associate His risen life with scenes in which He had spent so large a part of His earthly ministry; and there the greatest proportion of His followers was gathered, and He would have the quietest and securest opportunity of meeting with the five hundred brethren at once. The disciples little thought that this was a farewell visit to their homes, and that within a few weeks they must return to Jerusalem, to stay there for a time, and then to wander forth to all lands, from the ancient Indus on the east to the far-famed shores of Tarshish on the west.

I. It was in the early part of May when they returned to Galilee. They were in evident bewilderment as to their next step. What should they do? Should they continue to lead the artificial life which they had taken up during the Master's ministry? That seemed impossible and needless. Should they do nothing but wait? That appeared unwise when life was yet strong in them, and their means of livelihood were scant. It was of course possible to go back to fishing-smacks and fishing-tackle; but should they? And they hesitated.

But one evening came; the fragrance of thyme and rosemary and of a hundred flowers filled the air; the lake lay dimpled in the light of the setting sun; the purple hills that stood sentinel around seemed by their very peacefulness to promise that no storm should imperil the lives of those that ventured on the blue depths. There stood the boats, yonder lay the nets, in those waters were the finny tribes; the old instinct of the fisherman arose in their hearts, and found expression on the lips of the one from whom we should have expected it. "Peter said unto them, I go a-fishing." I see no harm in it. The Master never forbade it. He cannot mean us to loiter our time away. We cannot be preachers without Him. I shall go back to the life from which He called me three years ago, and if it pleases Him to come again, He can find us now, as He found us once, among the fishing-tackle.

The proposal met with an instant assent: "We also go with thee." And in a few moments Peter with six others had leaped into a boat, and they were preparing for the night's work with all the enthusiasm with which men throw themselves into a craft which for some time they have disused. But their ardor was soon checked. Hour after hour passed. The lights went out in the hamlets and towns. The chill night damps enwrapped them. The grey morning at last began to break, whilst again and again the nets were hauled up and let down, but in vain; not a single fish had entered them. "That night they caught nothing." Why this non-success? The night was the most favorable time! These men knew the lake well, and were experienced in their craft. They did their best, but they caught nothing! Why was this? Was it a chance? No, it was a providence; it was carefully arranged, disappointing and vexing though it was, by One who was too wise to err, too good to be unkind, and who was preparing to teach them a lesson which should enrich them and the whole Church forever.

The failure put an arrest on their temporal pursuits. Had they been successful that night, it would have been very much harder for them to renounce the craft forever; but their non-success made them more willing to give it up, and to turn their thoughts to the evangelization of the world. Then, too, our Lord surely meant to teach them that whilst they were doing His work, whether that work was waiting or active service, it was not necessary for them to be anxious about their maintenance; He Himself would see to that, though He had, for each meal, to light a fire and prepare it Himself. And, deeper than all this, there were surely great spiritual lessons to be gained respecting the conditions of success in catching men in the net of His Gospel.

It is difficult to understand how a man can call himself a Christian, and how he can face the awful possibilities of life, except he believes that all is ruled by One who loves us with a love that is infinite, and who wields all power on earth and in heaven. If, however, that be your fixed belief, you may find it often severely tested. "I have waited this livelong night; can this be Christ's will?" "I have done my best in vain; can this be Christ's will?" "I have labored without a single gleam of success; can this be Christ's will?" Yes, most certainly it is. It is His love which is arranging all, in order to teach you some of the sweetest, deepest lessons that ever entered your heart. There is not a cross, a loss, a disappointment, a case of failure in your life, which is not arranged and controlled by the loving Saviour, and intended to teach some lesson which else could never be acquired. Fitfully, curiously, without apparent art or fixed design, is the web of our lives woven; thread seems thrown with thread at random, no orderly pattern immediately appears, but yet of all that web there is not a single thread whose place and color are not arranged with consummate skill and love.

But what good can failure do? It may shut up a path which you were pursuing too eagerly. It may put you out of heart with things seen and temporal, and give you an appetite for things unseen and eternal. It may teach you your own helplessness, and turn you to trust more implicitly in the provision of Christ. It is clear that Christians have often to toil all night in vain, that Christ may have a background black and sombre enough to set forth all the glories of His interposition.

II. In the morning Jesus stood on the shore, but the disciples knew not that it was Jesus. It was customary for fish-dealers to go down to greet fishers on their return from the night's toil, in order to buy up fish. Such a one now seemed waiting on the sand in the grey light, and His question was such as a fish-dealer might put: "Children, have you any food?" It therefore never occurred to the disciples to think that it was Jesus. And indeed, after the miracle was wrought, it was only the keen eye of love that knew Him to be the Lord. How often is the Lord near us, and we know Him not! He is standing there in the midst of scenes of natural beauty though His foot leaves no impression on the untrodden sand, and His form casts no shadow on the flowers or greensward. He is standing there in that dingy counting-house, or amid the whirr of the deafening machinery, though He fills no space, and utters no word audible to human ears. He is standing there in that home, watching the sick, noting unkindness and rudeness, smiling on the little deeds done for His sake, though none ever heard the floors creak beneath His weight, or saw the doors open to admit His person. How much we miss because we fail to discern Him!

By acting thus He not only taught His disciples the reality of His presence, but He prepared them also for that new kind of life which they were henceforth to lead—a life of faith rather than of sense; a life of spiritual communion rather than of physical fellowship. He kept showing them that, though out of sight, He was still in their midst. By easy stepping-stones He joined Calvary and Olivet. By gentle progressive lessons those who had believed because they had seen were taught to walk by faith, not by sight, and to love One whom they did not see. And thus it came about that they trod no shore however desolate, went to no land however distant, dealt with no people however boorish, without carrying ever with them the thought, The Master is here!

But let me say here that if you would see Christ everywhere, you must be like John, the disciple of love. Love will trace Him everywhere, as dear friends detect each other by little touches that are meaningless to others. Love's quick eye penetrates disguises impenetrable to colder scrutiny. Not for the wise, nor for the few, but for the least that love, is the vision possible that can make a desert isle like Patmos gleam with the light of Paradise itself.

III. How great a difference Christ's directions made! Before He spoke they were disconsolately dragging an empty net to shore. The moment after He had spoken, and they had done His bidding, that net was filled with a shoal of fish so heavy that it was no easy matter to drag it behind the ship.

Great lessons await us here! We, like these, have embarked in a great fishing enterprise—we are fishers of men! Our aim is to catch men alive for Christ our Lord. For this we are ready to toil, to pray, to wait. But our success depends wholly upon our Lord. He will not give it us until we can bear it, and have learned the lesson of the night of fruitless toil. And if we are to succeed it must be in His realized companionship, and in obedience to His word.

There is a right side of the ship, and a wrong one; there is a time to plant, and a time to be still; to everything there is a season, and a time to every purpose under heaven. We do not know these. If we are left to ourselves, we may cast the net on the left side of the ship at the time when we should be casting it on the right, and on the right side of the ship when we should be casting it on the left. Christ alone knows, and He will teach us exactly how and when to act with the very best results.

IV. Christ's provision for the needs of His servants. I should imagine that the disciples were somewhat anxious about their bodily needs and their supply. They did not realize that if they were doing Christ's work, Christ would look after their real needs. Christ let them meet with non-success to show how fruitless their toil was. And in the morning, when He stood on the shore, He filled their nets with fish, and called them to fire and bread and fish, to show how easily He could supply all their need. Of course this does not apply to all promiscuously, but it does apply to those who give up time, and labor, and earthly toil, for the cause of Christ. If they are really called to the work, Christ seems to say to them: "Do the best you can for Me, and do not try in addition to make up for your time and labor by night work—you had better use the night for necessary rest; the longest night spent in unbelieving labor will not profit; but I in a single moment in the morning can more than make up to you for all you have spent." Christ never lets us be in His debt. If we lend Him a boat for pulpit, He weighs it down to the gunwale. If we give Him time, He makes up what we have lost. If we seek first the kingdom of God and His righteousness, He sees that all things else are added. It is vain for you to rise up early and to sit up late, to eat the bread of carefulness. He giveth His beloved when they sleep.

What delicate attentions to these men! Christ knew that they were drenched with spray, chilled with the keen air, and so He prepared a fire—so thoughtful is He of the tiniest matters that will alleviate discomfort and increase our pleasure. At the same time He is frugal of the miraculous. He will deal lavishly in miracles so long as needed, but not an inch beyond. He might have created fish enough on that fire to supply them all, but that was needless so long as a hundred fifty and three great fishes lay within easy reach; so Jesus said, "Bring of the fish which ye have now caught."

When Peter heard John say, "It is the Lord," true to his character he sprang into the sea and swam to shore, leaving the rest to drag the heavy net as best they could. Now he seems to remember his failure to bear his share in the toil; so he goes to the margin of the lake, lands the net, counts its contents, and examines the meshes, to find them unbroken, and then returns with fish enough to make a breakfast for them all. It was only when all this was done that Jesus said to them, "Come and dine." Then He came forward and took the bread and fish, and gave to them. All were convinced that it was Jesus, but they were dumb with amazement and awe; they would have liked to ask questions, but they felt that they need not; their senses were convinced almost in spite of themselves. "None of the disciples durst ask Him, Who art Thou? knowing that it was the Lord."

This, says John, was the third time that Jesus had showed Himself; not literally the third time that He had shown Himself to any one; but the third time that He had shown Himself to the disciples assembled in any considerable number. The first time was in the evening of the resurrection day; the second, when Thomas was there; the third, in the incident here recorded.

We all need our rest times, our times of learning, our times of fellowship with Jesus. Happy are we when Jesus says, "Come and dine," and leads us off to sup with Him in desert places! It may be in the loneliness of nature, or of the sick-bed, or of thwarted love; but, wherever it is, it is well if only He is there to feed us with His own dear hand.

The time will come when the night of this sunless world shall be over, and the morning of eternity shall break upon us; it may be that in the hour of death we shall find that our work has not been so fruitless as we feared: on the quiet beach we shall see Jesus standing and know that it is He. Then one last plunge through the chill flood, and we shall partake of the preparations which His love has made, and He will say, "Come and dine."

XXXV

Peter's Love and Work

"Thou knowest that I love Thee. . . . Feed my lambs."—JOHN xxi. 15.

That miraculous catch of fish on which we have dwelt was a parable to the disciples of the kind of work in which they were thenceforward to be engaged. They were to catch men. But there was one amongst them who must have wondered much how he would fare, and what part he would take when that work was recommenced. Might he have a share in it? He would seem to have forfeited all right. With oaths and curses he had thrice denied that he belonged to Jesus. He had given grievous occasion to the enemy to blaspheme. He had failed in a most important part of an apostle's character.

True, he had repented with bitter tears, and had received a message from the empty tomb; on that Easter morn he had heard his forgiveness spoken by the lips of his Lord, and he would not have exchanged that forgiveness for an imperial crown; but he was not quite at ease. His uneasiness betrayed itself in his plunge into the water to swim to Christ's feet, and in his rush to drag the net to the shore. He wished to be restored to the position in the Apostolate which his sin had forfeited; not because of the honor which it would bring, but because nothing less would assure him of the undiminished confidence and the entire affection of Jesus.

The Lord read his heart; and when the morning meal was done, He singled him out from the rest of His disciples, and asked him three times if he loved Him, and then thrice gave him the injunction to feed His flock. In addressing him our Lord calls him by his old name, Simon Bar Jonas, not by his new name, Peter; as if to remind him that he had been living the life of nature rather than of grace.

In considering this subject, it will be convenient to speak of the question, the answer; the command.

I. OUR LORD'S SEARCHING QUESTION—"Lovest thou Me?"

It is a very remarkable question.—We should have expected the inquiry, Dost thou believe Me? Wilt thou obey Me? Art thou prepared to carry out My plans? But lo! the risen Lord seems not anxious about aught of these, and only asks for love, and this from the rugged, manly, headstrong Peter. Yet as we hear the question asked, we realize it is the true one. He who has asked it has struck the right method of dealing with men; and if He only get the love, He will get easily enough the faith and the obedience as well.

In this startling question you have unbared to you the distinctive feature which makes Christianity what it is, and which makes it different from all other religions which have flung their clouds or their rainbows over human spirits. It is the religion of love: and a man may speak with a seraph's burning tongue to defend Christianity; he may give his goods to feed the poor in obedience to the precepts of Christianity; he may even burn at the stake rather than renounce Christianity as his intellectual creed; but if he does not love, he is no Christian. If a man love not the Lord Jesus, he is anathema.

But if only there be love—love to God, love to man—then though there may be many deficiencies in head and heart, there is the one prime evidence of Christianship. It was on such grounds that the Rev. Adam Gibb of Edinburgh once acted. He had once or twice dissuaded a young woman from joining the church, deeming her ill-informed, and unable to answer elementary questions; and on his third refusal she answered, "Weel, weel, sir, I may na', an' I dinna, ken sae muckle as mony; but when ye preach a sermon aboot my Lord and Saviour, I fin' my heart going out to Him, like lintseed out of a bag." Any one who has observed the process will know how lifelike the illustration was, and will not wonder that Mr. Gibb admitted her, and that she lived to be one of the fairest members of his church.

It is a universal question.—Its universality suggests that in Christ there is something universally lovable, and that every one has the power of loving Him, if only the rubbish is removed which chokes the springs of affection. There are different shades in love—the love of gratitude, where the rescued spirit sings the praise of Him who took it from the terrible pit and miry clay; the love of complacency, with which the holy soul admires Him who is fairer than the sons of men, and dwells with rapture on His majestic beauty and endearing goodness; the love of friendship, in which by constant intercourse a deep attachment arises between the confiding soul and the all-sufficient Saviour. And there are as many methods of manifestation of love as there are different temperaments. With some, it is silent; with others, it speaks. With some, it sits listening at Christ's feet; with others, it hurries too and fro to serve. With some, it is exuberant and enthusiastic; with others, it is still and deep. But whatever be the shade or the evidence, in each Christian heart there must be love to Christ, and the heart must be willing to give up its throne to the reign of Jesus as its Lord.

Often it carries a special emphasis.—Peter had grievously sinned. Jesus could not pass it by in utter silence. For His disciples' sake and His own, it was necessary to allude to, and to probe it. But each was performed as gently as possible. Thrice he had been warned, thrice he had denied, and now thrice shall he be asked if he really loves. And in asking him if he loved Him more than the rest, our Lord surely reminded him of his boast that if all the rest forsook Him, he never would. Christ delicately reminded him that his actions had not been consistent with his professions, at the same time giving him an opportunity of wiping out the record of failure by a new avowal of attachment. Thus He deals with us still. He does not drag our secret sins to light before our brethren and friends, and parade them before the sun; but He asks with deep meaning if we love Him, leaving conscience to apply the question. And is there not good reason for Him to ask it? How you have forgotten Him! You have been occupied with the world, pleasure, or even sin.

And there is nothing that breaks us down so quickly as this. Peter was grieved. An old man, eighty years of age, reared in connection with a church, once found his way to the penitent form, crying, "I've come here to be broke." Ah, there is nothing that so breaks us down as this!

The question must be asked as a preliminary to service.—Thrice He asked Peter, as if to be perfectly sure ere He sent him forth on a shepherd's work. All the self-denial, patience, tenderness, and delicacy of love are needed, as the Lord knew well, in dealing with men, who are naturally uninteresting, or perhaps repulsive, and hence our Lord saw the necessity that there should be love. But how could there be love to them? It was impossible to expect it; and so Christ introduced Himself, saying, in effect, "Dost thou love Me? Henceforth there will be little opportunity of doing anything for Me, thou canst not now shelter Me in thy home, or let Me use thy fishing boats, or share My toils; but as thou lovest Me, and desirest to show it, expend it on those whom I love, for whom I died, and whom I long to see brought into My fold. If only thou lovest, thou art fit for this."

You may not be naturally fitted to teach children, or shepherd adults; but if you love Christ you will do better than those more cultured. It is not science, nor intellect, nor eloquence, that wins souls; but love to Christ pouring over in love to man. Love will give you a delicacy of perception, an ingenuity, a persuasiveness, which no heart shall be able to resist. Love will reconcile the accomplished scholar to a life among savages, and will carry the refined and cultured lady up to the sultry attic, or down to the damp and airless cellar. Love will bear all, believe all, hope all, endure all, if only it may win wild wandering sheep for Christ.

II. THE CONTRITE REPLY.—It was very humble. Peter did not now boast that he excelled the rest, he did not even dare to stand sponsor for his own affection; he threw the matter back on his Lord's omniscience, and without mentioning the degree more or less, he said simply, "Thou knowest all things, Thou knowest that I love Thee." There is a delicate shade of meaning in the Greek. The words translated love are not the same. Jesus asks Peter if he cherishes toward Him love—spiritual, holy, heavenly. Peter declines to use that term, and contents himself with speaking of a simpler, more personal, more human affection. If I do not give Thee that love which is Thy due as Son of God, I at least give Thee that which befits Thee as Son of Man.

There are many who could not go even as far as this. Yet here are tests of love! Would you be able to enjoy Heaven if Christ were not there? Would you be willing to go to hell itself if you might have Him? Do you feel drawn out to Him in service? Do you do things which you certainly would not do except for His sake? Are you glad to hear of Him in sermon or talk, so that there is a warm feeling rising to Him at the mention of His name? Does it cost you pain to hear Him evil spoken of? Do you sorrow that you do not love Him more? Then you can challenge Him, saying, "Despite my worldliness, my faithlessness, my sins, Thou knowest all things, Thou knowest that I love Thee."

It was very confident.—"Thou knowest all things." Jesus is omniscient. He can see with microscopic eye the lichen on the grey stone, the enamel on the shell, the modest flower; and He can see the love that is in the disciple's heart, though it be but a tiny seed.

When we sin, we are tempted to believe that we have no love to Christ. But let this incident encourage us. It is impossible for any true lover of Christ to go on in a course of sin, but quite possible for him to be betrayed into a single sin. And if that has been your case, do not shun the Master; He still believes that it is possible for you to love, and He is willing even to reinstate you in His blessed service. Who is there, that does not long to speak more confidently of his love to Christ? Cease then to think of your love to Christ, dwell much on His love to you—"He loved me, He gave Himself for me." Think of its unwearied patience, its delicacy, its tenderness. Consider the character of Christ as unfolded in the New Testament. Commune with Christ as friend with friend. Above all, put away from your heart all that might grieve Him, and throw it open to the Holy Ghost, with prayer that He would shed Christ's love abroad. Then, almost unconsciously, it will arise, though it may not become palpable till some great crisis calls you to the front, and demands some heroic sacrifice, which you will give, not feeling it great.

III. THE DIVINE COMMAND.—In the miracle Peter had been commissioned to do the work of a fisherman, that is, of an evangelist; here he is commissioned to do the work of a shepherd, that is, of a pastor. Feeding and tending lambs and sheep. It is not every one that is able to care for the sheep; but there is hardly any one who loves, that cannot feed or tend the lambs. And even if you shrink from the former, what good reason have you to refuse to comply with the latter?

There are in this land hundreds of young lives whom the morning light awakes to hunger, filth, and wretchedness, and whom the evening shadows limit to rooms in which you would not care to keep your dogs. They are growing up without the least sense of decency, or the slightest reverence for God. Their existence is one long struggle against the constituted guardians of society; or if they do not resist, they are always eluding. In addition to these are the children of our homes and families and schools. "Feed My lambs!"

It is worthy of note that two Greek words are used in these injunctions. In the first and last, the Master says simply, Feed. In the middle He adds, Do the work of a shepherd. So that the lover of Christ has not fulfilled all his duty, when he has given his sacred lesson or instruction: he must go further, and be prepared to act as shepherd.

XXXVI

The Life-Plan of Peter and John

"What is that to thee? follow thou Me."—JOHN xxi. 22.

We are standing on the eastern shore of the Lake of Galilee. The morning breeze blows fresh in our faces; the tiny wavelets run up with a silvery ripple, and die on the white sand; across the expanse of water the white buildings of Tiberias and Capernaum gleam forth. With gunwale all wet and slippery a fishing smack is drawn up on the deserted shore; near it the nets unbroken, although they had been heavy with finny spoils; yonder the remnants of a fisherman's breakfast and the dying embers of a fire.

The Master has just reinstated His erring apostle and friend, and proceeded to describe the death by which he was ultimately to glorify God: "Verily, verily, I say unto thee, when thou wast young, thou girdest thyself, and walkedst whither thou wouldest; but when thou shalt be old, thou shalt stretch forth thy hands, and another shall gird thee, and carry thee whither thou wouldest not."

How different this forecast to what Peter would have chosen for himself! What a contrast between that yielding to the will of another, and that impetuous nature which so constantly betrayed itself! Take, for instance, the occasions that are offered in this chapter. As soon as he hears John's suggestion that the Lord is standing on the beach, he lets go the fish that he had spent all night to catch, the nets which it cost hours to make, the boat which was probably his own property, binds his fisher's coat about him, plunges into the water, and never rests till he has cast himself at his Master's feet. As soon as the Lord expresses His desire to mingle some of the recent haul with His own preparations for breakfast, he springs up, hastens to the margin of the sea, drags the net to land, counts its contents, and brings specimens to the little group gathered about the Master. Every movement so quick and energetic! To wish, is to act! To desire a thing, to do it! He makes us think of young manhood in all its vigorous, nervous life.

The Lord did not damp or repress His fervid disciple. He looked on him, to borrow the thought of another, with tender pity; as a parent, who has passed through many of the world's darkest places, beholds the child who is speaking of what he expects life to bring. Fresh from His own agony, the Lord knew how different a temper that would be which had been induced by prolonged suffering and patience: and He knew how necessary it was that that temper should be induced in His beloved disciple, so that he might become a pillar in His Church, and the tender sympathetic writer of that First Epistle, which is so saturated with a spirit of tender patience and sympathy for all who suffer.

Having uttered these cautionary words our Lord seems to have moved away, bidding Peter follow—a mandate which was intended to carry a deeper meaning. John followed them some few steps in the rear. Hearing footsteps, Peter turned and saw him, and with a touch of unworthy curiosity, hardly compatible with the seriousness of the statement Jesus had just made, said, "Lord, and what shall this man do?"

The question was objectionable. It savored too much of Peter's old, hasty, forward self. The

Lord would not become a mere fortune-teller to gratify his inquisitiveness. He put a check, therefore, on the unbefitting inquiry, and yet, in rebuking, answered it: "If I will that he tarry till I come, what is that to thee? follow thou Me."

It is not easy to explain certainly the import of Christ's reply. Some have interpreted it as meaning Christ's coming in death. But this can hardly be, for He would as certainly come to Peter dying amid the agony of martyrdom, as to John dying in a peaceful old age. Surely the period referred to must have been the fall of Jerusalem, only forty years distant, and to which our Lord so often referred as one phase at least of His coming. Then the old economy would fall and pass away; Christianity assume a world-wide importance, and the cross become one of the mightiest factors of human history.

When those words were repeated to them, some of the disciples interpreted them as meaning that John should not die, but they did not convey that meaning to John himself; he only saw in them a general intimation that his lot was in his Master's hands, and in any case would be a very different one from Peter's.

I. OUR LIFE-PLAN IS FASHIONED BY THE WILL OF CHRIST.—What royalty there is in those words, If I will! If Jesus were less than Divine, how blasphemous they would appear! What arrogance to suppose that He could regulate the time and manner of life or death! Yet how natural it is to hear Him speak thus. No one starts or is surprised, and in that calm acquiescence there is a testimony to the homogeneousness of Christ's character. It is of one piece throughout. There is a perfect consistency between His acts and words.

The ancients thought of their lives as woven on the loom of spiteful fates, whom they endeavored to humor by calling euphonious names. The materialist supposes that his life is the creature of circumstances, a rudderless ship in a current, mere flotsam and jetsam on the wave. The Christian knows that the path of his life has been prepared for him to walk in; and that its sphere, circumstances, and character are due to the thought and care of Him who has adapted it to our temperament and capabilities, to repress the worst, and educate the best within us.

We are ignorant of the place and mode of our death. Our grave may be in ocean depths with storm-blasts as our dirge, or the desert-waste with the sands as our winding-sheets. Like that of Moses in a foreign land, unknown and untended; or within the reach of friendly hands, which will keep it freshly decked with evergreens. But wherever it may be, it must befall as Christ has willed. We may die by some lingering agony, or the gentle slackening of life's silver cord. The temple may be shattered by an earthquake, or taken down stone by stone. But whether the one or the other, it will be determined by His will. He who makes the hue of each fading leaf different from that of any other in the forest has some new trait of godliness, some fresh feature of grace to illustrate and enforce in the dying hour; it is therefore written, "Precious in the sight of the Lord is the death of His saints."

There is no lasting happiness, no comfort, no peace, to be had in this life, apart from the belief that the so-called trifles, as well as the apparently greater incidents of existence, are included in the circumference of Christ's will, either executive or permissive. But in speaking thus, I discriminate between ourselves and our surroundings. I am speaking more particularly of the latter, and urge that even where they are apparently moulded by the carelessness or malignity of others, yet these are, unconsciously indeed, but really, effecting what He predetermined should be done. "If I will."

Bind this to your heart. It may be appointed for you to die in early prime, when the purpose of your life seems unfulfilled; or to live a sequestered life, banished to the Patmos of exile and suffering, dying after long years. But in any case, your Saviour has contrived and adjusted all. And He will send the Angel of His Presence with you, to help you, and to bring you to the place that He has prepared.

II. THE LIFE-COURSE OF ANY IS DETERMINED BY THE PECULIARITIES OF CHARACTER AND SERVICE.—Christ tells us that we are destined to a long future; and in doing so gives us the only satisfactory clue to the mystery of existence. If there be no life beyond death, life is a maze of endless wandering, to which there is no clue. But if there be—and after all there is no if in it—we can easily understand that the present needs to be carefully adjusted to our nature and our future niche in the great universe of God, that we may be able, to the farthest limit, to realize our Master's anticipations.

There is a conspicuous illustration of this before us. Peter was to be the apostle of sufferers, and write a letter, which should help, as perhaps no other writing has helped, all sufferers to the end of time; but he could never have penned it apart from the fiery trials through which his character was softened and sanctified. How could he have spoken of the humility, meekness, and patience of the suffering believer, had he not drunk deeply of the cup of suffering for himself and lived in constant anticipation of the martyr-death of which the Lord spoke?

John's work, on the other hand, was to declare, as he does in the Book of Revelation, that Jesus is the Living One, unchanged and unchanging, the King of earth and heaven. And how could he have produced that marvellous work, and received and reported those sublime visions, if he had not lingered on, in loneliness and exile, till Jerusalem had fallen before Titus and his legions, the Temple been destroyed, and the Jews scattered to every nation under heaven?

Neither of these men understood at the time what he was being prepared for. But as each now from heaven reviews the work he did, and the way in which he was prepared for doing it; as each compares the discipline through which he passed with the peculiarities of the people he was to address, and the testimony he was to deliver, he must be full of glad acknowledgments of the perfect adaptation of means to ends, of instrumentalities to results.

And what is manifestly true of them is equally so of each of us. Not always in this world, but in the next, we shall discern the admirable fitness of the discipline through which we passed, to prepare us for our position and ministry both here and hereafter.

III. WHILST GOD IS WORKING OUT OUR LIFE-PLAN, WE MUST GIVE OURSELVES TO PRACTICAL OBEDIENCE.—"Follow thou Me." The Master reiterated this command, both when He told Peter his destiny, and when His apostle was prying into secrets with which he had no immediate concern. Whatever threatens us, looming in the future, we must not be deterred from following our Master; and we are not to waste our time in speculation as to matters which lie beyond our ken, but apply ourselves to the practical duties, which lie ready to our hand.

But what is it to follow Christ? It is not to live an Oriental life beneath these Northern skies, nor wear an Eastern garb, nor speak in the Hebrew tongue. A man might do all these, and in addition wander like Him, homeless and outcast, through the land, and yet not follow in His steps. No! Following Jesus means our identification in the principles that underlay His life, in His devotion and prayer, in His absolute compliance with God's will, in His constant service of mankind, in the sweetness and gentleness and strength of His personal character. There is no path of legitimate duty into which we are called to go, in which He does not precede; for when He putteth forth His own sheep, He goeth before them, and His sheep follow. As of old, His disciples saw Him going before them ascending up to Jerusalem, and they followed Him; there is no path of arduous duty and suffering in which He does not still precede.

Following Christ involves almost certain suffering at first. When Peter asked what they would have, who had left all to follow Jesus, the Master did not hesitate to say that the bitter herb of suffering would mingle with all the dishes with which their table might be spread: and when James and John tried to bespeak the right and left seats of the throne, He spoke of the cup and baptism of pain. But afterward, when the cross and grave are passed, then the fullness of joy and the pleasures, which are at God's right hand forever-more!

We may follow Christ, and yet our paths diverge. Peter and John had been close friends. In them, the binary stars of love and zeal, labor and rest, action and contemplation, revolved in a common orbit. Together at the grave, in the boat, in the temple, in prison; but their outward fellowship was not permitted to continue; perhaps if it had, it would have been too absorbing. It is in silence and solitude that spirits attain their complete beauty, and so the Master is sometimes obliged to say to us, "What is that to thee? follow thou Me."

In following Jesus, with the shadow of the cross always on his spirit, Peter learned to sympathize with his Master's anticipation of death, which in earlier years had been incomprehensible to him, and had led him to say, "That be far from Thee, Lord"; and it gave him finally the opportunity of fulfilling his first resolve to go with Him to prison and to death. We often think ourselves strong to do and suffer long before patience had done her perfect work. We rush impetuously forward, and are overwhelmed. Then our Master has to lead us about, to take us round by another and longer route, to train us by toils and tears and teachings, till, hopeless of our own strength and confident in His, in our old age we cry, "I must put off this my tabernacle, even as our Lord Jesus Christ hath showed me."

If the old legend is true, Peter was crucified with his head downward, because he felt unworthy to be so like his Lord—following Him with humility and reverence. But whatever befalls us, whatever be the nature of our experience in life or death, let it be our one aim to glorify God. "And the God of all grace, who hath called us unto His eternal glory in Christ, after that we have suffered a little while, shall Himself perfect, stablish, strengthen us. To Him be the dominion forever and ever. Amen."

XXXVII

Back to the Father

"And there are also many other things which Jesus did."—JOHN xxi. 25.

Once more, as we learn both from the Gospel according to Matthew and the First Epistle to Corinthians, our Lord met the eleven Apostles, together with some five hundred brethren beside, on a mountain in Galilee, chosen partly for retirement and seclusion, and partly that all might see Him. The majority of these were alive when Paul wrote. "And Jesus came and spake unto them, saying, All power is given unto Me in heaven and in earth. Go ye therefore, and teach all nations, baptizing them into the name of the Father, and of the Son, and of the Holy Ghost, teaching them to observe all things whatsoever I have commanded you; and lo, I am with you alway, even unto the end of the age."

Only once or twice beside did the Lord appear. He was seen of James, and this interview seems to have determined this saintly man, who was his own brother either through a previous marriage of Joseph, or as born after his own birth, of Mary, to become a humble follower of Him, with whose existence His own was so mysteriously blended. Then He appeared once more to all the Apostles, and being assembled with them commanded them to wait in Jerusalem till the promise of the Father was fulfilled, that He would send them another Comforter, the Holy Ghost. "For John," He said, "truly baptized with water; but ye shall be baptized with the Holy Ghost not many days hence."

There seems to have been an interval at that point, during which the disciples had time to think over what the Lord had said. It had suggested to them the idea of the setting up of the Messianic kingdom, which had always been viewed as coincident with the bestowal of the Holy Ghost. "Lord," they said when they came together again, "wilt Thou restore at this time the kingdom to Israel!" The Lord would not gratify their curiosity, and at that moment it would have been useless to combat and explain their erroneous views. This must be left to the education of time, and circumstance, and that same Spirit. These things were kept in the Father's secret councils. It was not for them to know, but they should receive power.

Then, with the tenacity of affection for the scenes of His former life, He led them out as far as Bethany. And when they had reached the beloved spot, associated with so many sacred and tender memories, He lifted up His hands and blessed them; and while He blessed them, He was parted from them, and a cloud became both vail and chariot, parting them and receiving Him out of their sight.

Thence He ascended far above all principality, power, might, and dominion, through all heavens to the right hand of the Father, there to pursue His life of ministry and prayer for men, and specially for those He loved. And angels stood beside the little group of lovers, assuring them of His return in the same manner as they had seen Him go. And they worshipped Him, and went forth, and preached everywhere, the Lord working with them, and confirming their word with signs following.